Praise for Divorce For Dummies

Divorce For Dummies is truly one-stop shopping for the separated and divorced, offering legal, financial, and emotional help in a friendly, concise manner. Whether you're just thinking about splitting up or have been divorced for a couple of years, this book is for you. Like a wise friend who has been through the process, too, *Divorce For Dummies* dispenses useful, timely advice to people at all stages of divorce. And, you don't have to wade through 200 pages of legal jargon to get your questions answered — you can dip into the book for ten minutes and find tips and guidance that apply to your situation right now.
> — Diana Shepherd, Editorial Director, *Divorce Magazine*

What a helpful book! Direct and to the point with clear information for finding your way through the fact-versus-fiction of the legal system. An enormous help to legal advocates and those contemplating divorce.
> — Gail Irby, Executive Director, Family Crisis Center, Harlingen, TX

John Ventura has dedicated his career to helping Americans deal with life transitions. This time, he and Mary Reed lend their knowledge and gentle support to those who must make the difficult move from married life to being single. If there's a way to make divorce painless, John Ventura and Mary Reed have found it.
> — George Chamberlin, Talk Show Host, KSDO Radio, San Diego

Divorce For Dummies is that friend indeed when we're most in need. At a time when we are confused, afraid, and vulnerable, it's the safe place to find help. John Ventura and Mary Reed walk us through the toughest decisions many of us will ever make, with sensitivity and expert guidance. It's like having your closest friend and a top-notch family lawyer rolled into one, and available at all hours. Finally, a clearly marked map through the field of land mines that is divorce. I only wish *Divorce For Dummies* had been around when I was trying to find my way.
> — Ellen G. Sanchez, M.Ed., Family Life Educator

After 25 years as a matrimonial attorney and a financial family advisor, I can tell you, go straight to Chapter 2 of this book. You'll be on top of the game should there be a divorce, and better yet, if you follow the financial advice in *Divorce For Dummies,* you'll never feel dependent again.
> — Adriane G. Berg, Editor of *Wealthbuilder,* the monthly family financial guide, and host of WABC's *Money Show*

This book should be read at the first sign of trouble in a marriage. Chapter 2 on "Getting Smart about Your Family's Money Matters" and Chapter 20 on "Thinking Ahead: Postnuptial and Prenuptial Agreements" are especially significant. Before the final step is taken to a formal filing there should be a premeditated effort to financially protect yourself. I am a wounded veteran of two divorce wars with an 18-year history of child support payments; thank God it's over! I am sorry this book came along 20 years too late for me.
— Sam A. Listi, Architect and Developer

Reading *Divorce For Dummies* is like listening to a trusted friend and advisor who has all the right answers. It offers friendly, useful advice that will make a difficult time a little easier.
— Gerri Detweiler, Author of *The Ultimate Credit Handbook*

The authors combine heartfelt empathy with clear and sensible advice that addresses all types of divorces, whether they involve kids, lots of money or debt, cooperative spirits, or even violence. This expertly detailed and well-mapped journey leads us out of the maze of uncertainty, fear, and legalese surrounding divorce. It's like having a rewarding session with an experienced family law attorney, a great therapist, and your best friend, all at once. Read *Divorce For Dummies* and then rest confident that if bad gets worse, you'll know the right steps to take toward a very healthy new beginning.
— Paula Calhan Zeigler, Vice-President of CXR Co., Inc., and former legal assistant

John Ventura and Mary Reed handle the complex and delicate issues of divorce with ease and calming reassurance. This book is a valuable tool for couples considering divorce, or for those who have divorced, as it addresses many concerns and complications both before and after the process. Ventura and Reed have done a remarkable job of bringing the virtues of civility and savvy together while leaving no legal, financial, or emotional stone unturned.
— Lori Pridgen, Consumer Credit Counseling Service of South Texas

WARNING: The information in this book — especially on how to work efficiently with your divorce lawyer — may save you thousands of dollars in legal fees.
— Robert I. Kligman, Esq., Divorce lawyer, San Francisco

 ™

References for the Rest of Us!™

DIVORCE
FOR
DUMMIES®

by John Ventura and Mary Reed

Wiley Publishing, Inc.

Divorce For Dummies®

Published by
Wiley Publishing, Inc.
909 Third Avenue
New York, NY 10022
www.wiley.com

Copyright © 1998 Wiley Publishing, Inc., Indianapolis, Indiana

For general information on our other products and services or to obtain technical support, please contact our Customer Care Department within the U.S. at 800-762-2974, outside the U.S. at 317-572-3993, or fax 317-572-4002.

Wiley also publishes its books in a variety of electronic formats. Some content that appears in print may not be available in electronic books.

Library of Congress Cataloging-in-Publication Data:

Library of Congress Control Number: 98-84961
ISBN: 0-7645-5058-6

Manufactured in the United States of America
10 9

About the Authors

John Ventura is an attorney and a nationally known authority on consumer advocate law and financial issues. As a boy, he dreamed of becoming a Catholic priest so he could help others. To prepare for that career spent his high school years in a seminary. After graduation, John decided he could best pursue his dream by combining journalism with the law, so he earned a degree in both from the University of Houston.

Today, John operates three law offices in the Rio Grande Valley where he offers legal advice in the areas of bankruptcy, consumer law, and personal injury. His goal as an attorney and as an author is to provide individuals with the information and advice they need to make the laws work for them, not against them.

John is the author of eight books on consumer and small-business legal and financial matters, and the author of *Law For Dummies* (Wiley). He has written for *Home Office Computing* and *Small Business Computing* magazines and he writes a regular column for a Texas business journal. John also hosts a weekly radio program on legal issues.

John has been a frequent network TV show guest on CNN, CNN-fn, CNBC, the Fox News Channel, and the Lifetime Network, and has done numerous national and local radio programs. He has provided expert opinion for publications including *Money, Kiplinger's Personal Finance Magazine, Black Enterprise, Inc., Martha Stewart's Living, The Wall Street Journal*, and *Newsweek*. John and his family live on South Padre Island, Texas.

Mary J. Reed has ghost-written numerous books on money and legal matters and has been a regular contributor to *Home Office Computing* and *Small Business Computing* magazines. She is the owner of MR•PR, a public relations and special events firm based in Austin, Texas. Mary counts among her clients attorneys, publishers and authors, doctors, retail businesses, hospitals, nonprofit organizations, and restaurants, among others.

Prior to starting her own business, Mary was vice-president of marketing for a national market research firm, public affairs and marketing director for a women's health-care organization, and public relations manager for an award-winning regional magazine. She also worked as a policy analyst for a local official and as a management consultant in Washington, D.C., and Boston, consulting to both public- and private- sector clients. Mary holds a bachelor's degree in political science from Trinity College in Washington, D.C., and a master's degree in Business from Boston University.

When she is not busy reinventing her professional life, Mary fills her time with friends and family, travel, gardening, mountain biking, tending to her four cats, reading an endless stack of magazines and books, and actively participating in her husband's life-long passion for building and racing vintage Triumph motorcycles.

About the Special Contributor

Sandy Cartwright has been practicing law in Austin since 1993. Born and reared in Canada, he received his bachelor's degree in political economy from the University of Chicago. Moving south in 1985 for a break from the cold, he fell in love with the Texas Hill Country, and has lived in Austin ever since, completing his law studies at the University of Texas along the way.

In addition to litigating in the family law environment and being constantly perplexed by the strange things people do to, with, or despite their families and loved ones, Sandy can be found cooking, backpacking, traveling in South America whenever possible, and wrestling with home improvement projects that (he swears) become self-aware and plot against him.

Dedication

John's Dedication

To my in-laws, Ernest and Rose Gomez. Married 40 years — one of the lucky couples!

Mary's Dedication

To my parents. Your words and your deeds have taught me what a successful marriage is all about and have provided me with a model to strive for. Happy 50th anniversary!

Authors' Acknowledgments

Our thanks go to the project editor for this book, Nancy DelFavero. Her contributions to *Divorce For Dummies* are evident on every page. Thanks as well to senior copy editor Tammy Castleman and copy editor Elizabeth Kuball for helping to make us sound good.

Special thanks to attorney Sandy Cartwright. His dedication to this project and his from-the-trenches comments and critiques helped make this much more than just another divorce book. Sandy, we couldn't have done it without you.

Thanks also to Lynn Thompson, social worker and executive director with Big Brothers-Big Sisters of Austin, Texas. Her insights regarding the emotional impact of divorce on families have enriched this book.

Thanks also to Heather Stobaugh for her willing and enthusiastic help with the sometimes-tedious research.

And last, but certainly not least, thank-you to our spouses, friends, coworkers, and families. They demonstrated their love and support throughout the writing process, giving us encouragement when we didn't think we could write another word, making us laugh, and helping us remember what is really important in life.

Publisher's Acknowledgments

We're proud of this book; please register your comments through our online registration form located at www.dummies.com/register.

Some of the people who helped bring this book to market include the following:

Acquisitions, Development, and Editorial

Project Editor: Nancy DelFavero

Acquisitions Editor: Mark Butler

Copy Editors: Tamara Castleman, Elizabeth Netedu Kuball

Technical Editor: Lynn Thompson, LMSW-ACP

Editorial Manager: Mary Corder

Editorial Assistants: Paul E. Kuzmic, Donna Love, Michael D. Sullivan

Production

Project Coordinator: Karen York

Layout and Graphics: Cameron Booker, Lou Boudreau, Maridee V. Ennis, Angela F. Hunckler, Jane E. Martin, Brent Savage, Deirdre Smith, Michael A. Sullivan

Proofreaders: Christine Berman, Michelle Croninger, Henry Lazarek, Nancy Price, Rebecca Senninger

Indexer: Liz Cunningham

Publishing and Editorial for Consumer Dummies

Diane Graves Steele, Vice President and Publisher, Consumer Dummies
Joyce Pepple, Acquisitions Director, Consumer Dummies
Kristin A. Cocks, Product Development Director, Consumer Dummies
Michael Spring, Vice President and Publisher, Travel
Brice Gosnell, Associate Publisher, Travel
Suzanne Jannetta, Editorial Director, Travel

Publishing for Technology Dummies

Richard Swadley, Vice President and Executive Group Publisher
Andy Cummings, Vice President and Publisher

Composition Services

Gerry Fahey, Vice President of Production Services
Debbie Stailey, Director of Composition Services

Contents at a Glance

Cartoons at a Glance

By Rich Tennant

"Mother will be so disappointed when she finds out I'm going to be a divorcee. She always wanted me to be a widow."

page 5

HE DIDN'T REALLY COMMIT ADULTERY, BUT I AGREED TO PUT IT IN THE DIVORCE APPLICATION AS ONE LAST FAVOR TO HIM.

page 73

Following on the success of the **Elvis Presley Wedding Chapel** in Las Vegas...

I now pronounce you husband and wife. Thank you very much.

...the **Zsa Zsa Gabor Divorce Court.**

Congratulations darlings-you're divorced.

page 111

"You get an allowance? Is that like child support?"

page 183

"I don't know if we had irreconcilable differences or not. We never talked."

page 257

"They both traveled a lot and were big Internet users. Finally, three years and two modems later, they broke up due to insufficient bandwidth."

page 303

Cartoon Information:
Fax: 978-546-7747
E-Mail: richtennant@the5thwave.com
World Wide Web: www.the5thwave.com

Table of Contents

Part II: Divorce Preliminaries 73

Chapter 6: Putting Your Divorce in Motion 75

Chapter 7: Helping Your Kids Get through Your Divorce 89

Introduction

Nearly one-half of all marriages in the United States end in divorce. That adds up to more than a million divorces a year! Despite divorce having become so commonplace, most people are almost completely at a loss over what to do first if *their* marriages are breaking up. (An understandable situation — most of us go into marriage expecting the best but not usually prepared for the worst.)

Overwhelmed by confusion, anger, fear, and resentment, many divorcing spouses turn what could have been an amicable breakup into a cutthroat battle. Others panic over the changes occurring in their lives (and the lives of their children) and end up making costly mistakes that could have been avoided if they had more information about the divorce laws in their state. They end their marriages bitter, angry, and a whole lot poorer.

But divorce doesn't have to be about winners, losers, and huge legal bills. With the right information and advice (and the proper attitude), most couples can work out the terms of their divorce with a minimum of expense, hassles, and emotional upheaval. In this book, we tell you how it can be done.

Why You Need This Book

Divorce For Dummies helps demystify the divorce process, and it does so in plain English (and not a bunch of confounding legalese). Want to know what you'll find in the chapters ahead? Dip into this book and you can discover the following:

- What to do first before you file for divorce
- The difference between a fault and no-fault divorce
- Family law and divorce law basics, and how divorce laws may vary from state to state
- Facts to consider when you're deciding on division of property, alimony, child support, and child custody
- Mistakes to avoid, trade-offs to consider, and insights into effective negotiating
- Tips for finding an attorney who is competent *and* affordable

> ✔ What to expect if you successfully negotiate the terms of your divorce with an attorney's help, and what to expect if you must go to trial
> ✔ Divorce-related resources, including Internet sites, support groups, and divorce-related publications

We also offer you advice for keeping your emotions as well as your legal expenses under control. And, for the small percentage of you who are involved in hostile divorces and have to iron out your differences through a divorce trial, this book can prepare you for the courtroom experience. Plus, we offer advice for minimizing the potential negative effect divorce may have on your children, and suggest ways to rebuild a new life for yourself after divorce.

How This Book Is Organized

You can use *Divorce For Dummies* in either of two ways. You can read it cover to cover, and never skip a beat on the subject of divorce, or pick it up when you need an answer to a particular question or want to know more about a certain subject. For even easier reading, this book is organized into six parts:

Part I: Trouble in Paradise

This part of the book helps prepare you for dealing with a seriously troubled marriage and reviews your options if you're in a failing relationship. It provides information on how to build a solid credit record of your own, gather facts about your family's finances, and hone your money management skills before you get divorced. This part also offers an overview of family law — the type of law that governs marriage and divorce, and the responsibilities that parents have to their minor children. We close out this part with a chapter on separation as a way to save your marriage (or as a prelude to divorce).

Part II: Divorce Preliminaries

The second part of *Divorce For Dummies* tells you how to prepare yourself for the divorce process and has specific advice for the spouse who initiates a divorce and for the spouse who gets the bad news. It devotes a full chapter to an especially difficult task — telling your children that Dad and Mom won't be living together any more and helping your kids get through your divorce. And, last, this part provides advice on how to cope with the emotions you will inevitably feel and how to deal with the reaction of your friends and family to the end of your marriage.

Part III: Decisions, Decisions

Once your divorce has begun, you have to make some important and sometimes tough decisions: How will your marital property be divided up? Will you pay or receive spousal support? How will you handle child custody and visitation? What about child support? The answers to these questions should be easier to reach after you read the chapters in this part of the book.

Part IV: Working Out the Terms of Your Divorce Agreement

This part of the book is a must-read whether you and your spouse negotiate most of your divorce yourselves or you each hire attorneys to do most of the negotiating for you. You'll gain a greater appreciation for the benefits and the drawbacks of doing your own negotiating, and discover the benefits of using mediation to help settle your divorce. We tell you how to locate an affordable attorney, what you should expect from the attorney you hire, and what your attorney expects from you. For those of you headed for a divorce trial, the final chapter in this part tells you what to expect before, during, and immediately after your divorce is tried in court.

Part V: After Your Divorce Is Finalized

After your divorce is wrapped up, you still have paperwork to deal with and money matters to handle. Plus, you now face the prospect of getting by on your own. This part of the book helps you address those issues. Some of you may also face problems with your divorce agreement or with your spouse failing to adhere to the custody, visitation, child support, or alimony terms of your divorce. This part of the book reviews these and other common post-divorce problems and provides advice for dealing with them. Finally, we include a chapter that explains the value of prenuptial and postnuptial agreements in the event you marry again.

Part VI: The Part of Tens

The first chapter in this part points you to great Web sites where you can learn more about divorce, get your questions answered by divorce experts, and chat with other individuals going through divorce. The second chapter in this part offers advice for helping your kids cope in the aftermath of your divorce. Another chapter provides practical tips for how to put your divorce behind you and move forward. The final chapter offers suggestions for how to build and sustain a mutually fulfilling relationship in the future.

Icons Used in This Book

 This icon clues you in to something especially useful that can save you time, money, or energy as you're going through your divorce.

 Stop and read this information to steer clear of mistakes and pitfalls that are common in divorce.

 This icon calls your attention to areas of divorce and family law that may differ from one U.S. state to another.

 We use this icon to draw your attention to the somewhat technical but very important financial details of your divorce.

 This icon highlights gender-related social and financial issues facing both men and women who are divorcing.

 When you see this icon, we tell you where to point your Web browser to find information resources, download a helpful form, or even hook up with a support group.

 A low-tech (but high-touch) version of the Dummies Link, this icon points out publications, organizations, and government agencies that are good information resources.

 For those of you who like as much in-depth information on a subject as possible, you may want to make a point of reading this material.

 This icon highlights divorce scenarios that are so bizarre (yet true) that they made the news.

Part I
Trouble in Paradise

The 5th Wave   By Rich Tennant

"Mother will be so disappointed when she finds out I'm going to be a divorcee. She always wanted me to be a widow."

In this part . . .

*I*f your marriage is rocky and you think you're headed for a breakup, this part of the book provides information to prepare you for the divorce process. (Because divorce may not be an option for some of you, we also talk about marriage as well as divorce issues.)

We provide some solid advice for getting your finances together (whether or not you're divorcing), an overview of your legal rights and obligations during the divorce process, plus some basics on family law in general and divorce law in particular. This part ends with a chapter on separation, which many couples opt for as a last-ditch effort to save their marriages, or use in lieu of divorce.

Chapter 1

What to Do First When Things Start to Go Wrong

- -

In This Chapter

▶ Recognizing the signs of trouble

▶ Sticking it out

▶ Taking steps to improve your marriage and avoid a divorce

▶ Deciding whether to separate permanently or divorce

▶ Dealing with violence

- -

Marriages rarely die overnight. Almost always, the destruction of a marriage happens little by little, over time. Ideally, if trouble arises in your marriage, you and your spouse should be able to respond to problems before they cause serious damage to your relationship. You can then either work things out and stay married, or make a mutual decision to separate or get divorced. But, if your marriage is in really serious trouble, any discussion, cooperation, or compromise may be impossible, and you may have no option but to end it yourself, possibly against your spouse's wishes.

When you are having marriage problems, whether they are big or small, the sooner you face facts and decide what to do about them the better. Burying your head in the sand when it comes to marital woes won't make your problems go away. In fact, they'll probably just get worse. Furthermore, if divorce is in the cards, the sooner you acknowledge it, the more emotionally and financially prepared you'll be for what is to come.

You may find yourself replaying old arguments, resurrecting old hurts, crying a lot, or becoming consumed with anger when your marriage is in trouble. Those responses can quickly turn small problems into big ones and cause you to lose all perspective when it comes to your spouse and your marriage. Furthermore, when you let your emotions get out of control, it becomes difficult if not impossible for you to identify and realistically assess all of the options you have for dealing with your troubles.

To help bring some objectivity and common sense to your situation so that you can gain a true appreciation of just how bad (or not so bad) things really are, this chapter reviews some of the more common signs of a marriage in crisis and highlights the options you have for dealing with your relationship problems. Just knowing that you have choices can be reassuring and helpful. This chapter also addresses steps you can take if the pressures in your troubled relationship cause your spouse to turn violent.

Do You Have Cause for Concern?

When your marriage is going through tough times, you may find yourself wondering whether it's an instance of the "for better or for worse" your marriage vows alluded to, or whether your relationship is truly on the rocks.

Although no test exists that can tell you whether your problems are typical reactions to the stress and strain most marriages experience at one time or another, or whether they point to more-serious issues, troubled marriages do tend to exhibit many of the same characteristics. How many of the following statements apply to your marriage?

- In your mind, your spouse just can't do anything right anymore.
- You fight constantly.
- You've lost the ability or the willingness to resolve your marital problems.
- Resentment and contempt have replaced patience and love.
- You've turned from lovers into roommates.
- One or both of you is having an affair.
- You go out of your way to avoid being together and, when you are together, you have nothing to talk about.
- Your children are reacting to the stress in your marriage by fighting more, having difficulty in school, getting into trouble with the police, abusing drugs or alcohol, or becoming sexually promiscuous.
- You have begun having thoughts about divorce.

Don't panic if you find that your marriage exhibits some of these characteristics — you are not necessarily headed for divorce court. However, you do have cause for concern and it's time for you and your spouse, first separately and then together, to assess your options and decide what to do next.

Marital problems can trigger depression, feelings of vulnerability and powerlessness, anger, and sleep problems, any of which can impede clear thinking and sound decision-making. A mental health professional can help you deal with these disturbances so that you can move forward.

The Old-Fashioned Approach to Trouble — Stick It Out

Not all that long ago, the pressure to stay married was so great that when a couple's marriage failed, divorce was almost inconceivable, no matter how miserable the couple may have been. The reasons for shunning divorce were numerous: Society actively frowned on divorce; divorced women were looked upon as "damaged goods"; the anti-divorce sentiments of many religions influenced the behavior of married couples far more than they do today; being divorced was a lonely experience because there were far fewer single-parent families than there are today; and most women did not have careers outside the home or credit in their own names, so staying married was an economic necessity.

Although times have changed, many couples opt to stay married after their relationships have failed. These couples may have young children and feel it's important for them to be raised in a two-parent household, or they may be unable to afford a divorce right away. Some couples experience implicit or explicit pressure from their family, friends, or church to stay together, whereas other couples come to an understanding that allows them to lead separate lives but remain under the same roof. Finally, some couples whose marriages have ended don't divorce because they are afraid of what life will be like if they are single again. Fear of the unknown may motivate them to tolerate a situation that would be unbearable to others.

 If your home is full of tension and anger because of your marital problems, you may be doing your children more harm than good by staying together.

 Never stay in a marriage if your spouse is threatening to physically harm you or has already harmed you or your children! At the very least, separate and give your spouse an opportunity to get professional help. If you are fearful that leaving may trigger violent behavior in your spouse, contact your local domestic abuse shelter or the National Domestic Violence Hotline (800-799-7233) for help in developing a safety plan.

Trying to Work Things Out

When you decide to stay in your marriage, you have two basic options: You can try to improve your relationship; or you can grit your teeth, shut down your feelings, and put up with things the way they are. The first alternative is almost always the better choice. Three options for improving your marriage include taking a short break from one another, getting marriage counseling, and trying mediation. None of these alternatives are mutually exclusive, so you may want to give them all a try.

Take a short break from each other

Sometimes what you really need when you just can't get along and your emotions are running high is a short time apart — a day or two, a long weekend, maybe even a vacation on your own. At the end of your time apart, you may have a whole new attitude toward your relationship and a renewed commitment to it.

Use the time apart to calm your emotions, assess your situation, and put your marital problems in perspective. Think about whether you are giving your spouse adequate attention and affection. Try to assess why you are not getting along and your role in those difficulties. Analyze the kind of arguments you are having — what you tend to argue about, how often you argue, and when — to determine if any patterns emerge.

Don't use the time to go on a shopping spree or to merely entertain yourself, and avoid short romantic flings. And, don't try to forget your troubles with drugs or alcohol.

If you spend your time apart with a close friend or family member, choose that person carefully. Avoid anyone who does not like your spouse or resents your marriage. If you are looking for advice from the person you will be spending time with, the friend or family member should be impartial and someone whose judgment you trust.

There's a potential downside to spending even a short period of time apart when your marriage is floundering: You, or your spouse, may decide that you enjoy being away from each other so much that you want to make it permanent. Distance doesn't always make the heart grow fonder!

Get marriage counseling

Saving your marriage may require more than just taking a break from your spouse. If only it could always be that easy! It may take reestablishing or improving communication between the two of you so that you can begin a productive dialogue about what has gone wrong in your relationship and why and what you can do to improve things. However, when your marriage is in serious trouble, your emotions can run so high that a calm, rational discussion to identify the roots of your marital problems and what to do about them can be next to impossible. Instead, you either withdraw from each other to nurse your wounds in silence, or argue constantly.

Timing is everything when your marriage is falling apart. Do not wait until your marriage is damaged beyond repair to get professional help.

You may want to try to save your marriage by participating in a weekend-long, intensive "marriage encounter" sponsored by Marriage Savers. Although initially begun by a Catholic priest, most marriage encounter weekends are nondenominational. To learn more about Marriage Savers, call 800-795-LOVE (800-795-5683). Another option is Marriage Enrichment (800-634-8325). Both programs emphasize communication and reflection between couples.

When your marriage has derailed, getting it back on track can be tough because it's difficult if not impossible to step back and objectively assess what's going on and what needs to happen. That's when the help of a trusted and experienced therapist, marriage counselor, or religious adviser can provide invaluable assistance. The right adviser can help create an environment that promotes discussion and mutual understanding. He or she can also offer insights into your problems, help you and your spouse come to an agreement about what do about those problems, and even teach you new marriage skills.

Choose your marriage counselor carefully. Some states set few if any education and training requirements for individuals advertising themselves as marriage counselors.

If money is an issue for you, check your local phone book to see if there is a Family and Child Services, Inc. office nearby. This non-profit organization offers counseling on a sliding-fee scale for couples, families, and individuals. Just knowing that there is a way out of your situation without having to resort to divorce can take some of the pressure off and make it easier for you to address your marital problems.

If your spouse won't go with you to talk to a marriage counselor or religious adviser, go by yourself. You may learn things about yourself as well as new relationship skills that can help improve your current marriage or prepare you for a happier marriage in the future.

Your spouse's unwillingness to attend marriage counseling sessions with you may signal that he or she is no longer committed to your marriage.

Finding a qualified marriage counselor

Working with the right marriage counselor can help save your marriage or, at the very least, save you and your spouse months or even years of anguish trying to decide what to do about the problems in your relationship.

We offer you the following practical tips for locating a qualified marriage counselor:

✔ Seek out a marriage counselor or therapist who is a member of the American Association for Marriage and Family Therapy (AAMFT). To become a member, counselors and therapists must complete a rigorous training program. Call the Association directly for the names and phone numbers of the AAMFT members in your area (202-452-0109) or look in the Yellow Pages of your local phone book under Marriage Counselors or Therapists for AAMFT members.

✔ Get a referral from a friend or family member you trust.

✔ Schedule a get-acquainted meeting with several marriage counselors.

✔ Find out how long each counselor has been practicing marriage or family therapy, what courses he or she has taken in that field, and what professional licenses or certifications he or she has.

✔ Be sure that the person you decide to work with is someone both you and your spouse feel comfortable with. You may have to share intimate and emotionally painful information about yourselves with the counselor that you choose.

✔ To make sure that your counseling is covered by your medical insurance, ask your insurer for a list of the counselors who are preferred service providers.

Look into mediation

When very specific problems are playing havoc with your marriage, *mediation* can be a good way to address them. (For more on the subject of mediation, turn to Chapter 16.) For example, those problems may include arguments over who should do which household chores or how you should share child-care responsibilities.

Mediation is not appropriate if your marriage has a host of problems, or if your problems are emotionally complex. Like the tango, mediation takes two. So, if one of you is unwilling to give mediation a try, it's not a viable option for your marriage.

Mediation is about mutual understanding, cooperation, and problem solving; it's *not* about winning. Your mediation session is facilitated by a trained mediator who will encourage you to calmly discuss your problems and help you work together to identify a mutually acceptable solution to them. The mediator does not take sides, interject opinions, or find a solution for you.

During mediation, you and your spouse each have an opportunity to give your opinions and explain your side of the issue. When one of you is talking, the other is expected to listen without interrupting and remain calm and focused on the subject at hand.

Mediation is not a substitute for therapy. In fact, you may need to spend some time in therapy, by yourself or with your spouse, before you can use mediation successfully.

An important advantage of mediation is its low cost. A mediation session is relatively inexpensive and considerably cheaper than a divorce. To find a mediator experienced at helping couples resolve marriage-related issues, look in your local yellow pages under "Mediation."

Call the Academy of Family Mediators for more information about mediating marital problems and for information about family mediators in your area. You can reach the Academy at 800-292-4236.

When Sticking It Out Isn't an Option

Living together while you try to resolve your marital differences and save your marriage may be an unrealistic option for some people. Instead, you may decide to separate or live apart for a while.

Separating until you make a final decision

Separating can provide you with an opportunity to find out what it's really like to live in separate residences. Meanwhile, the door is still open for getting back together. Separation can also be a prelude to divorce.

Before you separate for even a relatively short period of time, it is a good idea to protect yourself by talking with a family law attorney beforehand, especially if you want spousal or child support. Also, the attorney can warn you about anything you could do to jeopardize your standing in a divorce should your marriage end.

You can opt for either of two types of separation — an *informal separation* or a *legal separation.*

> ✔ Couples who *separate informally* simply begin living apart. This may be an appropriate option if you and your spouse clearly anticipate that your separation is temporary and that you will eventually reconcile and not divorce.

✔ If you view your separation as the first step toward a divorce and have no plans for reconciliation, then a *legal separation* formalized with a legally binding separation agreement is best. A legal separation can be an arrangement that is ordered by the court or that you and your spouse agree to in writing.

A legal separation is often preferable for many financial and legal reasons:

- You formalize the terms of your separation, including whether or not one of you will help support the other financially while you are living apart; how you will deal with the issues of custody, visitation, and child support if you and your spouse share minor children; and how you will divide up the property you own together.

- Having everything spelled out minimizes the potential for conflict while you are separated.

- If one of you reneges on the terms of your separation agreement, it will be easier to get the court's help enforcing it.

- Fewer issues will have to be decided on if you end up eventually getting a divorce.

If you agree to help support your spouse while you are separated and want to claim your spouse as a deduction on your income tax return, you must legally separate.

If you can't work out a negotiated separation agreement with your spouse, the court will order one. Read Chapter 5 for more information about both informal and legal separations.

Dating others while you are separated is usually not a good idea because you can leave yourself open to charges of adultery.

Separating with no plans for divorce

If divorce is not an option for you due to religious, financial, or even health insurance considerations, you can opt for a permanent separation. If you do, formalize your new living arrangement with a written separation agreement.

The process for preparing such an agreement is analogous to what you would do if you were getting divorced. You and your spouse can work together to negotiate the terms of your separation and address, as appropriate, the division of your marital property, child custody and child support, and alimony. You can hire attorneys to help you negotiate an agreement, or to represent you before a judge who will decide the terms of your separation for you. The key difference between separation and divorce is that, when all is said and done, if you only separate, you're still married.

Legal annulments do not equal religious annulments

Legal annulments and religious annulments are two different animals. In some religions, if you divorce and want to remarry, your religion will not recognize your new marriage unless your old marriage is annulled. Religious annulments are most commonly associated with the Roman Catholic faith. If you get a religious annulment, you do not have a legal annulment, and vice versa.

Getting an annulment

A *legal annulment* is a court action that voids your marriage and proclaims that it was never legally valid in the first place. It's like the marriage never happened. Annulments were a much more common option when getting divorced had more of a social stigma attached to it.

Annulments are available in most states, but the process for obtaining one varies. To get a legal annulment, you have to use criteria established by your state to prove to the court that your marriage is legally invalid.

The most common criteria for an annulment include:

- ✔ Your spouse lied to you or misled you in some way and, had you known the truth, you would not have gotten married. For example, you want a family, but your spouse never told you that he is impotent or has AIDS.
- ✔ At the time of your marriage, your spouse was already married.
- ✔ Your spouse was not a legal adult when you got married.
- ✔ You were forced into marriage.
- ✔ Either or both of you were under the influence of alcohol or drugs at the time of the marriage.

An annulment will void your marriage, but if there are young children from that relationship, it will not modify or cancel in any way your parental responsibilities to your children.

Getting a divorce

Your final option when your marriage is failing is to get divorced. The following chapters of this book provide information that can help you get through the divorce process as painlessly as possible.

In some states, if you and your spouse decide to divorce, depending on the grounds for your divorce, you may have to live apart from one another for a certain period of time first, usually from six months to a year.

What to Do If Things Turn Violent

Sometimes when a marriage is falling apart one spouse begins to threaten the other with violence or becomes physically violent. If this happens in your marriage, take the threats or the violence very seriously. Ignoring them can literally be a matter of life or death!

According to 1994 U.S. Census data, female spouses experience ten times as many incidents of violence at the hands of their partners than do male spouses.

Call the police

Although domestic violence is a crime in all states, each state varies in regard to how it deals with the problem. Even so, if you are harmed by your spouse or threatened with harm, call your local police department. One or more police officers will be sent to talk with you and prepare a police report. If it is obvious that you have been abused, the police may arrest your spouse on the spot.

Although they are in a very small minority, some police officers believe that domestic violence is not a matter for the police — it's a private matter between a husband and wife. Therefore, if you call the police for help and the responding officers seem reluctant to prepare a police report, calmly request that one be prepared, and get the officers' names and badge numbers. If the officers continue to refuse, it will be helpful to have this information when you contact their superiors.

Get a protective order against your spouse

A *protective order* is a court order that can make it illegal for your spouse to enter or come within a certain distance of your home, your workplace, or your children's school or day care center. (In some states, you can also get a protective order against someone you are not married to.) If your spouse violates the terms of the protective order, he or she can be arrested. (The court that issues the protective order is a state-level civil court; it may or may not be a family law court.)

After you ask for a protective order, you will have to attend a court hearing. Depending on your state, your spouse may or may not be there. (Your spouse will have an opportunity to tell his or her side of the story at a second hearing.) During the hearing, the judge decides whether to grant you a protective order by talking to you and by reviewing any police reports relating to your situation. Frequently, the judge will order that the violent spouse enter an alcohol or drug addiction rehabilitation program, attend domestic violence prevention classes, and possibly get counseling as well.

It can be easier to get a protective order against your spouse if police reports are on file. The reports can also help if you file criminal charges against your spouse.

In some states, if you need immediate protection and the courts are closed because it's a weekend, evening, or holiday, your local police can issue a *temporary protective order.* However, it stays in effect for just a few days.

If you get a protective order but your spouse refuses to obey it, call the police immediately. In most states, your spouse can be arrested and criminally prosecuted. To make certain that the police will arrest your spouse if the situation requires it, keep a certified copy of the protective order with you at all times.

File criminal charges

If your spouse has already been physically violent with you, in addition to getting a protective order from the court, you should file criminal assault charges against your spouse. Taking both actions will provide you with different and overlapping protections.

Head for a crisis shelter

If you are afraid to remain in your home or apartment despite a protective order against your spouse, consider going to your local domestic abuse shelter. You can take your young children with you. If you are in a crisis situation (your spouse has just beaten you or is threatening to) and you can get to a phone, call the shelter's crisis hot line. The person answering the phone will calm you down, advise you on how to handle the situation, and call the police for you. If you don't have the shelter's crisis hot line memorized, dial 911.

If you are in an abusive relationship, the excellent book *Getting Free: You Can End Abuse and Take Back Your Life* by Ginny Nicarthy (Seal Press Feminist Publishing) can help you break away.

Your state may have an *anti-stalking law* that can help protect you if your spouse is following you, waiting for you outside your residence, making threatening or harassing phone calls, or displaying other behaviors in order to intimidate and frighten you.

Call the Domestic Violence Hotline at 800-799-7233 to find out about resources in your area for victims of domestic abuse and for individuals who are afraid that their spouses may become abusive.

Other safety measures you can take

In addition to memorizing the phone number of your local domestic abuse shelter, here are some other things you can do to protect yourself if your spouse has been abusive in the past and you are afraid you will be harmed again, or if your spouse is threatening you with violence for the first time:

✔ Hide an extra set of keys, some money, and some clothes in a safe place in case you need to get out of your home quickly.

✔ Always have in mind a safe place to go that your spouse does not know about.

✔ If you have children, tell them that if you say a certain "code word" that's a signal for them to run to a neighbor's house or call the police.

✔ Tell everyone you know about the abuse. Sharing this information with others diminishes the power of some abusers.

✔ Join a support group. The people on the other end of the National Domestic Violence Hotline can help you find a group in your area or you can call your local domestic abuse shelter for information. Joining a group may give you the resolve you need to deal with your situation in a decisive manner.

✔ Testify in court against your spouse.

Chapter 2

Getting Smart about Your Family's Money Matters

. . . .

In This Chapter

▶ Knowing what your family owns and owes

▶ Getting educated about money management issues

▶ Understanding the importance of having your own credit

▶ Staying employable

. . . .

*W*e'd all like to believe that till-death-do-us-part wedding vows guarantee that every marriage will last forever. But these days the reality is that one in two marriages ends in divorce. So it makes sense for every married and about-to-be-married person to be prepared not only for the possibility that his or her marriage may end in divorce but also for the financial consequences that can follow. At a minimum, your preparation should include the following:

✔ Becoming familiar with your family's finances

✔ Learning how to manage your money

✔ Working to maintain a positive credit history in your own name

✔ Building and maintaining marketable job skills

Understandably, you may view marrying with the possibility of divorce looming over your happy union as pretty cynical. But, when you understand how *not* being prepared for the end of your marriage can affect you and your children, you'll be convinced that the advice we give you on what you can do to minimize the impact of divorce on your life is wise (albeit unromantic).

Consider this: Your lack of preparation may force you to stay in a bad marriage because you can't support yourself or because you don't have the financial resources to live on your own. And, without the right preparation, you may be at a disadvantage when it comes time to work out the financial details of your split. Plus, when you are single again, you may have a hard time building a financially secure life for yourself.

If practice makes perfect when it comes to being prepared for life after divorce, Elizabeth Taylor Hilton Wilder Fisher Burton Burton (they *were* married and divorced twice) Warner Fortensky would have a lock on it. But even glamorous Hollywood legends can benefit from the information in this chapter, which tells you how to increase your financial savvy so that you can be a full partner in your marriage, ready for whatever married life brings to you, including divorce.

This chapter also offers advice about protecting yourself from the financial fallout of divorce and preparing to earn your own living or make more money after a divorce. If you are a stay-at-home spouse or if you put your career on the back burner during your marriage, pay special attention to this information.

If you think a divorce may be in your future, the sooner you can put the advice in this chapter into action, the better prepared you'll be, financially and legally, for life on your own.

Traditionally, married women were less apt to work outside the home than married men, relied on their husbands for financial support, and tended to take a back seat to them when it came to financial affairs. Although things have changed dramatically over the past few decades, many women, regardless of their income and education, continue to view money matters as a "male thing." Often, a wife's lack of financial savvy costs her dearly when she gets divorced. Statistics show that women are more apt than men to have a lower standard of living after divorce. The reasons for this difference in their standard of living are several: Women tend to have lower-paying jobs, are more apt to end up with the children, or may lack the financial know-how or credit record they need to build a good life for themselves after they are divorced.

Between 1970 and 1990, the divorce rate for women between the ages of 40 and 50 increased 62 percent! Because the rate of remarriage for women in this same age bracket is lower than for men, it is especially important that older women are knowledgeable about their finances and have their own credit.

It Takes Two to Manage (Or Mismanage) Money

Don't rely entirely on your spouse to pay your household bills, reconcile your checkbook, make investment decisions, and so forth. You need to share these responsibilities. At the very least, you should know what bills need to be paid, how much is in your checkbook, and where your money is invested. Here's why:

- Your spouse may resent having to shoulder all the responsibility for managing your family's finances. This resentment can cause troubles in your marriage.

- Your spouse may not be a good money manager. You and your children may be harmed by your spouse's bad decisions. In addition, your spouse's financial mismanagement may damage *your* credit history, not just your spouse's.

- If your spouse becomes incapacitated by a serious illness or accident, you may be unprepared to manage your family's finances and, as a result, you may make costly financial mistakes.

- You'll have fewer arguments over money because both you and your spouse will be fully aware of your financial situation.

- If your spouse is engaging in an extramarital affair or has a problem with gambling, drinking, drugs, or even 1-900 phone calls — all of which cost money — you are more apt to feel the drain on your pocketbook if you share financial responsibilities.

- If you and your spouse negotiate your own divorce agreement, you may not be prepared to make good decisions.

- If your divorce is not amicable and your attorney lacks the information he or she needs to handle your divorce, that information will have to be acquired through the *discovery process,* which makes your divorce more expensive. (The formal discovery process helps the parties of a divorce get the facts of the lawsuit so that neither side takes the other by surprise. The process can involve depositions and interrogatories, in which individuals are questioned by attorneys, the production of documents, and psychological examinations, among other things. To find out more about the discovery process, see Chapter 4.)

- If your spouse manages your family finances and initiates the divorce, he or she is free to do things with your finances that can harm you. For example, your spouse can waste your marital property — cash and other assets that you own together — or hide them from you so that they aren't included in your divorce negotiations. For more on hiding assets, read Chapter 10.

- After your divorce, you may be without the financial resources and information you need to build a new life for yourself.

A Maryland woman spent so much time chatting online — as much as 21 hours a day — that she completely neglected her family. A victim of Internet Addiction Disorder (yes, it has a name), she's now divorced. Guess who got stuck with her online bills?

The daughter of the "R" in H&R Block, learned the hard way just how dangerous it can be if a married woman does not take charge of her own finances. She trusted her first husband to manage her money, including her trust fund, but he lost a substantial amount of it in risky investments. After she divorced him, she not only mismanaged *her* money but was also hit with huge IRS bills for taxes her former spouse had not paid. Faced with the depletion of her trust fund, she finally took the time to became financially savvy. Along the way, she also wrote a book called *Prince Charming Isn't Coming* (Viking) to help other women avoid similar financial nightmares.

Financial Fundamentals: What You Must Do First

To play an active, informed role in the management of your family's finances, you must have certain information about your household finances, as well as basic money management skills and the other resources important to your financial life and well-being.

Take an accounting of what you have and what you owe

You don't have to be a CPA to take an accounting of your family's financial worth. Get yourself a notebook and make a list of the following:

- Your total household income and the source(s) of that income.

- The checking and savings account numbers that you and your spouse use and the bank(s) in which those accounts are held.

- Your family's significant assets and the approximate value of each.

- How your *joint assets* are titled or deeded — joint tenancy with right of survivorship, tenancy by the entirety, tenancy in common, or community property (which are described in the sidebar "Joint property and your rights to it," later in this chapter).

An *asset* is a thing of value. Depending on the type of asset, you can use it to purchase something else, you can sell it, or you can use the asset to collateralize a loan. An asset can be tangible — such as cash, real estate, vehicles, antiques, fine jewelry, or art — or intangible — such as stocks, bonds, or retirement benefits.

- Your family's debts — whom you owe and how much.

- ✔ Where financial and legal documents important to your family are stored, including bank records, tax returns, wills and other estate planning documents, titles and deeds, loan agreements, insurance policies, and documentation pertaining to any IRAs, stocks, bonds, and mutual funds you or your spouse may own, as well as paperwork related to the retirement plans either of you participate in.

- ✔ What your credit histories say about you and your spouse.

- ✔ The names, addresses, and phone numbers of your family's CPA, banker, attorney, financial adviser, and stock broker.

- ✔ Basic information about your spouse's business, if your spouse is self-employed, including its legal form, assets, and liabilities.

Have an understanding with your spouse that you agree to fully share all of your household's financial information with each other and that all financial records are kept in a place that is readily accessible to both of you.

Make sure that any assets owned by you and your spouse are in both of your names.

Draw up a spending plan and stick to it

Knowing how to manage your debts and assets is essential so that you have enough money to pay your bills each month, don't take on too much debt, and accomplish the most with any money you may have left over. Being a good money manager means knowing how to do the following:

- ✔ Develop and manage a household spending plan. (See the sidebar "Savvy budgeting tactics" later in this chapter to figure out more about spending plans, and see the table coming up for a sample form designed to help you keep track of your finances.)

- ✔ Manage your checking account. If you don't keep track of how much money is in your checking account by recording each check you write and recording all account deposits and withdrawals and then reconciling your account balance with your monthly bank statements, you can lose money in "bounced" check fees.

- ✔ Use credit wisely. Although credit can help you purchase necessities you couldn't afford otherwise, using credit too often or not understanding the terms of credit before you apply for a credit card or get a loan from a bank, credit union, or finance company can land you in the poorhouse.

- ✔ Make sound investment decisions with stocks, bonds, mutual funds, real estate, and so on. Even if you use professional stock brokers, financial counselors, and real estate agents to help you manage important investments, you should know enough about your investments to intelligently evaluate their advice.

Sample Form for a Household Spending and Savings Plan

Fixed Monthly Expenses	Dollar Amount
Rent or mortgage	_____
Car payments	_____
Other installment loans	_____
Insurance	_____
Children's allowances/activities	_____
Day care	_____
Monthly dues	_____
Cable TV and subscriptions	_____
Total	$ _____

Variable Monthly Expenses*	Dollar Amount
Groceries	_____
Utilities	_____
Telephone	_____
Gasoline	_____
Clothing	_____
Credit card payments	_____
Out-of-pocket medical/dental	_____
Magazines and books	_____
Church or charitable donations	_____
Haircuts and grooming supplies	_____
Online service expenses	_____
Restaurant meals	_____
Miscellaneous	_____
Total	$ _____

Estimate the entire year's expenses and divide by 12 for the monthly amount.

Periodic Expenses*	Dollar Amount
Tuition	_____
Auto registration and license	_____
Insurance	_____

Periodic Expenses*	Dollar Amount
Taxes	_____
Household repairs	_____
Birthday and holiday gifts	_____
Entertaining	_____
Subscriptions	_____
Total	$ _____

*Estimate the entire year's expenses and divide by 12 for the monthly amount.

Total Monthly Household Expenses (The three previous totals from this table combined)	$ _____
Net Monthly Household Income	$ _____
Surplus or Deficit (Net Household Income minus Total Monthly Expenses)	$ _____
Surplus Allotted for Savings	$ _____
Surplus Allotted for Investments	$ _____

For help developing and using a budget, pick up *The Budget Kit* by Judy Lawrence (Dearborn Financial Publishing, Inc.). You can also purchase a companion CD-ROM for Windows.

And now for a quick lesson in property law

When you get divorced, your state's property laws entitle you and your spouse to a share of the assets you acquired — together or separately — during your marriage and to a share of the income you both earned while you were married. Those assets and income are called your *marital property*. Exactly how your marital property is eventually divided up depends in part on whether you live in an equitable distribution state or a community property state (the two types are distinguished later in this section).

No matter what state you live in, property and income you bring to your marriage are considered your separate and individual property. That property is yours to keep in your divorce.

Savvy budgeting tactics

A spending plan, better known as a budget, is a basic money management tool. It helps you plan how to spend your household income each month so that you don't come up short when it's time to pay your bills and also have enough left over to cover your day-to-day living expenses. A spending plan also helps you allocate income to help pay for things that are important to you and your family, such as a down payment on a home, your children's college education, family vacations, a new car, or your retirement.

Developing a spending plan isn't difficult. It's simply a matter of recording your monthly household expenses, tallying them up, and then comparing them to your monthly household income.

To get a comprehensive picture of your monthly expenses, review your checkbook register, your bank statements for automatic debits to your account, your ATM withdrawals, and your cash receipts. To get a true picture of your expenses, look at several months' worth of information.

Some expenses are fixed, whereas others are variable or change every month, and other expenses occur periodically throughout the year. (To budget for periodic expenses, divide the total annual cost of each periodic item by 12. That gives you a monthly cost to include in your budget.)

Your total net monthly household income is the actual amount of money available to spend (gross income less taxes and other deductions). That income can include wages and salaries, investment income, or child support.

Try using a form like the one in the table in this chapter to record your income and expenses. If the total amount of your monthly expenses exceeds your total household income each month, you need to reduce your expenses to avoid serious financial trouble.

If your budget shows that you have a surplus of cash at the end of the month, then you can pay off your debts more quickly, put more money into savings and investments, or spend some of the money on things you or your family really want or need.

One final comment about spending plans: Developing one may not be difficult, but living with one can be really tough if you don't exercise self-control. In the end, a spending plan is only as good and as useful as the discipline you put behind it.

Share and share alike

If you live in a *community property* state, each of you owns an undivided one-half interest in the value of your marital property regardless of whether your income alone purchased most of what you own, whether your spouse made significantly more than you did, or whether, throughout your marriage, your spouse stayed home to care for your young children. However, in a divorce, a judge can order that you receive more or less than your one-half interest (see the next section "Fairness is relative"). You and your spouse can agree to something different, too.

Most states are equitable distribution states except for the following nine, which are community property states:

Arizona	New Mexico
California	Texas
Idaho	Washington
Louisiana	Wisconsin
Nevada	

If you live in a community property state, a creditor has the right to collect from your share of your marital property if your spouse fails to pay on the debts he or she acquired during your marriage.

Fairness is relative

Equitable distribution states use the concept of "what is fair" to decide how a couple's marital property and debts should be divided between them when they get divorced. "What is fair" varies from divorce to divorce, although each equitable distribution state uses certain criteria to guide the division. The most-common criteria include

- ✔ How much each of you earns and could earn in the future
- ✔ Your current standard of living
- ✔ The value of the separate property each of you may own and the value of your marital property
- ✔ The contribution each of you made to your marriage (by the way, being a full-time homemaker or stay-at-home parent has financial value)
- ✔ The employee benefits to which each of you may be entitled
- ✔ The length of your marriage
- ✔ Your age and your health
- ✔ Whether or not you have children from your marriage who are *minors* (children under the age of 18 or 21, depending on the state) and your custody arrangements for those children

If your divorce is a fault divorce, judges in some states will take that fact into consideration when deciding how your marital property and debt should be split between you and your spouse. Those states that do consider fault will seriously penalize the spouse at fault.

Judges in community property states may use these same factors in determining whether divorcing spouses should leave their marriage with more or less than their presumptive one-half share of marital property.

If you and your spouse while living in a community property state acquire property in that state, and then move to an equitable distribution state, the property you take with you from the first state to the second is presumed to be community property and would be treated as such if you later divorced. The opposite would be true if you moved from an equitable distribution state to a community property state. Obviously, the more often you move between different types of states during your marriage and the more you acquire in each of those states, the more complicated the details of your property settlement agreement will be if you divorce.

Some equitable distribution states believe that a spouse's contribution to the end of a marriage should influence the division of marital property in some cases. For example, if your marriage is ending because you committed adultery, you may end up with less marital property that you may be entitled to otherwise depending on your state.

Both community and separate property states treat inheritances and gifts a spouse may receive during marriage as separate, not marital property. How a personal injury cash settlement is treated in a divorce depends on the state; some view the money as separate property and others do not.

If you *commingle* property that you bring to your marriage you may unwittingly convert it into marital property! Commingling happens when you mix your separate property with your spouse's, or when you mix your separate property with marital property. For example, you and your spouse open a joint bank account and deposit your separate funds in the account. Then, you use the money to pay your joint bills or to buy things that you both want. Your funds are now commingled.

Joint property and your rights to it

You can own joint assets in any number of ways. How you own that joint property affects your rights when it comes time to split it up.

- ✔ **Joint tenancy with the right of survivorship.** If your spouse dies, his or her share automatically goes to you, no matter what your spouse's will or trust says, and vice versa.

- ✔ **Tenancy by the entirety.** Similar to joint tenancy, but only spouses can own property this way.

- ✔ **Tenancy in common.** You have no legal claim to your spouse's share of the asset

and vice versa. Therefore, your spouse can do what he or she wants with his or her share of the asset — give it away, sell it, trade it, use it to collateralize or secure a loan, or encumber it with some sort of claim.

- ✔ **Community property.** Only certain states permit this kind of joint ownership. In those states, each of you has an undivided one-half interest in the property you acquire and the income you earn during your marriage, no matter whose name is on the ownership papers or who earns the most money.

How to Learn What You Need to Know

If you review the list of "financial-ought-to-knows" in the previous section of this chapter and come up lacking, don't panic. You can get up to speed in several ways. Start with your spouse. Ask him or her to sit down and describe your family's finances in as much detail as possible, show you where key documents and other important records are kept, and answer your questions.

If your spouse seems threatened by your sudden interest in the family finances, try alleviating that concern with an explanation of why you want to know. Explain that if you know more about your family's finances, your spouse will not have to shoulder all the burden for managing your money. Also, you will be better able to make wise decisions for the family if your spouse becomes incapacitated or dies.

Review your family's financial records and documents. Don't overlook information stored on your home computer. Many households use Quicken or some other personal finance software to help them manage their money.

If you don't know where your family's tax returns are filed and your spouse won't tell you, you can obtain copies by writing to the IRS, assuming that you filed joint returns. The IRS has a Web site for taxpayer assistance, with specific information depending on the state you live in. Check out www.irs.ustreas.gov/prod.

Money management and personal investment classes are a good resource for increasing your financial skills and knowledge. Your local college or university may offer such classes for little cost. Also, many investment companies and financial advisers offer investment seminars as a way to attract new clients or develop additional business from their current client base. These seminars are usually free, and no purchase is required. However, these advisers often assume that their audience has a better-than-average knowledge of investing, not to mention better-than-average money to invest.

Another possible source of financial education is the nonprofit Consumer Credit Counseling Service (CCCS) office in your area. Some of these offices offer low-cost to no-cost money management classes, including classes on how to develop and use a budget.

If you, or you and your spouse, owe a lot of money and are having trouble paying your bills, CCCS staff may be able to help you work out more affordable payment plans with your creditors so that you can get out of debt. The less debt you have going into a divorce, the less potential for problems after your divorce. If you don't find a listing for a CCCS office in your local phone directory, call (800) 388-2227.

If you can't find the class that fits your needs, call your family banker, CPA, broker, or financial adviser.

Magazines such as *Money* and *Kiplinger's Personal Finance Magazine* offer solid, easy-to-understand financial information and advice on a wide variety of consumer-related subjects. Although you won't become another Warren Buffett just by reading an issue or two, over time, you can increase your consumer IQ about subjects like choosing a bankcard, buying a mutual fund, living on a budget, buying a car, purchasing real estate, and avoiding consumer scams.

Your local YWCA or community college may offer the Women's Financial Information Program (WFIP). The program provides middle-aged and older women with financial skills and know-how to build their money management self-confidence.

Bookstore shelves are overflowing with titles about personal finance and investing. Even if you're a financial neophyte, you can find many books written for people just like you.

We don't mean to be self-serving but *Personal Finance For Dummies* by Eric Tyson (IDG Books Worldwide, Inc.) is a darn good book! We also recommend *Making the Most of Your Money: A Comprehensive Guide to Financial Planning* by Jane Bryant Quinn (Simon & Schuster) and *Your Wealth Building Years: Financial Planning for 18 to 38 Year-Olds* by Adrienne Berg (Newmarket).

These days, every network morning show seems to feature a regular segment on money management. Also, a number of cable networks are completely devoted to personal finance and investment subjects, including CNN Financial and CNBC (Consumer News and Business Channel). The Lifetime Network airs a regular financial program called *Bloomberg Personal.*

If you would prefer to get your financial education by staring at a computer screen instead of a TV screen, many excellent Web sites are devoted to personal finance issues. Here are a couple of the better ones:

- ✔ The Financial Pipeline (www.finpipe.com). The goal of this site is "to provide financial information to all levels of consumers and investors." A unique feature of the site is that consumers can obtain more in-depth information about the subject they're interested in by clicking on a <u>KNOWMORE</u> bar.

- ✔ Consumer World (www.consumerworld.org). Assuming that you are not put off by this Web site's lack of aesthetics, its more than 1,500 links will lead you to a wide variety of consumer information.

- ✔ The Federal Trade Commission (FTC) publishes numerous easy-to-understand publications designed to help everyday people understand their legal rights when it comes to spending money and using credit. The text of more than 100 publications is available at this site. Point your browser to www.ftc.gov.

> ✔ Go to the Moneyblows page to learn about some of the best books on working, earning, investing, and spending. You can also find specific information on consumer finance, debt, investments, and tax issues at this Web site. Go to www.moneyblows.com.

Although a financial seminar or adviser can certainly inform you of the pros and cons of different money management philosophies, you and your spouse may not agree about things like how much to spend and how much to save and what is an acceptable amount of credit card debt. A marriage counselor can help you resolve those disagreements. Differences about money can affect the quality and financial stability of your marriage and can impact your life long after your divorce.

Maintaining Your Employability

Even though two-income families are becoming the norm in today's society, many women, and a growing number of men, choose to be full-time home-makers and stay-at-home parents for at least some point during their marriage. If you are one of them, be aware that in today's fast-changing work world, your job skills can quickly become rusty or even obsolete and you may lose many of your professional contacts as well.

To protect yourself while you are out of the job market, do what you can to keep your job skills up-to-date, and also develop new ones, if possible, even if you have no immediate plans to work outside of the home. You may also want to begin preparing for a new career. Your local trade school, private or community college, or university are all potential sources of training and education.

At the very least, learn how to use a computer, if you are not already computer literate. Most white-collar and many blue-collar jobs assume or require that you have computer skills.

Don't lose yourself in your marriage by always making your needs secondary to your family's. Taking care of and developing yourself is not necessarily selfish. By doing so, you gain the confidence and the resources — both inner and financial — to rescue a failing marriage, end a bad marriage, or take care of yourself if you are widowed. In other words, hope for the best but be prepared for the worst.

Working part-time is another option for building and retaining your job skills and professional contacts. A part-time job helps you build a résumé. Plus the money you earn can fund a checking or savings account in your own name, provide extra income to help pay your family's bills, help finance your children's education, or even underwrite monthly dates with your spouse.

Being prepared to enter the work world as quickly as possible has assumed greater importance now that life-long spousal support has virtually become a thing of the past. The more quickly you can land a good job and earn a good living, the better off you will be.

Building a Positive Credit History

Your *credit history* is a record of how you manage the credit accounts that you maintain in your name or that you share with your spouse. Those accounts may include national bank cards, bank loans, debit cards, lines of credit, and so on.

One or more of the "Big Three" national credit bureaus — Equifax, Experian (formerly TRW), and Trans Union — has your credit history stored in a computerized database; smaller regional or local credit bureaus may also be maintaining a credit file on you.

When you apply for a bank loan, credit card, or some other form of credit, the creditor reviews your credit history to make sure that you show no signs of problems and that you do not have too much credit. If problems do exist, obtaining credit at reasonable terms — or any credit at all — may be difficult.

Creditors look not only at how much credit you are servicing but also at your credit limits. In other words, if you have a credit card with a credit limit of $1,000, even if you are not carrying a balance on that card, the fact that you *could* run one up is something that creditors consider when evaluating whether or not to extend credit.

Having good credit in your own name (not just *joint credit* that you share with your spouse) plus your own trouble-free credit history are essential in preparing for the possibility of divorce. Here are some of the most important reasons why:

- ✔ Without your own credit history, it can be difficult — maybe even impossible — for you to obtain a bank loan or a credit card, purchase a home, or rent a car, if you get divorced. Also, because some employers and insurance companies review credit histories as part of their decision-making process, you may even find it tough to get the insurance or job you need! Although you can build your own credit history after your divorce, the process takes several years.

- ✔ When you and your spouse share joint credit, both of you are legally responsible for those accounts. That means that if your spouse mismanages that credit, your credit history, as well as your spouse's, is damaged.

- ✔ If your divorce agreement requires that your spouse pay off certain debts you were both liable for and if your ex-spouse fails to meet that obligation, the creditor can try to collect the money from you.

Selecting the best credit card

If you plan on paying your credit card balance in full each month, go for a card that offers you a *grace period* of at least 25 days. (A grace period is the time you have to pay the card balance before you're charged interest.)

If you expect to, at times, carry a balance on your credit card, shop for one with a low annual percentage rate (APR). You should also pay attention to how that APR is calculated. Most companies base their APR on an *average daily balance,* including new purchases. That method works out better for the credit card company than it does for you. The most consumer-friendly APR calculation method is the *adjusted daily balance method*. The average daily balance *not* including purchases method is second best. Steer clear of cards that use the *two cycle average daily balance* method to calculate APRs — they cost you a bundle in finance charges. Information about the APR calculation method should be included in a credit card offer's fine print.

Don't automatically go for the card with the highest credit limit. Using a credit card to finance a major purchase is an expensive financing alternative. You are better off saving up for what you want to buy or getting a bank loan. Also, having a high credit limit can jeopardize your opportunity to obtain an important loan for other credit in the future.

Don't be tempted by credit card offers touting special benefits such as product rebates, frequent flier miles, and so on. To take advantage of these offers, you'll probably have to charge a lot on the credit card first, and some cards with added benefits tack on high APRs, a short grace period, or other unfavorable terms of credit.

Avoid cards with a high annual fee or an annual fee that escalates after a certain period of time.

Avoid cards that charge you high penalties if you don't make your payments on time, or if you don't use your card often enough.

Be cautious of credit card offers with especially low interest rates. The rate may be intended to do nothing more than get you to agree to begin using the card or to transfer the balance on your current card to the new card. Frequently, the low rate lasts for just a short period. When that period ends, you may be charged a much higher rate of interest.

Steer clear of cards that increase the annual rate you pay if you are late with your payment or if you exceed your credit limit.

To obtain an up-to-date list of the credit cards with the lowest interest rates, contact CardTrak at (800) 344-7714. As of this writing the list costs $5.

✔ If, prior to your divorce, you or your spouse close all of your joint accounts and you later tell those creditors that you would like credit with them in your own name, they can require that you reapply for credit if the joint accounts were based on your spouse's income. If you don't already have a credit history that reflects credit in your own name, you will likely be denied the credit you want.

Some single men and women with their own credit and bank accounts close them when they marry, open joint bank accounts with their spouses, and apply for joint credit. There is no law saying that, when you get married, you and your spouse must merge your finances.

 If you live in a community property state — Arizona, California, Idaho, Louisiana, Nevada, New Mexico, Texas, Washington, or Wisconsin — you and your spouse are viewed as an economic unit. Therefore, if your spouse fails to pay one of his or her individual debts, the creditor can try to get paid by coming after *your* share of the marital property, and not just your spouse's share.

Establishing a Credit History of Your Own

Before you begin the credit-history process, request a copy of your credit report from each of the Big Three credit bureaus (listed in the previous section of this chapter). It would also be good to know what's in your spouse's credit report, but your spouse has to agree to order it. However, your credit reports alone provide you with information on most of your joint debts as well as your individual ones. They just won't tell you about your spouse's individual or separate debts.

Review your credit reports carefully for errors and omissions. If you find any problems, complete the investigation request form that should have come with each report by following the instructions on the form.

Contacting the Big Three

You can order a copy of your credit report from each of the Big Three credit bureaus by calling any of the following phone numbers (when you call, you hear recorded ordering instructions):

Experian, 800-682-7654

Trans Union, 610-690-4909

Equifax, 800-685-1111

If you have ever been denied credit, employment, or insurance due either in whole, or in part, to information in your credit report, you are entitled to a free copy of your report. Otherwise, you probably have to pay for any reports you order.

A credit report costs around $8 in most states. A few states require that credit reporting agencies provide state residents as many as two free credit reports a year. Some states have also capped the price of a credit report at something less than the usual $8 fee.

Two good resources for building a credit history are worth checking out. These books tell you how to read your credit report, how to make good credit decisions, and how to deal with problems in your credit record: *The Credit Repair Kit,* 3rd Edition, by John Ventura (Dearborn Financial Publishing, Inc.) and *The Ultimate Credit Handbook* by Geri Detweiler (Plume).

If all of your credit is in your spouse's name, request that each of the Big Three credit bureaus establish a credit file in your own name, too (Susan Smith, not Mrs. Robert Smith, for example). If you live in a community property state, you should also ask that your history reflect the payment history on the credit accounts in your spouse's name that you are contractually liable for. Ask the creditors to begin reporting information on these accounts in your name as well as your spouse's. Assuming that these accounts have positive payment histories, having them in your credit file may help you build your own credit history.

If you used to have credit in your maiden name, make sure that this credit is a part of your credit history. If it's not, ask that the credit bureau add that information.

If some of the joint accounts in your credit history reflect late payments or even defaults due to your spouse's mismanagement of those accounts, try to distance yourself from that negative information by preparing a 100-word statement explaining the reason for the negatives. Send the statement to each of the Big Three credit bureaus (see the nearby sidebar, "Contacting the Big Three"). The statement you provide becomes a permanent part of your credit record.

Being an *authorized user* on your spouse's accounts will *not* help you build your own credit history. That's because being an authorized user means that you get to use the credit but you have no legal responsibility for the account.

The federal Equal Credit Opportunity Act (ECOA) says that joint accounts opened prior to June 1, 1977 must be reported to credit bureaus in both your names.

After you clear up any credit record problems and contact the credit bureaus about reporting certain accounts in your name as well as your spouse's, continue the credit-building process by applying for a small ($500, for example) *unsecured* bank loan. If you can't get one, apply for a *cash-secured* loan. (If you are approved for an unsecured loan, the bank's only requirement is that you promise to repay what you borrow according to the terms of the loan. But, if you can obtain only a cash-secured loan, you are required to keep a certain amount of cash in a savings account at the bank or to purchase a certificate of deposit [CD] from the bank. If you don't pay off the loan, the bank can take the money in your savings account or your CD as payment.)

Ordinarily, when a consumer is building a solid credit history in his or her own name, the consumer pays back the loan over a period of 12 months. However, depending on your marital situation, you may not have that much time. Therefore, let the degree of crisis in your marriage dictate how quickly you pay back what you borrow.

If the bank won't loan you money without a cosigner, don't ask your spouse to cosign the note — you will end up linking your credit to your spouse's. Ask a relative or close friend to cosign instead.

After you pay off a loan, you should take a few more steps to secure a good credit history:

- ✔ Order a copy of your credit report from each of the Big Three credit bureaus to make sure that they reflect your loan payments. If they don't, ask the bank to report your payment history to the credit bureau it works with. Next, apply for a retail store charge card and an oil and gas card in your own name. These are relatively easy types of credit to get. Don't charge many purchases on these cards and make all of your payments on time.

- ✔ You may have to apply for a second loan, one that is unsecured or that is not cosigned, before you can get a credit card in your own name.

- ✔ After you establish a good payment history with your retail charge card, and oil and gas charge cards, apply for a national bankcard. If the bank that granted you your loan offers a bankcard at competitive rates, apply for it.

- ✔ If you can't qualify for a regular national bankcard, apply for a secured card. You will have to collateralize or secure the bankcard by opening a savings account with the company issuing you the card, or by purchasing a certificate of deposit (CD) from it. If you default on your payments, the company can withdraw money from your account balance or cash in your CD to cover your charges. Make the secured card a stepping stone to an unsecured card by not exceeding your credit limit and by making all of your account payments on time.

For an up-to-date list of banks that offer secured and unsecured bankcards, call Bankcard Holders of America at 540-389-5445.

The Credit Choice Web site has information that can help you find the right credit card to meet your needs. Surf over to

www.creditchoice.com/index.htm.

Use your full name, not your spouse's name, whenever you apply for new credit. For example, avoid Mrs. Robert Smith, and use Ms. or Mrs. Lois Smith.

Chapter 3

Family Law Basics

• •

In This Chapter

▶ Covering the evolution of family law

▶ Understanding the legal side of marriage obligations

▶ Finding out the role of state family law courts

▶ Examining your parental rights and obligations

• •

*T*he rules of the game for marriage, separation, and divorce, as well as those that apply to parent-child relationships, fall under the heading of *family law*. Among other things, family law establishes the ground rules for what makes a marriage or divorce legal, sets out the obligations of one spouse to another, and defines the basic responsibilities that parents have toward their children, such as supporting them financially even after the parents' marriage has ended.

This chapter provides an overview of the laws that apply to beginning and ending a marriage. It also offers a brief historical perspective on how those laws have evolved to accommodate and reflect society's changing values. This chapter also explains how family laws can vary significantly from state to state.

Check out Family Law Advisor at www.divorcenet.com for easy-to-understand advice and information on a variety of divorce-related legal and emotional issues. Although some of the material is specific to the State of Massachusetts, most of the information at this Web site is applicable to anyone getting divorced (in fact, the site offers a state-by-state resource center). New material is posted each month.

Changing Laws for Changing Times

In the past few decades we've witnessed dramatic changes in our society's life-styles, values, and attitudes. Among those changes was the movement of women out of the house and into the work world. In turn, fathers began playing a more active role in the care and raising of their children. As a result, lawmakers and family law courts began to reevaluate their attitudes toward both child custody and alimony.

In response to the changing roles of women in our society and other changes that began in the 1960s, states began revising their laws in regard to families, and judges began interpreting existing family laws in new ways. For example, as a growing number of women became less financially dependent on their husbands, fewer ex-wives began receiving life-long alimony or any alimony at all. (Today, alimony of any kind is less common in divorces, and men as well as women may receive it.)

Changes in custody and child support decisions

Prior to the early 1970s, a couple's having minor children was a heavy deterrent to divorce. Therefore, most divorced couples tended to be childless, or their children were grown adults. But, by the 1970s, all that had changed and since then most divorces have involved minor children.

Another change that occurred during the '70s was that lawmakers and courts moved away from the presumption that mothers should get sole custody of their children in a divorce and began basing custody decisions on what was in the best interest of a couple's children. This change opened the door to a wider variety of custody arrangements, including fathers and mothers sharing custody and fathers having sole custody. In fact, in nearly all states, mothers and fathers are now presumed to have an equal right to the custody of their children.

Attitudes toward child support also changed as a result of what was occurring in society. Before the early 1970s, fathers were generally presumed to have an obligation to support their minor children. However, with a growing number of women earning their own money, the courts began to consider the support of minor children a responsibility of both men and women.

The option of joint custody is available in all 50 U.S. states except South Carolina.

Fault versus no-fault divorces

Another change in family law that we've witnessed is the emergence of the *no-fault divorce*. This kind of divorce allows couples to divorce more quickly, less expensively, and (it's hoped) with less rancor than when fault is involved.

One state's strategy for saving marriages

The State of Louisiana has become so serious about reducing its divorce rate that in the summer of 1997 its legislature passed a law requiring that couples preparing for marriage opt for either a traditional marital contract or a new *covenant contract*.

Couples who sign this new, more-binding kind of contract agree to stay married and not get divorced unless they can prove that their spouse has committed adultery, has physically or sexually abused the other partner or one of

the children, has abandoned the marriage for at least one year, or has been convicted of a felony and been imprisoned. Furthermore, before they can divorce, the couple that signs a covenant contract must prove that they have been separated for at least two years, unless there is a proven adultery.

No-fault divorce is still available to couples in Louisiana who do not sign this new type of marital contract.

In most states, proving fault used to be an economic boon for the spouse making the allegation when it came time to divide up a couple's marital property and make spousal support decisions. Today, however, fault is less apt to influence the outcome of a divorce and judges are more likely to recognize that just as it takes two to build and sustain a marriage, it usually takes two to ruin one as well.

Most states currently permit no-fault divorces, but an effort is being made in some states to swing the pendulum back to the days when a *fault divorce* was the only option. The goal of those who support fault divorce is to reduce the divorce rate by making it harder and less pleasant to end a marriage. Proposals have also been made to impose waiting periods on couples who want to get divorced.

FindLaw's family law site links you up to literally thousands of organizations, laws, publications, and other family law resources. Plus, it has a keyword option that makes it easy to locate specific information. Bookmark this one at www.findlaw.com/01topics/15family/.

Getting Hitched

People typically think of marriage as a romantic relationship and most marriages do start out that way. However, marriage is also a financial and a legal relationship. In fact, the financial and legal aspects of marriage last long after the romance dies, and those aspects of marriage become paramount if you decide to legally separate or get divorced.

A license to marry

Whether you get married in a church or synagogue, in a courthouse, or by an Elvis impersonator in a Las Vegas wedding chapel, to be legally married you must obtain a *marriage license* from your state and file it with the appropriate government office — usually your county clerk's office — within a certain number of days after your marriage. Your marriage license represents your state's permission to marry.

A common law marriage represents an exception to the licensing requirement. More about this informal way of getting hitched is covered in the sidebar "Common law marriages: More common that you may think" on the following page.

To obtain a marriage license you must meet some very basic state-established standards:

✔ In most instances, you also have to be a legal adult (18 or 21 years of age, depending on your state), and you have to take blood tests in order to prove that you do not have certain diseases.

✔ You will not be issued a marriage license if you are planning to marry a close relative such as your parent, sibling, grandparent, child, grandchild, great-grandchild, aunt or uncle, or niece or nephew, nor will you get one if you are already married to someone else — that's called *bigamy*.

Depending on your state, you may also be barred from tying the knot with your first cousin, stepchild, or stepparent, among other relatives.

Your contractual obligations

After you sign and file your marriage license, you and your spouse have a legally binding marital contract with one another. With that contract you agree to assume a number of important financial and legal obligations to one another. The contract also entitles you to certain legal rights as spouses. Some of those obligations and rights include the following:

✔ You have an obligation to support one another financially.

Your state's laws do not say how you must provide the financial support or how much support you have to provide. Furthermore, if you are a stay-at-home spouse, your state likely views the work you perform in taking care of your home, raising your children, or supporting your spouse's career as contributing financially to your marriage, although not all states do.

Common law marriages: More common than you may think

Surprise! You may be married even if you didn't tie the knot in a formal civil or religious ceremony. Depending on your state and whether or not you meet certain criteria, you may have a *common law marriage*. Note, however, that not all states recognize such marriages.

To have a common law marriage, you must live with one another for a certain period of time (which varies from state to state) and you must hold yourselves out as though you are married, or are intending to be married (for example, by signing hotel registers as Mr. and Mrs. So-and-So, or by opening a joint checking or savings account as Mr. and Mrs.).

As common law spouses, you have the same legal rights and responsibilities as couples who are formally married. And, to end your marriage, you have to go through a legal divorce process just like any other married couple. However, if at the time of your split, your common law spouse claims that you are not really married, you will have to document the nature of your relationship.

On the other hand, if you and your partner live in a state that recognizes common law marriages and you decide to split up, as long as you both agree that you do not have a common law marriage, you do not have to get a formal divorce.

If you have questions about whether or not you are common-law married, get in touch with a family law attorney.

- ✔ You have an obligation to share your estate (that is, everything you own) with your spouse when you die. The law in most states says that your spouse is entitled to a minimum of one-third of your estate, even if your will provides for less.

- ✔ When you divorce in most states, your entire will or just those parts that relate to your former spouse are voided automatically.

- ✔ You have the right to file a joint tax return and to enjoy the tax benefits of filing jointly.

- ✔ You have an equal responsibility to pay any debts that you and your spouse incur jointly.

- ✔ You have the right to a share of the property and income you and your spouse acquire and earn during your marriage if you get divorced. Exactly what your share will be depends in part on whether you live in a community property or a separate property state.

- ✔ You don't have to comply with the property laws of your state when you and your spouse negotiate a prenuptial or postnuptial agreement.

- ✔ You have the right to certain retirement and government benefits including disability and pension income and Social Security.

    ✔ You have the right to visit your spouse in a hospital intensive-care unit and in jail.

    ✔ You have the right to make decisions about your spouse's health and medical care when your spouse is too ill or too seriously injured to make those decisions on his or her own.

A Word on Family Court

If you are involved in a family law dispute or are getting legally separated or divorced, your legal issue falls under the jurisdiction of the family court in your area. The judge presiding over that court specializes in family law.

If some aspect of your separation or divorce ends up in court, the judge rules on the issue after a hearing or trial. A jury trial is usually not an option.

If your spouse is physically abusive and you get a protective order to keep him or her away from you, that matter is taken up in family court. However, if you file criminal charges against your spouse, those charges are heard in criminal court. If the court decides that your spouse is guilty of assault or battery, he or she may spend some time in jail.

Separation, Divorce, and Your Parental Rights and Obligations

Each state has its own laws and processes for ending a marriage just as it does for beginning one. However, those laws that apply to legal separations and divorces tend to be considerably more complicated and time-consuming than the ones relating to marriage. For example, before your divorce can be final, you have to decide how to divide up your marital property and debt and whether or not spousal support will be paid. (Chapter 9 covers the subject of property division, and Chapter 10 covers spousal support in greater depth.)

If you have children under the age of 18, you also have to make decisions regarding child custody, visitation, and support. The federal government even gets involved in the end of your marriage because it has passed laws relating to the payment of child support. Although love may have been all you needed to begin your marriage, you need considerably more to end it. The following sections cover some of the basic considerations you need to keep in mind with regard to children in a pending divorce.

The least you owe your children

If you are the parent of minor children, you have very specific legal obligations to them. You must provide them with food and clothing, medical care, and a place to live. You must also make sure that your children receive at least a minimal education (college is not required) in a public or private school or at home. These obligations remain, regardless of whether you and your spouse separate or divorce. Usually, your parental obligations remain until a child is a legal adult — 18 or 21 — depending on your state.

You as a parent have rights, too

Having children isn't a one-way street. You, and not just your children, have legal rights, including the right to choose where, when, and how you fulfill your legal obligations to your children, within limits. For example, your state won't care if you raise your children as vegetarians, but it will intervene if it has reason to believe that you are starving them; in fact, you may lose custody of your children as a result. And, although your state won't tell you what pediatrician to use (your HMO may, however), if your state decides that you are withholding lifesaving medical treatment from your child, the authorities will intervene.

Depending on the outcome of your custody negotiations, you may lose some of your parental rights when you get divorced (for example, the right to have your children live with you or even your right to spend unsupervised time with them).

A brief history of child custody law

Prior to the mid-1800s, children were considered little more than property. When a couple split, the husband typically got the property, including the kids. At that time, fathers also needed their children's labor to work the family's farmland.

As breadwinners did less and less farm work and more and more factory work, fathers began spending extended amounts of time away from their children. Consequently, mothers assumed greater responsibility for the day-to-day care of their children. By the mid-19th century mothers, and not fathers, were more apt to get custody of the children when that decision was left to the state courts.

Courts began to apply the *tender years doctrine* to their custody decisions. From then on, the courts viewed mothers as the primary nurturers of their children and assumed, therefore, that children were better off living with their mothers after divorce, even if that woman was only nominally fit for the job of child rearing.

Beginning in the 1960s, state laws began to view each parent as equally capable of raising their children after divorce. As a result, the current laws of most states do not necessarily favor mothers over fathers in custody battles (but, in reality, mothers are more apt to get custody of their children). Shared and joint custody arrangements have also become more common since the 1960s.

According to the Children's Rights Council, in the laws of 14 states and the District of Columbia, there exists the presumption that *shared parenting* or joint custody is warranted. Those 14 states are California, Florida, Idaho, Iowa, Kansas, Louisiana, Minnesota, Mississippi, Missouri, Montana, Nevada, New Mexico, Oklahoma, and Texas.

Fathers taking on new roles

Women are not the only ones who have been busy reinventing themselves and affecting family law in the process. Many men have begun playing a more active role in the upbringing and nurturing of their children. Some dads, supported by the father's rights movement, have become increasingly outspoken about the inequities of a divorce system that they view as pro-female. As a result, a growing number of divorcing fathers are more aggressively asserting their legal rights when it comes to child custody and visitation decisions.

According to the 1995 U.S. Census Bureau "Household and Family Characteristics" report, 15 percent of fathers have custody of their children and are single parents — *triple* the number there were in 1970.

The Web site sponsored by the Fathers' Rights Foundation won't get any awards for design, but it does offer divorcing or divorced dads plenty of good information on issues they'll be facing. You can find the site at www.fathers-rights.com.

Full-Time Dads is an essential newsletter for any dad who considers his children to be his top priority. It is chock-full of helpful advice and information written by people who should know — other full-time dads! (You full-time moms may find this newsletter helpful, too.) To view sample issues, point your Web browser to www.slowlane.com/ftd/. A year's subscription is $18. For more information call 908-355-9772.

Chapter 4

Divorce Law Basics

. . . .

In This Chapter

▶ Meeting the minimum requirements for a divorce

▶ Understanding the difference between fault and no-fault divorce

▶ Examining the three basic kinds of divorce

▶ Finding out what happens if your divorce ends up in court

▶ Finalizing a divorce

. . . .

*Y*our divorce may be your first encounter with the legal system (except for that appearance or two in traffic court). Understandably, the prospect of dealing with lawyers, courts, and legal mumbo jumbo can be fairly intimidating.

One of the best ways to steel yourself for what's to come and boost your self-confidence is to find out about the laws that apply to divorce and the legal processes involved in getting a divorce. With that in mind, this chapter provides an overview of the basics of divorce law and some of the key decisions you need to make to comply with the requirements of the legal system.

Not Just Anyone Can Get Divorced

To get a divorce, you have to meet some minimum state requirements. The most common are:

  ✔ **Residing in your state for a certain period of time.** A handful of states have no residency requirement — your obvious destination for a "quickie divorce" — but most states require that one or both of you be a resident for a minimum amount of time before you can either file a petition for divorce or before your divorce can be granted. Six months is the most common residency requirement, but it may be weeks, months, or even a year, depending on your state.

> ✓ **Getting divorced in the state where you live.** That is, you must get divorced in the state you call your permanent home — and not in the state where you got married.
>
> ✓ **Being separated.** Some states require that before you can be divorced you must live apart from your spouse for a certain period of time. The theory behind this requirement is that, with enough time, you and your spouse may have a change of heart and reconcile.

Pointing the Finger at Your Spouse — Fault versus No-Fault Divorce

According to the American Bar Association, 31 states (as of this writing) allow couples to get an old-fashioned *fault divorce.* When you file this kind of divorce, you have to provide a very specific reason, or *grounds,* for wanting to end your marriage. Providing grounds for a divorce means accusing your spouse of asocial behavior, such as adultery, physical abuse, mental cruelty, drunkenness, drug addiction, or insanity.

You also have to prove that the grounds actually exist. At its most extreme, proving fault can lead to spying on or videotaping your spouse, taping your spouse's phone conversations, using private detectives, putting friends on the stand to testify about your spouse's misdeeds, and so on. A fault divorce can certainly provide the grist for a lurid soap opera.

Currently, all states recognize some form of *no-fault divorce,* a kinder, gentler type of divorce. When you file for a no-fault divorce, you do not need grounds for divorce. In essence, you simply have to acknowledge that things "just didn't work out." Common grounds for obtaining a no-fault divorce include "incompatibility," "irretrievable breakdown," or "irreconcilable differences." Because you don't need to prove fault, this kind of divorce is usually less expensive, quicker to complete, and easier on spouses and their children than most fault divorces. Therefore, a no-fault divorce is the more popular type of divorce.

Some states permit no-fault divorces only in those instances in which a couple has been legally separated for a minimum period of time — sometimes as long as a year and a half.

Fault used to play a major role in alimony decisions but that is no longer a consideration in many U.S. states. However, about half of the states do allow fault to be considered in division of property negotiations. In those states, fault will have a large impact on the final details of a couple's divorce and on the amount the spouse who is *not* at fault will eventually receive.

Which states have the highest divorce rate?

According to the U.S. Census Bureau, approximately 50 percent of all American marriages end in divorce. However, divorce rates vary from state to state. For example, Nevada, home of the "quickie divorce," gets the prize for having the highest divorce rate of all, followed by Indiana, Tennessee, New Mexico, and Alabama. The states with the fewest number of divorces per capita include New Jersey, Connecticut, Pennsylvania, Maryland, and Massachusetts, which has bragging rights as the state with the lowest divorce rate in the country.

Why are the states with the lowest divorce rates located mostly in the Northeast and Middle Atlantic, while the states in the South and Southwest are among those with the highest divorce rates? Religious differences and population levels may offer some explanation. It's also interesting to note that, with some exceptions, states with the highest divorce rates also tend to have a more-transient population. Couples who are more mobile may be less likely to have strong family ties and deep social roots in their communities — resources that can help them weather their marital woes.

The following list ranks states by number of divorces per capita (according to U.S. Census data).

1. Nevada
2. Indiana
3. Tennessee
4. New Mexico
5. Alabama
6. Wyoming
7. Arkansas
8. Mississippi
9. Arizona
10. Idaho
11. Oklahoma
12. Texas
13. Florida
14. Kentucky
15. Colorado
16. Georgia
17. Washington
18. North Carolina
19. Missouri
20. Oregon
21. Delaware
22. Kansas
23. Utah
24. Montana
25. Alaska
26. Vermont
27. West Virginia
28. New Hampshire
29. Virginia
30. South Carolina
31. Hawaii
32. Maine
33. Louisiana
34. Michigan
35. Ohio
36. South Dakota
37. Nebraska
38. Illinois
39. North Dakota
40. California
41. New York
42. Iowa
43. Wisconsin
44. Rhode Island
45. Minnesota
46. New Jersey
47. Connecticut
48. Pennsylvania
49. Maryland
50. Massachusetts

Resolving Basic Divorce Issues

You and your spouse have to decide on a number of fundamental issues before your divorce is final. (If you get a legal separation before you divorce, you still have to work out these same issues.) Your decisions must include:

- ✔ **How will your marital property and debts be divided up?** Complex laws, including state property laws and federal tax laws, plus numerous interpretations of those laws, can make deciding who gets what a complicated undertaking, especially if you and your spouse have managed to amass a considerable amount of assets.

- ✔ **Will one of you pay spousal support or alimony to the other? If so, how much will the payments be and for how long will they continue?**

- ✔ **If there are minor children from your marriage, how will custody, visitation, and child support be handled?** This issue can be one of the most emotional in a divorce. Some spouses fear that if they don't get custody, they will no longer play a meaningful role in the lives of their children; others may view fighting for the kids as a way to get back at their spouses.

Responding to a federal government mandate, all states have guidelines for determining the minimum amount of child support that should be paid in a divorce.

If you and your spouse can work together to resolve these issues, your divorce can be relatively quick and inexpensive. But, if you can't, or if your divorce has complicating factors (your marital property or debt is substantial, for example) bringing your marriage to an end can take time and money. In a worst-case scenario, you must look to the courts for help.

If you are an older woman who never worked outside the home during your marriage or has not done so in many years, you may have difficulty finding a well-paying job after you are divorced. Therefore, getting an adequate amount of alimony for a long enough period of time is essential to your maintaining an acceptable post-divorce lifestyle. However, if your divorce is rancorous, your spouse may fight against paying you the alimony you think you need.

In a divorce settlement that has set corporate boardrooms abuzz, a Connecticut state court judge awarded the wife of a corporate executive an estimated $17 million in cash and real estate, plus alimony of $250,000 a year. The award includes a portion of the husband's executive benefits, including a deferred bonus and vested and unvested stock options. During the couple's divorce trial, the wife's attorney argued that she deserved a share of her husband's executive benefits because, as a "corporate wife," she actively supported his career, gave him business advice, threw business-related parties, and attended business social functions with him. She is using part of her divorce settlement to fund a foundation for marriage equality. Meanwhile, the husband was contemplating a new marriage, but said he planned to ask his new wife-to-be to sign a prenuptial agreement.

The Rules of the Divorce Court Game

The divorce laws and guidelines of your state provide a framework and set boundaries for resolving the basic issues that must be decided before your marriage can be ended. In other words, those laws and guidelines are actually quite flexible, within certain limits:

- ✔ As you work your way through the divorce process, you and your spouse have a considerable amount of leeway when you decide on most of those issues, as long as you are both *in agreement*.

- ✔ As you address the division of your marital property, spousal support, and child custody and visitation, assume that a *family law judge* is looking over your shoulder. This means that whatever you decide about those matters should be fair to you both, given the laws of your state, and your decisions should reflect an appreciation of what the judge would probably decide if your divorce were to end in a trial.

- ✔ Among other factors, *local norms* and cultural values can influence the final outcome of a divorce. A judge in a more socially conservative part of a state may decide the same issue — alimony or which parent gets custody, for example — quite differently than a judge in a more socially liberal part of that same state (and vice versa).

Second-guessing family law judges can be tricky because judges have considerable discretion in how they interpret the law. Furthermore, although we like to think that all judges approach legal issues with unbiased minds, the truth is that their decisions are at times colored by their own prejudices, preferences, and real-life experiences. For example, if your divorce goes to trial, the judge who hears your case may have just been divorced and may feel that he or she was "taken to the cleaners" by his or her ex-spouse. Or the judge's daughter may be a single, divorced mom who struggles to make ends meet because her ex-spouse is not meeting his support obligations.

You can appeal a judge's decision, but appeals are hard to win. Plus, appealing means spending more money on an attorney and then, if you win your appeal, more money on a new trial.

Divorce law helps resolve legal and financial issues. The law will not resolve the anger, guilt, fear, or sadness you may feel. Don't look to the legal system to do that for you. You'll be left feeling disappointed and frustrated when your divorce is over.

One Objective (But Many Ways to Get There)

The goal of any divorce is to end a marriage. However, that goal can be achieved in many ways. You can work together to make your divorce as easy and inexpensive as possible, or you can turn your divorce into an expensive battle full of anger, unreasonable demands, and uncompromising behavior.

Just what path your divorce takes is up to you and your spouse. Here are your basic options:

✔ **Option 1 — The Cooperative Divorce.** You and your spouse work out the terms of your divorce together and then one of you files a no-fault divorce. Or, you hire attorneys to help you work out the details, but you still keep things friendly.

✔ **Option 2— The Contested Divorce.** You and your spouse can't agree on all of the key issues in your divorce. You may be able to avoid a trial by resolving your differences with the help of attorneys or through a dispute resolution technique such as *mediation* (see Chapter 16 for more information on mediation). Both fault and no-fault divorces can be contested.

✔ **Option 3— The Courtroom Divorce.** At this point you lose control of your divorce. It is now in the hands of a family law judge. Luckily, only about 5 percent of all divorces are resolved this way.

Your divorce can actually be a combination of two or even all three divorce options we just listed. For example, you and your spouse work some things out together, then you hire attorneys to negotiate other aspects of your divorce, and then a judge resolves the issues on which you're deadlocked.

Many states have an abbreviated divorce process available for couples who have been married for a very short period of time, who have no young children from their marriage, and who have amassed little or no marital property and debt.

Using collaborative law to get divorced

A relatively new option for working out the terms of your divorce outside of court in a friendly manner is available through a process called *collaborative law.* You, your spouse, and your respective attorneys (who must be trained in the collaborative law process) sit down together to reach a divorce settlement. Unlike mediation, with collaborative law no neutral third party is involved. After you have hammered out an agreement, your divorce is filed. The benefits of this approach include:

✔ Lower costs

✔ Less stress for you, your spouse, and your attorneys

✔ Creative solutions to divorce issues

✔ Increased cooperation between spouses

✔ A positive foundation from which to build a post-divorce relationship if you and your spouse share young children

The drawback to using collaborative law to negotiate your divorce is that if you and your spouse are unable to come to an agreement and need the court's involvement, the lawyers you have been working with must withdraw from your case and you'll have to find new attorneys. Essentially that means you have to start the divorce process all over again.

You can find lawyers practicing collaborative law in only a handful of states: California, Minnesota, Ohio, Oregon, and Texas. However, lawyers in many other states are now expressing an interest in using the collaborative process.

Many couples committed to working things out themselves with minimal help from attorneys also use *mediation* as a way to help them structure their divorce agreement negotiations and minimize the opportunity for emotions to get in the way of reason. (See Chapter 16 for more on mediation.)

The cooperative divorce

A *cooperative divorce* is the divorce option that is easiest on your pocketbook (and on your emotions). With cooperation, filing a *divorce petition* (the legal paperwork that initiates a divorce) will be little more than a formality and no reason exists for the nonfiling spouse to respond to the petition.

First, you and your spouse work together to structure a divorce agreement that you both think is fair. After you've drafted an agreement (with or without the help of attorneys), your divorce should move along relatively quickly because much less bureaucratic red tape and legal paperwork exists to slow its progress. After any final changes in your divorce or marital settlement agreement have been made, the agreement is filed with the court and the petitioning spouse may have to make a brief court appearance. Not long after, your divorce is official.

The messy divorce

If your divorce is contested or if it involves fault, lawyers are almost certainly involved and a response is filed. The response is just the start of the legal paperwork and formalities that you and your spouse can expect as your divorce inches its way along.

More legal formalities and paperwork mean that the messy divorce takes longer to complete than the cooperative divorce. The messy divorce also costs a whole lot more.

The litigated divorce

The litigated divorce (an extreme version of the messy divorce) is more emotional, time-consuming and expensive, and involves more paperwork and legal red tape than either the cooperative or the messy divorce. It can exhaust both your emotional and your financial resources. Also, the animosity between you and your spouse most likely won't go away after your divorce is final, and you may have difficulty even carrying on a polite conversation when it's all over with.

If you have children, your anger toward one another may seriously harm their short- and long-term emotional well-being. If both of you want to be actively involved in the lives of your children after your divorce, you will no doubt run into one another at after-school games, recitals, graduations, weddings, and other events. The last thing you want is for your estrangement to overshadow or color these important events in your children's lives.

In the 1970s, clinical psychologist Judith Wallerstein began studying children of divorce in northern California. Wallerstein chronicled her findings in two books: *Surviving the Breakup: How Children and Parents Cope with Divorce* (Basic Books) co-authored with Joan Berlin Kelly, and *Second Chances: Men, Women and Children a Decade after Divorce* (Houghton Mifflin Company) co-authored with Sandra Blakeslee.

Research shows another important drawback to a litigated divorce: Spouses whose divorces are decided by a judge are less likely to be happy with the final outcome of their divorce and less committed to making the terms of their divorce work than couples who arrive at a negotiated divorce settlement.

If your divorce ends with a trial, you are more apt to find yourself revisiting the final terms of your divorce in your lawyers' offices and in court. Doing so not only takes money and time but also means that you never really put your divorce and your failed marriage behind you. Even more important, a litigated divorce and the rancor that you and your ex-spouse may feel for years to come can have a very damaging effect on the physical, mental, and emotional health of your children for years to come.

Most marriages have very complex histories. Therefore, no matter how much time a family law judge may spend trying to understand your marriage, the judge may still not have a complete grasp of the intricacies of your divorce case.

Initiating the Divorce Proceedings

No matter which legal path your divorce takes, every divorce starts out the same way — one spouse files a *complaint* or *petition* with the court. If you do the filing, you are the *plaintiff* or the *petitioner* and your spouse is the *defendant* or *respondent*. In your petition, you establish the facts and the issues of the divorce, as you see them, and you indicate what if anything you want from your spouse — spousal support, child support, custody of the children, and so on.

When you file a divorce petition, you are actually initiating a civil lawsuit against your spouse. As the *petitioner,* you pay at least the initial court costs of your divorce, and if your case ends up in court, you present your side first.

Ordinarily, both parties in a divorce pay their own legal and court costs. However, you can try to include in your divorce agreement a provision that your spouse will reimburse you for all or a portion of those costs.

Serving the papers

After a petition is filed, your spouse must be formally notified of your action. This can be accomplished in a number of ways:

 ✔ Your spouse can sign a *waiver of service,* which means that he or she will not be formally *served* with a notice that you have filed. You'll probably use this method if you and your spouse handle your own divorce or if you hire an attorney and your divorce is amicable.

 ✔ Your spouse will be formally served by a sheriff, constable, or private process server. This method is most likely if your divorce is hostile.

The sheriff can serve your spouse at home, at work, or wherever he or she can be found. If the papers can't be served, perhaps because your spouse is evading the sheriff, a private process server can be hired. Your spouse will have a tougher time alluding this person because private process servers wear street clothes and aren't as easy to spot.

Depending on your state, after the papers have been served, your spouse usually has 20 to 60 days to file a response (also known as an *answer*) to your lawsuit. Your spouse also has the option of not responding, which often happens when a divorce is a no-fault one and uncontested.

Normally, the court cannot order your spouse to pay temporary spousal support or child support while the terms of your divorce are being worked out until your spouse has been served.

If you and your spouse are not already legally separated but will begin living apart now that your divorce has begun, it's best to have a written agreement that details your living and financial arrangements and how you will handle child-related issues during the divorce process.

Divorce by default

If your spouse can't be served, don't worry, you won't have to stay married indefinitely. In most states, you can publish a legal notice in your local newspaper or in the newspaper your spouse is likely to read if you are no longer living in the same town.

The published notice informs your spouse that you have filed for divorce and outlines your spouse's legal rights. Should your spouse fail to respond within a certain period of time, the court gives you a default divorce.

Negotiating your way out of a stalemate

At any time during your divorce, you and your spouse can reach an agreement about the issues being contested. In fact, good attorneys should be actively trying to help you reach a negotiated divorce settlement. Every key issue you can resolve outside of court saves you money and time.

If you and your spouse have reached a stalemate about how to handle child custody and visitation, the court may require that you both attend a mediation session before you can go to trial. The goal of the session is to break your standoff. A growing number of states are making this requirement. Many states have expanded the mediation requirement to encompass other unresolved divorce-related issues as well.

The good news is, it works: An estimated 70 percent to 80 percent of all divorces that go to mediation are resolved through this non-court dispute resolution process. (See Chapter 16 for more on mediation.)

What Happens after You Decide to Litigate

When your divorce is not cooperative, you, your spouse, and your attorneys will work your way through a very specific legal process. At its most extreme, the process culminates with a court-ordered judgment after a trial. However, at any point during the process, you and your spouse can reach an agreement regarding all of the issues in your divorce and avoid a trial.

So that you understand some of what's to come, the following information offers a brief overview of each stage in the divorce process if your divorce goes all the way to court.

Pretrial motions

Depending on the circumstances of your divorce, sometime between the filing of the petition and response your attorneys may file *pretrial motions* asking the court for temporary court orders for spousal support, child custody and support, and visitation.

Pretrial motions are written or oral requests made to the court prior to a trial asking the court to take a specific action. *Temporary court orders,* or *pendente lite* orders, are written rulings by a judge on a disputed issue that will be in effect for a limited period of time. This period of time is spelled out in the court order.

Temporary court orders can, for example, determine who can stay in the family residence while your divorce is ongoing, or they can freeze assets so that neither you nor your spouse can spend, sell, or attempt to hide your marital or separate property.

Your attorneys may also ask the court to issue an *injunction,* which is a specific type of court order. An injunction bars a particular action. For example, an injunction may prohibit your spouse from removing marital property from your home.

Discovery

Attorneys use the *discovery* process to help them determine the facts of a case. Depending on what they want to learn through discovery, the attorneys may use a variety of formal legal tools, some of which are described in this section. The discovery process can take just a short time, especially if the facts of your divorce are clear and undisputed, or it can last many months.

Voluntarily providing your spouse's attorney with the information he or she requests is less-painful than going through the formal discovery process. Plus you'll end up saving time and money.

Discovery can be formal or informal depending on whether

- ✔ Your attorney has to force your spouse's attorney to provide certain information related to your divorce using the formal tools of discovery (or if your spouse's attorney has to do the same).

- ✔ The two attorneys agree in writing to willingly exchange all the information they need to work out the terms of your divorce.

- ✔ Your attorneys need to formally acquire additional information related to your divorce from other sources.

- ✔ Your divorce is amicable (in which case less need exists for formal discovery) or contentious.

In some states, formal discovery is *limited*. For example, your attorney may be able to use discovery only to get at the financial facts of your divorce.

Informal discovery

Informal discovery occurs when your attorney asks your spouse's attorney (or vice versa) for financial, legal, medical, or other information and the information is provided voluntarily. The particular types of information your attorney asks for depends on the issues involved in your divorce.

Ideally, most of the discovery in your divorce will be informal because formal discovery can be both time-consuming and expensive, depending on just how much formal discovery either attorney does. Your attorney or your spouse's attorney may have to complete extra paperwork, formulate questions to ask your spouse or others, conduct interviews, and then review and analyze all of the imformation.

Formal discovery

Depositions, interrogatories, requests for the production of documents, and subpoenas are all *formal discovery* tools. The following list tells you what each of these terms means:

- ✔ **Subpoena:** A legal document requiring someone to provide testimony about something or someone at a court hearing or trial. Anyone who ignores a subpoena faces legal penalties.

- ✔ **Deposition:** A statement by a witness, taken out of court and recorded by a court reporter. The witness is under oath.

- ✔ **Interrogatories:** Written questions prepared by the attorney of the plaintiff for the defendant or vice versa. The answers to the questions are provided under oath. Interrogatories deal specifically with issues that are being disputed in a lawsuit.

✔ **Notices to produce documents and other information:** Depending on the issues that have to be resolved before your divorce can be final, any number of individuals may be involved in the discovery process:

The information provided by accountants, appraisers, business associates, bankers, and so on may be used to help resolve questions regarding the value of your marital property, spousal support, or child support, for example.

Social workers, therapists, baby-sitters, neighbors, the parents of your children's friends, your friends or your spouse's friends, the police, social service agencies, and others may be included in the discovery process.

A *notice to produce documents* is also known as a *request for production of documents and other tangible things*.

Proper deposition deportment

Your spouse's attorney may ask you to give a *deposition* as part of the formal discovery process in your divorce. Although you may wish you didn't have to, unless you want to risk being held in contempt of court and even spend time in jail, you have to comply with the request. Because you'll probably be nervous come deposition time, we provide you with some tips on how to manage the situation.

✔ **Tell the truth, even if it hurts.**

✔ **If you do not understand a question, say so.** Ask that it be repeated or restated.

✔ **Give your answer and nothing more — no extra facts and no elaboration.** Providing more information than you are asked for may hurt your case.

✔ **Be polite and don't argue with your spouse's attorney.**

✔ **If you have a break during the deposition, just sit quietly.** Don't let your guard down and begin chatting up the attorney who is asking you questions, or talking to the court reporter or anyone else who may be in the room. You may end up saying something you wish you could retract (but by then, it's too late).

✔ **Excuse yourself to discuss matters with your attorney if you need to ask him or her a question or if you need time to compose yourself.**

Your attorney is with you when you give your deposition. If your attorney tells you not to answer a question, don't answer it. A tactical and legitimate reason for your remaining silent probably exists.

Formal discovery is most common in divorces involving spouses who are unwilling to cooperate with one another. However, even if your divorce is amicable, your attorney may do a limited amount of formal discovery in order to

- ✔ **Narrow the scope of your negotiations by identifying exactly where you and your spouse agree or disagree, and the particulars of your agreements and disagreements.** The more that you know you agree on, the less you have to negotiate or litigate later, and the less your divorce costs.

- ✔ **Assess the strengths and weaknesses of your position versus your spouse's.**

- ✔ **Assess how well your spouse is likely to perform on the stand if your case goes to trial and your spouse is called to testify.**

- ✔ **Get your spouse to admit to certain activities or to establish certain facts.** If your divorce goes to trial and your spouse provides testimony while on the stand that differs from what he or she said during the discovery process, your attorney can use the discrepancy to undermine your spouse's credibility.

Pretrial conference or hearing

If it looks like you're headed for court, you get your first dose of what's to come at the *pretrial conference* or *pretrial hearing*. During this informal meeting, a judge (who may or may not be the same judge who hears your case at the trial) listens to the attorneys involved in your divorce as they present information about the entire case or information about just the issues that have not yet been resolved. If you and your spouse are at the hearing, the judge will probably question you and your spouse about some of the information your attorneys present.

The pretrial conference serves two purposes:

- ✔ The judge encourages you to settle with one another by providing you with his or her perspective about the probable outcome of your trial. This information may be sobering enough to make you swallow your pride, bury your anger, and cut whatever deal you can with your spouse.

- ✔ Or, if the judge can't convince you to settle your differences, the pretrial conference provides the judge and attorneys with an opportunity to review the issues that your trial will address.

The Judge's Ruling on Your Case

After listening to your attorneys' opening and closing statements, hearing testimony from you and your spouse and from any witnesses involved in your divorce trial, and reviewing any documents and other written information entered as evidence, the judge rules on the issues in your case.

The judge may announce his decision immediately at the end of the trial, or he may take time to consider all the evidence and announce his decision at a later date. (By the way, only about 5 percent of all divorces are settled in court.)

Entering the Judgment

When your divorce becomes final, the court enters a judgment making the terms of your divorce official and formally pronouncing that your marriage has ended. Your legal rights and obligations as spouses end and you are both single again.

If you and your spouse have been able to reach an agreement about the terms of your divorce, that agreement becomes your judgment. Typically the judgment includes a property settlement agreement and if you have minor children, an agreement regarding custody, visitation, and child support. It may also include a spousal support agreement. The judge attaches your negotiated agreement to the other legal paperwork required to make your divorce official or issues a judgment that includes everything in the agreement. If you have not been able to negotiate an agreement, the judge issues an order detailing the terms of your divorce.

The judgment ending your marriage may be called a *Decree of Dissolution of Marriage,* a *Dissolution Order,* or a *Dissolution Judgment* depending on where you live.

Chapter 5

Separation: A Healthy Breather or a Prelude to Divorce?

Separation is more than just a matter of living apart from your spouse. It is an important step with legal, financial, and emotional ramifications that requires plenty of advance planning. Separation can be the beginning of the end to your marriage, or the start of a better-than-ever union. Either way, don't take the decision to separate casually.

Before separating, you need to fully understand the pros and cons of such a change in your living arrangements. You and your spouse should also be clear about the direction you anticipate your separation will take you — toward reconciliation or to divorce court. Otherwise, you may be setting yourself up for disappointment and more heartache.

This chapter can help you analyze your reasons for separating and alert you to some potential drawbacks of living apart from your spouse while you're still married. It also explains the steps you must take to protect your legal rights and financial well-being after you separate. If you're using separation as a way to save your marriage, this chapter also provides you with sound advice about how to engineer a successful reconciliation.

You're Married, but Then Again, You Aren't

Separation is the equivalent of marital limbo. You are no longer living with your spouse, and you may even feel single again, but you are *still married*. However, your relationship has changed. When you live apart, you see one another less frequently and you are less accountable to one another for your comings and goings and what you do and don't do at home. After separating, you and your spouse may try "dating" each other in an effort to put the spark back in your marriage, or you may avoid any contact with each other unless it's absolutely necessary.

Depending on the state you live in and the type of fault divorce you may have filed, dating your spouse (and especially having sex with your spouse) while you are separated can jeopardize your grounds for divorce. The courts will understandably question the credibility of your fault allegations. Therefore, if you are separated, and are thinking about dating your spouse, consult your attorney first. However, if you are informally separated with the intention of reconciling, there is probably no real danger in dating your spouse.

Spousal inheritance, pension rights, and death benefits remain intact during a separation.

Why Should You Separate?

Couples separate for many reasons. Sometimes those reasons are well reasoned and logical; other times, they are based on fear or misguided hope. Sometimes, you and your spouse have no other option. Among the most common reasons for separating are the following:

- You want to find out what living on your own feels like.

- You need time to assess your commitment to your marriage, away from the day-to-day stress and responsibilities of the relationship.

- You want to get your emotions under control and analyze your marriage from a new and different perspective.

- You want to send your spouse a strong message that things have to change if you are going to stay married. (For example, your spouse has a substance abuse problem and has been unwilling to deal with it.)

- ✔ You are afraid to tell your spouse that you want a divorce, so you compromise by suggesting that you separate. You hope that your spouse will come to realize that living apart isn't so bad after all and you can ease your way into a final break.

- ✔ Your spouse wants a divorce, but you don't. By agreeing to separate, you hope to delay or even prevent the end of your marriage.

- ✔ Your state says that you can't get divorced without separating first.

- ✔ You anticipate an amicable divorce, but living with your spouse until your divorce is official is emotionally impossible.

- ✔ You and your spouse are estranged and can no longer continue living under the same roof.

- ✔ Your spouse has become physically violent and you are afraid for your or your children's safety.

- ✔ In most states you can get a court order for a legal separation faster than one for a divorce — an important consideration if you need to resolve issues related to child custody and support, spousal support, and so on as quickly as possible, and you aren't able to work these issues out with your spouse.

- ✔ You can't afford to get divorced yet.

- ✔ You have religious objections to divorce.

If you are a Roman Catholic and are contemplating divorce, you may want to visit the following Web site first. It's chock-full of excellent information.

`www.divorceinfo.com/catholic.htm`

Joseph P. Kennedy II and Sheila Rauch Kennedy ended their 12-year marriage in 1991. Two years later, Kennedy asked his former wife for a religious annulment so that he could remarry in the Catholic Church. Objecting to the annulment, Sheila Kennedy (a non-Catholic) not only took her battle all the way to the Vatican, but also penned a book, *Shattered Faith,* which takes a hard look at the issue of annulment.

If you want joint or full custody of your children and you anticipate a custody battle, staying actively involved in your children's lives by living with your family throughout the divorce process can be a good idea. Even though the laws in most states are gender neutral when it comes to child custody, many family courts continue to favor mothers over fathers.

Securing a religious annulment

If you are a divorced Catholic and want to remarry in the Catholic Church, you must obtain an annulment. Although the annulment process differs somewhat from church diocese to diocese, what follows is an overview of the basic annulment process:

✔ You first have to contact your parish priest about your desire for an annulment. A marriage tribunal (a Church court usually composed of at least three judges assisted by outside experts) then asks to meet with you to talk about your personal background, courtship, the problems in your marriage, the reasons for your divorce, and your life after divorce. (The tribunal may instead ask you to provide the same information by completing a written questionnaire.)

✔ You will be asked to provide the names of witnesses who can talk about their impressions of your marriage. They may also be interviewed by the tribunal or asked to complete written questionnaires.

✔ You'll have to provide the tribunal with certified copies of your marriage license, divorce decree, baptismal certificate, and other documents related to your annulment request.

✔ Your former spouse must be notified that you are seeking an annulment. He or she has the right to provide proof that no grounds exist for declaring that your marriage was invalid.

✔ After reviewing all the evidence, the tribunal will determine whether, according to Church policy, you have grounds for an annulment. If your request isn't granted, you can appeal the decision. If you lose your appeal, you can take your request all the way to the top to the Vatican in Rome.

From start to finish, an annulment can take anywhere from eight months to several years. Just how long it takes depends on your diocese, the degree to which your witnesses cooperate, and how quickly you provide all the information the tribunal requests.

The Drawbacks of Separating

Although separating certainly has its pluses, living apart from your spouse can have its drawbacks, too. So, before you agree to separate, determine if any of the following situations apply to you. Also, consult with a family law attorney who is experienced at handling divorces and separations.

✔ Your individual living expenses will increase after you and your spouse separate.

✔ If you are the spouse who moves out of the house, your new digs may not be nearly as plush as your former home.

✔ If you view your separation as temporary and anticipate living together again, your children may have a hard time understanding that "Daddy and Mommy are just spending some time apart."

✔ Separating may only be delaying the inevitable. You may be doing nothing more than prolonging the pain of your failed marriage and postponing the process of getting on with your life.

✔ If you do not have your own source of income, you may not have enough money to live on.

✔ Depending on your state, if you separate legally, and then later get divorced, you may end up paying for certain expenses twice.

✔ In some states, if you separate against your spouse's wishes, you may give your spouse grounds for a fault divorce.

✔ You can be held responsible for your spouse's debts and legal problems even though you are no longer living together. And, you may still be treated as a married couple with regard to pensions, life insurance, and contractual obligations. However, a carefully worded separation agreement written by a family law attorney can help address these issues.

✔ You may be charged with abandoning or deserting your marriage if you separate, which can weaken your position in your divorce negotiations and reflect badly on you when you're before a judge. A well-worded separation agreement can effectively deal with this issue.

When it comes to *legal* separations, state laws vary greatly. In some states, those who want to separate through a legal process may be out of luck.

If your spouse agrees to pay certain marital debts while you are separated and fails to do so, your creditors may have a legal right to come after both of you for payment. Furthermore, if your spouse gets into debt while you are separated, you can be held responsible for the debt even if you have a written agreement to the contrary. If you end up paying on that debt, you can later sue your spouse for reimbursement.

Depending on your state, your separation can affect what is and isn't marital property. If you separate legally as a prelude to divorce, then the property and debts you acquire during your separation may be considered yours and yours alone. But, if you are not legally separated, the property and debts you acquire during your separation may be considered marital property and debts.

If you are contemplating a separation, consult with a family law attorney first in order to gain a clear understanding of the pros and cons of separating given the laws of your state and the particulars of your situation.

Talk It Over Before You Separate

In addition to consulting with a family law attorney before you and your spouse separate, the both of you together should discuss the reasons for your separation (assuming that you can have a calm and productive conversation) and make it clear why you are separating — as a prelude to a divorce or as a last-ditch effort to save your marriage.

Neither of you should be harboring any illusions about the final outcome of your separation. That way, you can focus on achieving your goals for the separation. If you and your spouse are uncertain whether separating is your best move, a mental health professional may be able to help.

Initiating a Separation

If you are separating on an informal basis, you are separated as soon as you or your spouse moves out of your home. It's as easy as that. However, if you are getting a legal separation, one of you may have to file a *petition for separation* with the family court in your area.

After the terms of your legal separation have been worked out, your separation agreement must be filed with the same court where you filed your petition for separation. Remember that in some states you can obtain a legal separation *only* as a preliminary step to getting a divorce.

The court does not become actively involved in your separation unless you and your spouse are unable to negotiate an agreement either by yourselves or with the help of attorneys. If you cannot come to an agreement, a hearing is held, after which a family law judge decides the terms of your separation and issues a court-ordered separation agreement.

Think before you walk

Walking out in a huff definitely makes a strong statement about your feelings toward your spouse and your marriage. But if you stay away from home for an extended period of time (and just what constitutes an "extended" period depends on your state), your act of bravado may be viewed as desertion or abandonment and the spouse you left behind may have the last laugh.

If you walk out, you may have put yourself in a legally disadvantageous position for working out the terms of your separation or divorce, especially if your case is decided by a family law judge. Furthermore, in some states, if you desert your spouse, you forfeit your legal right to your share of your marital assets. That's a hefty price to pay for making a dramatic exit.

Traditionally, the spouse who wants the separation is the one to move out of the couple's home. However, if your spouse is the primary care giver of your young children, you should consider being the one to move so that the lives of your children are disrupted as little as possible.

Protecting Yourself When You Separate Informally

You can separate on an informal basis or, depending on your state, you may be able to separate legally. Although a legal separation is usually best, if the following statements apply to you, an informal separation may be what you need.

- ✔ You and your spouse both earn a good living and can comfortably support yourselves.
- ✔ You have no minor children from your marriage.
- ✔ You do not share joint accounts or jointly owe a great deal of money.
- ✔ You are confident that your separation will be relatively brief and amicable.

If you opt for an informal separation, you should nevertheless set ground rules for your time apart and make them part of a written agreement that you both sign and date. (Make sure that you both keep a copy of your final signed agreement.) An informal separation agreement can help protect you from the potential repercussions of a civilized separation turned sour.

Identify any issues that may disrupt the peacefulness of your time apart and determine ahead of time the best way to deal with those potentially disruptive conflicts. Working out solutions to possible problems in advance minimizes the potential for disagreements and misunderstandings during your separation. If problems do arise, instead of relying on your individual recollections of who-promised-to-do-what in order to resolve your differences, you can refer to your written agreement. Plus, you won't be pressed into hammering out a solution in the heat of the moment if you already have one on paper.

If your spouse mismanages your finances while you are separated, your credit history (and not just your spouse's) may be damaged. Therefore, include in your separation agreement provisions stating that, during your separation, your spouse will *not* include your name on any new financial or banking accounts and will *not* sign your name on any documents whatsoever, especially financial documents.

What to cover in your written agreement

When you and your spouse prepare your separation agreement, be sure to ask yourselves the following questions:

✔ How will you share the money in your joint bank accounts?

✔ What will you do about your joint credit cards?

✔ Who will remain in your home?

✔ How you will pay off your preexisting debts?

✔ Who will be responsible for paying the debts either of you may incur while you are separated?

✔ Will one of you pay alimony to the other?

✔ How will you share responsibility for the care of your children?

✔ When will your children stay with each of you?

✔ Will one of you pay child support to the other and, if so, how much will the payments be and when they will be paid?

Formalizing a Legal Separation Agreement

If you are separating permanently as an alternative to divorce, you absolutely must have a written legal agreement that spells out the terms of your separation. To protect yourselves, everything should be in black and white and enforceable by law.

A legal separation agreement is absolutely necessary if you and your spouse are so estranged from one another that communication and cooperation are impossible or if you don't trust your spouse to live up to his or her verbal promises.

Even if your separation is amicable and you both hope to reconcile, or if you want financial help from your spouse while you are living apart, or if minor children are involved, formalizing those arrangements in a legal written agreement is essential. Then, if either of you fails to live up to the terms of the agreement, you can ask the court to help enforce it.

The longer you live apart, the greater the chance that your relationship with your spouse will deteriorate. Your spouse may become involved in a new romantic relationship, for example, and abandon your reconciliation plans. Or, as time goes on, you may find it harder to cooperate with one another. At times like these, having a written separation agreement can help prevent a total breakdown of your relationship.

If you and your spouse can't come to a negotiated separation agreement, a family law judge will decide the terms of your separation.

A legal separation agreement can also serve some very practical purposes, especially in regard to your finances:

- ✔ To claim alimony payments as a deduction on your federal tax return, those payments must be part of a legal separation agreement.
- ✔ A well-written separation agreement can help limit your liability for any debts that your spouse may rack up during your separation.
- ✔ A separation agreement can provide for the continuance of certain spousal benefits, including health insurance, and continued access to credit if you and your spouse share joint accounts or you are an authorized user on your spouse's accounts.

Alimony pendente lite and *separate maintenance* are legal talk for spousal support payments during separation. If your spouse claims your alimony payments on his or her tax return, then you have to report them as income.

Not every state in the United States recognizes legal separations.

What should and shouldn't be in a legal separation agreement

A legal separation agreement addresses most, if not all, of the same issues that a divorce agreement covers including, when appropriate, child support, child custody and visitation, and spousal support. It can also address the division of marital property and debts. In fact, if you separate and then decide to divorce, all or some of what you include in your separation agreement can be converted into your divorce agreement.

Try the art of compromise

Give and take usually works better than strong-arm tactics when you are working out the terms of your separation. In other words, don't expect to get everything you ask for. You can refuse to compromise in an effort to have everything your way, but that approach is likely to backfire — you may end up in court where you will lose all direct control over the terms of your separation because the judge will have the final word. That said, you should be aware of provisions that can be helpful to include in your separation agreement and provisions that you should avoid if possible.

Hang on to your liquid assets

Be sure that your agreement gives you ready access to the liquid assets you and your spouse own. You may need them during your separation to help pay bills, put food on the table, or cover unexpected expenses, especially if your income is low and you will be receiving little or no spousal support.

A *liquid asset* is cash or something that can be quickly converted to cash. That includes CDs, the cash advance on your credit card, a checking account overdraft, as well as money market accounts and bond funds that allow you to write checks against your investment.

Separation etiquette

If Emily Post wrote rules of proper behavior for separated spouses, they'd have to include the following do's and don'ts. Ignoring the rules of separation etiquette can turn an amicable split into a hostile one, derail any plans for reconciliation, and even weaken your position when it comes time to negotiate your divorce.

Take heed of these separation don'ts:

✔ Don't get involved in a serious relationship, especially if the relationship means that you spend less time with your young children or that you neglect them when you and your new romantic interest are with your children. If your spouse finds out about your love affair, that information is likely to increase the hostility your spouse may already be feeling toward you.

✔ Don't bring a romantic interest home for the night when your children are staying with you.

✔ Don't bad-mouth your spouse, ever! If your children hear what you say, they are likely to repeat your comments to your spouse. Plus, nothing short of spousal abuse will send a judge into a tirade more quickly than learning that you've been saying disparaging things about your spouse.

✔ Don't do things that you know will be hurtful to your spouse. Ultimately, the person you hurt most may be yourself!

✔ Avoid sexual relations with your spouse without first understanding the potential ramifications of doing so according to the laws of your state. In some states, if you have sex with your spouse while separated, and if you have already filed for a fault divorce, you may lose your grounds for divorce. Furthermore, you may mislead your spouse into thinking you want to reconcile.

And, while you're at it, keep in mind these separation etiquette do's:

✔ Keep the lines of communication open between you and your spouse.

✔ If your children are living with you, allow your spouse to spend plenty of time with the children (unless your spouse has been abusive or you suspect that he or she has sexually molested the children). If you are legally separated, your agreement states when and where your spouse can see the children.

✔ Meet all of your obligations to your spouse and children without fail.

Be careful about what you sign

Question anything in a separation agreement that you do not understand. And, don't agree to any provision in your agreement because "it's good enough for now" or because you "can live with the arrangement for a while." Separation agreements often become *divorce* agreements and once something is in a separation agreement, it can be difficult, if not impossible, to have that provision voided or modified, unless you and your spouse agree to the change, or the problems it caused were obvious and significant.

Give yourself some room to maneuver by clearly indicating in writing that the separation agreement in no way binds you to the same terms in your final divorce agreement.

If You Kiss and Make Up

Some of you will breathe a huge sigh of relief after you have separated, but others may begin to miss certain aspects of married life. If you are the one who moved out and you are now living in a smaller place, surrounded by rented furniture and just a few items from your home, you may miss the old familiar comforts. If your spouse took care of most of the cooking (and boiling water sums up your culinary skills), you may quickly tire of fast food and scorched meals.

If your children are still young and they are not living with you, you will probably miss them; and if you are the parent with primary responsibility for the children while you are separated, you may feel overwhelmed without your spouse around to help. Or, you may have decided that you truly love your spouse and are willing to do what's necessary to repair your marriage.

For any or all of these reasons, you and your spouse may decide that living together is better than living apart. And, like many couples who reach that conclusion, you will reconcile and end your separation.

A mere nine days after musician Greg Allman and actress Cher were married in 1975, she filed for a legal separation. One month later the couple reconciled. Three months after that, Allman asked for a divorce but the couple later reconciled. A year after the birth of their son, Allman and Cher separated yet again, but actually didn't get divorced until 1979. Phew!

Reconcile for the right reasons

Be sure that you are reconciling because you really want to, not because you feel guilty, are scared to be alone, are tired of doing your own laundry, or for other reasons that may not be the right ones.

Initially, after you've reconciled, you may feel a sense of exhilaration and renewed hope for your future as a couple. But sooner or later, the old problems in your relationship are likely to resurface and you may respond to them in the very ways that contributed to your marital troubles in the first place.

Fortify the relationship with counseling

Despite your happiness at being together again, both of you may be harboring negative feelings toward one another, such as anger, hurt, doubt, and distrust, as a result of your separation. Although these feelings may be quite natural under the circumstances, they can get in the way of rebuilding your marriage. Therefore, if you are really serious about staying together and repairing your marriage, begin seeing a therapist or marriage counselor, if you aren't already doing so.

If you and your spouse get back together again after separating, you are more apt to make your marriage work if you begin therapy or counseling while you are still in the honeymoon phase of your reconciliation when you're more motivated to make it work.

Some people regress emotionally when they go through a traumatic experience such as divorce — it's almost as if they become teenagers again. With no one to come home to and no reason to come home, they begin spending too much money, drinking too much, doing drugs, or engaging in promiscuous behavior. Although these behaviors may temporarily numb feelings of grief and fear, they can lead to long-term problems. If you think your behavior is becoming self-destructive, don't wait to seek the help of a mental health professional. If you don't get help, odds are that you will end up separating again and maybe even getting divorced.

Part II
Divorce Preliminaries

The 5th Wave   By Rich Tennant

In this part . . .

Your marriage is definitely over and now it's time to take action. Chapter 6 gives you advice for breaking the news to your spouse, help in determining what you want out of your divorce, and estimates of what divorce will cost you (both personally and in dollars and cents). Chapter 7 tells you how to help your kids cope with the changes your divorce will bring to their lives. And, finally, to ease some of the stress and pain, Chapter 8 provides suggestions on how to deal with your emotions.

Chapter 6

Putting Your Divorce in Motion

. . . .

In This Chapter

▶ Telling your spouse that you want to call it quits

▶ Figuring out your financial situation

▶ Determining what you want from your divorce

▶ Estimating the cost of your divorce

▶ Protecting your assets in case your divorce gets ugly

. . . .

*W*hen you definitely know that you're headed for a split, you can't begin preparing for the divorce process too soon. You need at least a general idea of what's to come in order to intelligently negotiate a fair divorce agreement. If you head into your divorce unprepared, you're likely to feel overwhelmed and panicky. Taking a proactive stance will help alleviate some of the natural anxiety you're feeling about your divorce.

In this chapter we offer you practical advice for breaking the news to your spouse and words of compassion for those of you who hear your spouse say, "I want a divorce." This chapter also provides advice for getting your money matters in order and information you need to help ensure that you get a fair and adequate divorce settlement.

We also provide an overview of the factors that influence the cost of your divorce — many of which you can control — and some general fee ranges for simple and complex divorces. You'll also find some words of advice if you're anticipating a hostile divorce and suggestions for planning for what's ahead.

We know of at least two magazines devoted entirely to the subject of divorce. Toronto-based *DIVORCE* magazine publishes editions for readers in California, New York, New Jersey, and Chicago, as well as Toronto. *Marital Status*, based in Baltimore, was available only in Maryland as of this writing, but the publisher has plans to expand distribution to 21 states.

Breaking the News to Your Spouse

Couples in troubled marriages usually try just about everything to resolve their problems. But, for some couples it becomes obvious that things are simply not going to get any better, and they decide to call it quits. But that's not always the way it works. Sometimes, only one spouse is ready to end the marriage and takes the other by total surprise with the news that he or she wants out.

If you are the one who wants to end your marriage, the way you break the news to your spouse can have a big influence on whether your divorce will be amicable or contentious. It can also help set the tone for your post-divorce relationship, an important consideration if you have minor children.

Maintaining your composure

Telling your spouse that you want a divorce isn't easy, particularly if the news comes as a total shock or if your spouse has been hoping that some-how, some way, you can work out your marital problems and stay together. The following suggestions may help you ease into that conversation and help your spouse accept the news as calmly as possible:

- ✔ Quietly and slowly tell your spouse your reasons for wanting to end your marriage. Review what you consider to be the problems in your marriage, what you may have done to try to fix them, and why you feel that your efforts have not worked. Even if you've covered this same ground many, many times before, go over it again.

- ✔ Avoid blaming your spouse for the end of your marriage (as difficult as that may be). Avoid accusatory or derogatory language, and try to steer clear of starting an argument.

- ✔ As much as possible, speak in terms of how you feel. It's hard to argue with someone about his or her feelings. If your spouse does try to argue with you, reiterate your feelings and intentions, over and over if necessary.

If a calm conversation is impossible because your spouse is simply too upset about the idea of divorce, tell your spouse you would like to talk again later. Your next conversation will probably be a little easier to take. You may need to have a few conversations concerning your intention to divorce before your spouse finally accepts the news.

Making sure your spouse hears the news from you first

Your spouse should learn about your divorce plans from you first and not through the rumor mill (from mutual friends, relatives, or even your kids). That's a cruel way for anyone to find out that his or her marriage is ending and a sure way to make for a bitter divorce.

If you have already filed for divorce, tell your spouse that you've done so before he or she receives the divorce papers. If you can't tell your spouse in person or with a phone call, write your spouse a letter. It's preferable that you compose the letter, not your attorney. An attorney's letter is too impersonal and your spouse may be angered that you didn't bother to write it yourself. If your spouse holds a grudge, it can make your divorce negotiations even more difficult.

Waiting until your spouse is ready to begin negotiations

Don't expect to begin negotiating your divorce agreement as soon as you tell your spouse the news. It may take weeks or even months before negotiations can begin. Be patient and move slowly. Remember, you've probably been thinking seriously for some time about divorce and may have even begun preparing for that change. Therefore, you're probably much more prepared to end your marriage than your spouse is.

Your spouse's initial reaction is more likely to be anger, shock, and disbelief rather than the desire to get cracking on the divorce proceedings. Give your spouse a chance to let the news sink in and time to do some preparation before you actually set your divorce in motion.

If you move too fast, feelings of guilt or remorse on your part, or feelings of anger or abandonment on your spouse's part, may result in bad decisions that you both will regret later. You may concede too much to your spouse or be too willing to compromise. Your spouse may make unreasonable demands out of anger and spite. Feeling pressure from you, your spouse may panic, hire an attorney right away, and turn your divorce into a hostile battle when it could have been an amicable split if you had waited longer.

However, waiting for the right time may not be possible or practical in some cases. Given the particulars of your situation, you may not be able to hold off until your spouse is ready to cooperate. Your spouse may never be ready, or you and your spouse may be so estranged that being civil to one another and working cooperatively is impossible.

When your spouse is ready, have a general discussion about the issues in your divorce — particularly whether you want to do the negotiating yourselves or hire attorneys to do it for you — and try to develop a general time table for beginning your divorce. Unless both of you feel in control of your emotions and ready to talk, don't push to iron out the details of your divorce right away.

Depending on your state and whether you are getting a fault or no-fault divorce, you may need to live apart from your spouse for a period of time before filing for divorce.

Pulling Together Your Money Stuff

From the law's perspective, your divorce is about dollars and cents. In fact, money is at the heart of every major issue — spousal support, division of property, child support, and sometimes even custody — that must be resolved before your divorce can be finalized.

Complete and accurate financial information is essential to your obtaining an equitable divorce settlement. You need this information whether your divorce is amicable or rancorous, and whether you negotiate a settlement agreement with your spouse or place your family's future in the hands of a judge.

Keeping cool if your spouse initiates the divorce

Even if the writing has been on the wall for months or even years, finding out that your spouse wants a divorce can send you into an emotional tailspin of shock and disbelief. As time goes on, you may vacillate between feelings of anger and sadness, or anger and depression.

The sooner you can face facts and move forward, the better off you both will be. Although feeling sorry for yourself is an understandable response to finding out that your marriage is ending, especially if you didn't want it to end, painting yourself as a victim and wallowing in self-pity are not healthy responses to your situation. Obsessing over "the unfairness of it all," and how you've "been wronged," and "what could have been" will prevent you from working out a reasonable divorce agreement.

The "poor me" refrain will eventually drive away most of your friends and family members at the time when you may need them the most.

As you work through your emotions and begin dealing with the practical realities of your divorce, avoid angry recriminations and do not insult your spouse. And, don't go out of your way to either spend time together or to remain apart; do what makes you feel most comfortable.

Without adequate financial information you may not get either your fair share of marital assets or a reasonable amount of spousal support, and you may also come up short in child support. (Chapter 2 has more information on financial preparedness for every married person. This chapter provides information on handling your finances when divorce is definitely in the offing.)

If your spouse holds all the financial cards, deciding when to raise the stakes, when to hold, and when to fold is a guessing game. If you guess wrong, you may end up with less than you deserve.

Inventorying what you own

One of the first things you should do in preparation for your divorce is to develop a comprehensive picture of your financial situation. You should determine exactly what you and your spouse own and what your assets are worth. In short, you must inventory and value all of your significant assets.

If your divorce is amicable and you and your spouse are committed to an equitable settlement, together you can create an asset inventory by assembling documents proving that you own certain items and what they are worth. Such documents may include vehicle titles, deeds of record to real property (such as your home or other buildings you may own), and records of ownership of financial instruments (such as stocks or bonds). Working together will save time and help ensure that you don't overlook anything. In this case, two heads definitely *are* better than one.

Your family's CPA, banker, financial adviser, or investment counselor can help you pull together the information and documentation you may need for your asset inventory.

To create a comprehensive portrait of your finances, make a list of all your household assets and note a current market value for each. *Current market value* is the amount you can get if you sell an asset at the present time. You may have prepared an inventory of your assets after reading Chapter 2. However, that inventory may need updating once your divorce becomes a reality — you or your spouse may have sold assets or purchased new ones, the value of your assets may have increased or decreased, and you may have paid off debts or acquired new ones.

The assets you need to inventory can include any of the following:

✔ Bank accounts

✔ Certificates of Deposit (CDs)

✔ Deferred compensation plans including IRAs, SEPs, 401(k)s, stock option plans, profit sharing plans

- ✔ Business interests
- ✔ Fine art and other collectibles
- ✔ Fine jewelry
- ✔ Your home and other real estate
- ✔ Household furnishings
- ✔ The cash value of your life insurance policies
- ✔ Money market accounts
- ✔ Stocks, bonds, and mutual funds
- ✔ Vehicles (including recreational vehicles such as boats, jet skis, motorcycles, or snowmobiles)

Property that you owned prior to your marriage or that you inherited during your marriage is your separate property and will not be part of your divorce. For more information about marital property versus separate property, turn to Chapter 2.

Use the worksheets at the Divorce Hotline Web site (www.divorcenet. com) to itemize and inventory your family's assets and debts. The worksheets can help you make sure that you are not overlooking anything significant. Budgeting worksheets are also available at that Web site.

To make certain that your inventory list is comprehensive, look through your home safe and bank safe deposit box for titles to property, deeds, securities, wills, or other documentation related to your ownership of property.

Inventorying what you owe

Your family's financial portrait is only half-finished until you inventory and value your household debts, which may include:

- ✔ Balances on lines of credit
- ✔ Credit card debts
- ✔ Mortgages
- ✔ Notes you may have cosigned
- ✔ Other types of personal loans, including student loans and business loans for which you or your spouse are personally liable

Gathering miscellaneous financial documents

To inventory your assets and debts, you will need to refer to a variety of other financial and legal documents in addition to checking and savings account registers and bank statements. Those documents include:

- ✔ Copies of your tax returns for the past five years
- ✔ Real estate tax bills
- ✔ Copies of all life insurance policies in which either of you is listed as a primary or contingency beneficiary or owner
- ✔ Broker's statements and account statements for your stocks, bonds, and mutual funds
- ✔ Copies of any financial statements you prepared separately or together when applying for a loan
- ✔ A copy of your will and your spouse's will and any other estate planning documents
- ✔ Profit-and-loss statements and balance sheets for the closely held business you, your spouse, or the both of you own together and copies of related partnership agreements or articles of incorporation
- ✔ Copies of any prenuptial or postnuptial agreements you may have signed

After you locate all the documents you need, keep them all together in a safe place. If you hire an attorney to help negotiate your divorce, your attorney will need all of that information and more. The more information you and your spouse willingly share with each other's attorneys, the less information your attorney will need to secure through the formal discovery process, and the more money you'll save. (We tell you about discovery in Chapter 4.) It's also a good idea to make copies of all the documents you gather together just in case your spouse takes the originals.

Creating an income and expenditures worksheet

Assuming that you and your spouse will be negotiating child support, spousal support or both, you need figures on the annual gross and net income (actual take-home pay) you and your spouse each earn through your work, investments, pensions, inheritance, child support from a previous marriage, bonuses, and other sources of income. And, you must know how you both spend that income.

To determine how much money is coming into and going out of your household, first create a worksheet called "Income" by drawing three columns on a sheet of paper — one column for your income, one for your spouse's income, and one for any joint income you may receive. List each source of income in the appropriate column. Underneath each income source, record the monthly and annual amounts for each. Then add up the dollar figures in each column to create monthly and annual income totals.

Next, create a second worksheet called "Expenses" and draw three columns as you did for the Income sheet — one column for your expenses, one for your spouse's, and one that reflects your joint expenses. For each regular expense item entered, estimate how much you spend monthly and annually on each item.

If your spouse will not cooperate with you in the budget development process, you may have to take your best guess for certain types of income and expenses by using bank statements, check stubs, check registers, and credit card receipts.

Planning Now for Your Life after Divorce

An important aspect of planning for divorce is thinking about what life will be like after your marriage has ended and what you want out of your divorce. You may want to also ask yourself the following:

- ✔ How much will you need for living expenses after you are divorced? (Think about developing a post-divorce budget that projects the income and expenses you anticipate.)

- ✔ What adjustments are needed in order to make ends meet and live a happy life on your own?

- ✔ If after your divorce you plan to work outside the home for the first time or reenter the job market after not working for several years, what job skills do you need to be marketable?

- ✔ Where can you get those job skills? How long will it take to get them and how much will that education cost? (Remember to factor educational expenses into your post-divorce budget and any transportation and child care costs you may incur while you are developing your job skills.)

Although it can be tough to think about these things when you are preoccupied by more immediate issues, having at least a general plan for your post-divorce life helps you better define your divorce priorities and determine what you really want from your divorce and what you are willing to give up. This preparation is essential to working out the terms of your divorce.

Deciding on goals and priorities

Write down your divorce goals and priorities in their order of importance. Then, put the list away in a safe place. After a month or so when you've had some time to think, take another look at your list. You'll probably find that you want to add, subtract, or reorder a few items.

When you are thinking about what you really want out of your divorce try to be reasonable. Avoid asking for the impossible just to hurt or upset your spouse. You risk setting yourself up for disappointment and making your divorce more difficult than it needs to be.

Determining what you want out of your divorce

Spend some time thinking about the kind of divorce you want and what you are willing to do to get that divorce. Be prepared to articulate your desires to your divorce attorney. For example, are you willing to go all the way to a trial to get the top items on your divorce priorities list? Is a negotiated settlement of paramount importance? Is having sole custody of your children absolutely important? What would you be willing to give up to get more spousal support or support for a longer period of time?

If you're clear about the kind of divorce you want, you'll be better able to select an attorney who can help you achieve it. You'll also be able to provide your attorney with direction and feedback during the divorce process. If you hire a divorce lawyer with little or no thought to your goals and priorities, terminating your marriage may end up being more stressful, lengthy, and expensive than you ever imagined.

How Much Do You Have to Spend to End Your Marriage?

The thousands of dollars you spent on your wedding and honeymoon may be a mere pittance when compared with the cost of your divorce. How much it will cost to end your marriage depends on a number of factors:

- ✔ Whether your divorce is amicable and cooperative, or bitter and contentious.

The more you and your spouse can agree on, the less you will have to spend on attorneys, legal fees, and court costs. If your divorce is contentious, your attorney may have to file numerous pretrial motions. It will take your attorney one to two hours to prepare each motion and another one to two hours to argue each motion before a judge, and you will have to pay for all of that time.

✔ The state you live in and whether you reside in an urban or rural area.

✔ The reputation and experience of the attorney who represents you.

More experienced attorneys or attorneys with winning reputations can command bigger retainers and fees than lawyers who have not been practicing as long or who do not have established reputations.

✔ How many of your divorce terms you and your spouse can work out together.

✔ Whether you and your spouse get into a custody battle, which can be very expensive.

✔ The amount of marital property and debts you need to divide up and the complexity of those assets and debts.

Depending on the debts and assets involved, you may need to hire an appraiser, CPA, or other professional to help with your divorce.

✔ Whether your spouse is hiding any of your marital assets.

✔ Whether you and your spouse are willing to settle your divorce outside of court or whether one or both of you is determined to go to trial.

✔ The legal strategy of your attorney and your spouse's attorney.

Pinpointing the cost with multiple estimates

To get a better idea of the likely cost of your divorce, get estimates from several divorce attorneys. When you are interviewing potential attorneys, ask for fee estimates based on several different divorce scenarios. That will help you to decide whether to hold out for a particular property settlement or custody arrangement, or specific amount of alimony.

By using the attorneys' estimates, you can do a very basic cost-benefit analysis comparing the value of what you may gain should you pursue a particular goal compared with how much it would cost you to get it. However, no attorney can guarantee that you'll get the outcome you want, regardless of how much money you spend.

The least it will cost

If your divorce is extremely simple — you and your spouse have little or nothing to negotiate, you have no minor children, no marital property, few debts, neither of you is asking for alimony, and you are willing to complete most, if not all of the paperwork yourself — you can get divorced for just a few hundred dollars, maybe even less.

Even if you own marital property or owe marital debts, your divorce may cost you no more than a few thousand dollars, assuming that you and your spouse can work out the terms of your divorce together after an up-front consultation with your individual attorneys. Your attorneys should nevertheless review your final agreement. (Chapter 13 provides helpful information if you and your spouse want to do most of your negotiating.)

The most it will cost

Be prepared to spend a whole lot more money on your divorce if you and your spouse fight one another every step of the way, or if the issues in your divorce are complicated and the active involvement of your attorneys from start to finish is essential. In this case, you may be looking at legal bills in the five figures, or even more. For example, at the end of a prolonged child support battle, your legal bills may be as high as $30,000 to $40,000. If you and your spouse go to battle over the custody of your children, those bills could *triple*!

The hourly rate of an experienced family law attorney can range from $150 to $300 or more. Some attorneys will handle a very straightforward and amicable divorce for a flat rate as low as $500 per case.

Do what you can to avoid a custody battle. Not only will it be extremely expensive, but the battle may cause your children to suffer long-lasting emotional damage. If you are considering a custody fight, analyze your motivations, perhaps with the help of a mental health professional. After some serious reflection, you may decide that you are confusing your own needs with your children's or that you are using the issue of custody as a way to express your animosity toward your spouse.

Anticipating a Hostile Divorce

If you suspect that your divorce will be a knock-down, drag-out fight, or if you are certain that your divorce will not go smoothly, you need to take some defensive measures.

Opening a savings account in your own name

If you are sharing a savings account with your spouse, withdraw only some of the money in the account — maybe half, depending on your needs and the amount in the account — and deposit it in a new account in your own name at a different bank. Open your own checking account in the same way.

 After your spouse learns that you have taken money out of your joint account and placed it in your separate account, expect some fireworks that will make your divorce agreement negotiations more difficult. If you withdraw an unreasonable amount of money (and just what "unreasonable" constitutes is something your attorneys have to decide), you may end up getting less in your property settlement.

 Beware of leaving too little in your checking account to cover your monthly expenses, especially if the checking account you share with your spouse usually contains just enough funds to pay the monthly bills. Bounced check charges and angry creditors are among the last things you need right now!

Closing out your joint accounts

Close out any joint credit card accounts you maintain with your spouse. If you can't close a joint account because of an outstanding debt that cannot be paid off immediately, write the creditor to explain that you won't be responsible for any additional debts on that account beyond the current outstanding balance. Also, if you and your spouse have a line of credit with a bank or credit card, cancel or reduce any lines of credit that you may share. Be sure to inform your spouse of what you have done.

 Individual credit — credit in your own name — is essential to your having a life on your own. Building a credit history takes time. If you don't have individual credit when you close your joint accounts, you may have to wait several years before you have access to credit at the best terms. (See Chapter 2 for more on building your own credit history.)

Finding a safe place for your important personal property

If you are concerned that your spouse may try to damage, destroy, or steal any of your personal property in anger or out of a desire for revenge, find a safe place to hide your valuables. That can be a safe deposit box in your name, the home of a trusted friend or family member, your office file cabinet, or any other place your spouse can't access.

If your spouse steals or damages your personal property, you may be able to sue your spouse for theft or destruction of property. Your attorney can use evidence of your spouse's destructive behavior as leverage during your divorce negotiations or divorce trial.

Protecting your mutual assets from being wasted by your spouse

If your spouse is angry about your divorce or wants to get revenge, he or she may try to use up your joint assets rather than allow you to get a portion of those assets in your divorce. If you are concerned that this may happen, consult a family law attorney right away about what steps you can take to safeguard your joint assets. For example, the attorney will probably advise you to avoid maintaining large cash balances in your joint checking accounts or will file a temporary restraining order and request an emergency hearing regarding the property in question.

Identifying sources of ready funds

Protecting your legal rights when you are involved in a hostile divorce takes money, and lots of it. If you anticipate that your divorce will be hostile, start identifying the financial resources you have at your disposal right now. Those resources may include your separate property (such as your savings account, stocks, bonds, or mutual funds), borrowing against your retirement fund, getting a second mortgage on real estate, borrowing money from family members, and anything else along those lines.

Talk with a CPA or your financial adviser about the tax consequences and other implications of selling stocks or mutual funds, borrowing against the funds in your retirement account, or taking a second loan on the real estate you own.

Chapter 7

Helping Your Kids Get through Your Divorce

. . . .

In This Chapter

▶ Determining when the time is right to break the news

▶ Talking to your children all at once or one-on-one

▶ Preparing for your children's response (and their questions)

. . . .

*R*emembering to put your children first can seem like an awfully tall order, especially if the breakup of your marriage is full of conflict. After all, you have your own emotions to deal with, financial and legal matters to resolve, and worries about what the future may bring. Nevertheless, your children depend on you for the care and support they need to be happy and secure kids who'll grow into well-adjusted adults.

In this chapter, we help you address your children's personal needs during your divorce and offer advice for minimizing any emotional trauma they may experience. We also offer some guidance on when and how to tell your children about the end of your marriage and alert you to some of the ways your kids may respond to the news.

Remaining Sensitive to Your Children's Feelings

When you get divorced, you and your spouse are not the only people affected by the change in your marital status. Your divorce means the end of family life as your children have known it, something that has been important to them and that they have probably always taken for granted.

If you don't attend to your children's needs during your divorce (and afterward), you risk making your kids the innocent victims of your marital breakup. Studies have shown that children who are victimized by divorce are more likely to have trouble in school and with the law, which means that you may end up spending money later on for therapists, tutors, and attorneys' fees.

Research also shows that parents who openly express their hatred, anger, feelings of betrayal, or desire for vengeance — feelings that many couples have toward one another during divorce, and sometimes long after — unwittingly program their kids to be unhappy adults with troubled marriages of their own. An even more damaging situation occurs when couples manipulate their children in order to gain the upper hand in custody negotiations or to get back at the other spouse.

Your divorce may also mean that your children experience a change in economic circumstances, or they may have to move out of their home and neighborhood, attend a new school, and make all new friends. Therefore, unless you are aware of what to do and what not to do in regard to your children while keeping an eye on their moods and behaviors, your divorce can be emotionally devastating for them, even if it is a good thing for you.

If your children have gone through a divorce before, don't assume that it's easier for them the second time around. The second divorce may trigger the very same emotions they experienced during your first divorce. Their lives are again disrupted by changes in their lifestyle and the discomfort of living with two adults who are preoccupied with the end of their marriage.

What your kids may be fearing (and not telling you)

During and after their parents' divorce, children (especially the younger ones) often become fearful that terrible things will happen to them, or believe that they are in some way responsible for the breakup of their parents' marriage. Some of the more-common fears and misconceptions kids have about divorce include the following:

- The parent I no longer live with will leave me forever.

- My parents' divorce is my fault.

- If I am really good, my parents will get back together.

- I have to choose between my parents. I can't have a relationship with both of them after they are divorced.

- My mother's (father's) new boyfriend (girlfriend) or husband (wife) will replace my real parent.

- My stepbrother or stepsister is going to replace me.

Understanding the thoughts that may be going through your children's minds can keep you alert to any signs that your kids are having trouble coping with your divorce.

Strategies for Breaking the News to Your Children

Children often fear that they will lose one of their parents in a divorce or that their parents will abandon them and they will have to fend for themselves. Therefore, both of you need to convey in your words and deeds that you will always be there for them.

Make sure that your reassurances and promises are more than hot air. Otherwise, your children will become distrustful of you and cynical about your reliability and honesty.

Agree on what you're going to say

It is best if you and your spouse can take the time to determine what you are going to say about your divorce before you talk with your children. Get your story straight so that you don't contradict one another or argue while you are breaking the news to your kids. If you need help deciding what to say to your children, talk things over with your religious advisor or schedule an appointment with a mental health professional.

Unfortunately, some of you will not have cooperative spouses. That means that you and your soon-to-be-ex will probably have separate conversations with your children. Before you do, for your children's sake, try to come to an agreement about exactly what you will tell them. If you don't, you risk sending them conflicting messages about your divorce and its possible impact on them.

Tell them as a couple

If at all possible, you and your spouse should tell your children about your divorce together, even if it requires putting your animosity aside for a while. You will convey to them that although your marriage may be ending, you can cooperate as their parents, and that they still have a family — just a different kind of family — and you will both remain actively involved in their lives.

Play fair with each other

You should both agree that when you talk with your children neither of you will blame the other for your breakup or encourage your children to side with one of you against the other. Both behaviors are unfair to your children and can inflict irreparable emotional harm. When you criticize their other parent, your comments can backfire on you — your children may side with the parent you have maligned, and not with you.

For valuable advice on how to help your children cope with your divorce, check out *The Divorced Parent* by Stephanie Marston (Pocket Books).

Be honest, realistic, and avoid emotion

Be honest with your children about why you are getting divorced, but remember to keep their ages in mind and avoid sharing the lurid details behind your split. Tell them as much as they need to know and no more. If you haven't been able to hide the discord in your marriage, you may want to acknowledge what your children already know by saying something like, "We know that you've heard us fighting a lot, and here's why. . . ."

Don't hide the fact that life is going to be different for everyone in the family because of your divorce. Prepare your kids for some of the changes to come. Then reassure your children that your divorce has not and will not change your love for them and that you will continue to be involved in their lives. But don't promise them things you can't deliver.

Be very clear with your children that your divorce has absolutely nothing to do with them. Otherwise, they may feel somehow responsible for the divorce and assume that if only they had behaved better or gotten higher grades you would not be ending your marriage.

Try not to get emotional when you tell your children about your divorce. Watching a parent cry or get very upset can be frightening for children. Don't add to their anxiety with histrionics and overly dramatic behavior. You're likely to make them more concerned about your emotions than their own. As a consequence, they may not let you know exactly what they are feeling.

Ways you can help them absorb the news

If your children are having trouble coping with the news of your divorce, all they may need to turn their frowns into smiles is some cuddling and a little extra attention. But sometimes it's not that simple. When your children need more than what you can give them, consider involving a school counselor, mental health professional, social worker, relative, or another adult who's especially close to your children. Participating in a support group may also be helpful to older children.

Tell your children's teachers, baby-sitters and other caregivers, the parents of their close friends, and any other adults they see regularly about your divorce plans. Your heads-up will help them to understand that any significant changes in your children's behavior may be traced to your divorce. Ask these adults to keep you informed of any such changes.

Contact your state's family law court, a family law attorney, mental health professional, or a social worker who works with children and families to find out if any public or private resources (such as classes, workshops, and support groups) are available in your area that can help your kids cope with your divorce. These same resources may also offer counseling for divorcing parents.

In some jurisdictions, divorcing parents are required to take parenting classes taught by mental health professionals. In these classes they learn about children's reactions to divorce, effective parent-child communication, and resources that can help parents and their children.

Watch your own behavior around your children

Monitor your own behavior around your children. What you choose to do (or don't do, as the following list will tell you) can either help reassure them that things will be okay or can add to their anxiety about the future.

- ✔ Don't fight with your spouse when your children are around.
- ✔ Don't say negative things about your spouse to your children or to someone else within hearing distance of your children.
- ✔ Don't get overly emotional around your children about your divorce or your life after the divorce. You risk increasing their insecurity and fear about the future.
- ✔ Don't use your children as liaisons between you and your spouse.
- ✔ Don't interfere in your children's relationship with your spouse by trying to manipulate them into thinking of you as the "good parent" and your spouse as the "bad parent."
- ✔ Don't pressure your kids to choose sides.
- ✔ Avoid making dramatic changes in their daily routines. As much as possible, keep everything in their lives just as it was. Children generally don't like change, and divorce is change enough.

✔ Don't attempt to assuage your guilt over how your divorce may affect them — or try to get them to align with you solely and reject their other parent — by giving them special gifts or privileges or by relaxing your discipline with them.

✔ Avoid making your children your confidantes. Keep your adult worries and concerns to yourself or share them only with other adults.

✔ Don't look to your children for comforting. It should work the other way around.

✔ Don't expect your child to become "the little man" or "the little woman" of the house. Your kids are kids, not surrogate spouses.

When to Tell Your Children

Most of us tend to put off doing things that are unpleasant or that we don't feel confident about. So, you may come up with countless reasons to delay telling your children about your divorce plans. However, make sure that you tell them before anyone else does. They need to hear the news from you, in your own words. And, in the same breath, you need to reassure them that you will always love them and take care of them.

The right time to talk with your children about the changes to come depends on their ages and on the circumstances of your divorce. For example, if your spouse announces that he or she has already filed for divorce and is moving out the next week, you need to tell your children about the split sooner, and not later.

Telling the older kids

Bear in mind that preteens and teens usually need to be told sooner than very young children (assuming that you have some control over the timing of your conversations with your children). Older children need to be told sooner because they are more likely to learn about your divorce plans by overhearing a conversation or by coming across divorce-related papers. Also, older children are better at sensing that "something is up." Therefore, once you are certain that you will be divorcing and have worked out at least some of the details, especially those that affect your children, have a talk with your preteens and teens as soon as possible.

Do not discuss your divorce plans with your older children until you have talked the plans over with your spouse. It is unfair to make your kids your divorce confidantes and try to seek their advice and counsel. That is an inappropriate and unhealthy role for your children to play. If you need advice and counsel, talk to a trusted friend or family member, your religious advisor, or a mental health professional.

Telling the younger ones

When it comes to toddlers and elementary-age children, avoid telling them about your divorce plans too far ahead of the date when you and your spouse plan to begin living apart. Young children tend to have a different sense of time than adults and older children have. For them, a week can seem like a month and a month can seem like a year. If you tell your younger children prematurely, you risk intensifying the anxiety they have over knowing that their lives are going to change in ways they don't yet understand.

Parent News is a comprehensive online newsletter for divorcing and divorced parents. It covers a wide range of subjects from helping with your kids' homework to family-friendly books and movies, and also features informative articles and news updates about issues affecting parents. Head to http://parent.net for more information.

Regardless of their ages, whenever possible don't wait until just before you and your spouse begin living apart to break the news to your children. Instead, tell them far enough ahead of the day you plan to separate so that they have time to process your news, ask you questions, spend time with both of you in a relaxed manner, and enjoy your affection. All of those things are essential preparation for the changes ahead.

For a sensitive and comprehensive overview of the stress that children commonly feel when their parents are going through a divorce, and detailed advice on what parents can do to help their kids, head to the following Web page:

```
http://muextension.missouri.edu/xplor/heguide/humanrel/
              gh6600.htm
```

Telling Them Individually or All Together

Should you tell your children about your divorce all at the same time, or have separate conversations with each of them? In this section we give you arguments in support of either approach.

As a group

If your children are close in age and maturity, telling them all together has important benefits.

- ✔ **It can help foster a "we're all in this together" attitude among your children.** That feeling can be both a comfort and a source of strength to your kids.

✔ **If all of your children learn about your divorce at the same time, then each of them knows exactly what his or her siblings know.** This may not seem important to you, but if you tell each of your kids separately, they may worry that they don't know what their siblings know or that you are going to treat them differently than everyone else in the family.

Each child alone

If your children have significant disparities in their ages or levels of maturity, it's advisable to have individual talks with them so you can tailor an appropriate message.

Be sure to tell each child that you are having a similar conversation with his or her siblings. Unless your children are very young, they are probably going to talk with one another about what you have told them. Therefore, your message about why you are getting a divorce and what is going to change or stay the same in their lives should be consistent. If you tell each child something different, you'll only add to their anxiety and confusion.

Anticipating Your Children's Response to the Announcement

You can't predict exactly how your children will react to the news of your divorce. Their reaction depends on their ages and maturity levels, their personalities, and their relationship with you, among other things. Interestingly enough however, you may find that their emotions mirror yours and may include any or all of the following:

✔ Disbelief

✔ Anger

✔ Fear

✔ Sadness

✔ Depression

✔ Rejection

To help monitor how well your children are dealing with the news of your divorce, try to spend some extra time with them (but not in an interfering way). The time you spend together gives your kids the opportunity to express their feelings and concerns about their daily lives.

The art of "active" listening

If you have never before practiced *active listening* with your children, now is the time to start. Active listening requires your being attuned to the feelings behind your children's comments and questions, and then letting them know in a nonjudgmental way that you heard what they were saying.

Active listening does not involve preaching or lecturing, and doesn't necessarily involve analysis or problem-solving. Its purpose is to encourage your children to open up to you and to tell you what they think about your divorce.

Active listening promotes a feeling of love and trust between you and your children, something they need in order to deal with their parents' divorce.

After your children find out about your divorce plans, they may begin to feel isolated and cut off from their friends. They may feel as though they're the only children whose parents ever got divorced and may be embarrassed about what's happening to them. On the other hand, if you and your spouse fought openly and often during your marriage, or if violence or substance abuse colored your relationship, your divorce may be a relief to your children and represent a positive change in their lives.

Although your children may appear to be coping, don't assume that they're not having trouble in school or at play, or won't have trouble later on. Stay attuned to their mood swings or any changes in their behavior that may be a sign of emotional problems.

If you separate before your divorce is final, your children should visit the parent who moves out as soon as possible so that they can be assured that they have easy access to both of you. However, if your children refuse to visit their other parent or act reluctant to do so, don't force them. Also, make sure that they have their other parent's new address and phone number.

Recognizing the Signs That Your Kids Are Having Trouble Coping

If you're divorcing, you need to be familiar with the more common signs of emotional distress in children and stay alert for those behaviors so that you can intervene as soon as possible. When kids behave in the following ways, they're asking for help.

Toddlers to kindergarten-age children may

- Revert to infantile behavior, such as bedwetting, thumb-sucking, biting, and crying.
- Have trouble sleeping in their own room or have nightmares.
- Develop behavior problems at home or with other children.
- Become fearful of leaving you.

Elementary-age children may

- Get sick more than usual or act sick so that they can stay home from school (headaches and stomach aches are particularly common).
- Choose one parent to be angry with and choose another to cling to for comfort.
- Begin spending more time alone in their rooms and less time playing with friends.
- Participate in fewer classroom activities.

Adolescents and preteens may

- Withdraw from friends and family.
- Develop nonspecific illnesses or nervous habits such as nail-biting and facial tics.
- Spend more time alone in their rooms.
- Express anger toward the parent they think is responsible for the divorce.
- Try to play surrogate spouse to the parent they feel has been wronged.
- Develop behavioral problems (such as getting into fights) at school, outside of school, or at home.
- Engage in rebellious behavior such as shoplifting or vandalism, skipping school, smoking, drinking, doing drugs, or becoming sexually promiscuous.

Although you may have no cause for alarm if your children are under stress for a short period of time, if your child's obvious discomfort is prolonged or grows worse, you do have cause for concern. Alcohol and drug abuse, delinquency, or criminal actions require immediate attention because those behaviors can put your child and others in danger.

What Your Kids Will Want to Know

After you tell your children about your divorce plans, give them an opportunity to ask questions. If they ask you something that you can't answer, say so by admitting that you don't know or it's too soon to tell. When appropriate, tell them that you will give them an answer by a certain date or as soon as you can.

Questions you'll probably hear first

Your children's initial questions will probably relate to how your divorce will change their lives and what will stay the same. For example, depending on their ages, they may want to know

- ✔ Where will they live?
- ✔ Will they still go to the same school?
- ✔ Will you and your spouse still live in the same town?
- ✔ Will they spend time with each of you?
- ✔ Will you continue to coach their soccer or Little League team?
- ✔ Can they continue their music or dance lessons?
- ✔ How will you share parenting responsibilities?
- ✔ Can they still go to camp next summer?
- ✔ Will there be enough money?
- ✔ Where will their dog or cat live?

Don't be surprised if your children don't ask you many questions at first. Learning that you are getting a divorce will probably come as quite a shock, even if they already knew that you and your spouse are having marital problems and even if they have plenty of friends with divorced parents. They may need to let the news sink in before they're ready to ask you questions.

What you'll hear from the older kids versus the younger ones

Your older children may come to you with questions after they have shared your news with friends, especially if their friends' parents are divorced and their friends tell them what the divorce experience was like for them.

Your younger children may have a hard time grasping the concept of divorce and realizing that you and your spouse will always continue to love them and care for them. You kids may ask you the same questions over and over, which can really tax your patience. Understand that right now they need constant reassurance.

You can help your younger children deal with your divorce by reading them age-appropriate books that deal with the subject. We recommend the following titles to help your younger children acknowledge and express their fears and worries about your divorce and the changes that are occurring in their lives: *Dinosaurs Divorce: A Guide for Changing Families,* by Marc Brown and Laurence Krasny Brown (Little, Brown & Co.), and *At Daddy's on Saturdays* by Linda Walvoord Girard (Albert Whitman & Co.).

Opening up a dialog if your kids don't come to you first

Let your children know that you are willing and available to talk with them about your divorce and answer their questions whenever they want. If your kids seem reluctant to ask you any questions, take the initiative by talking with each of them individually about your divorce and asking them if they have any questions about it.

Obviously, if you have always enjoyed an honest, open relationship with your children, they will be more willing to discuss their fears and concerns than if you never before expressed an interest in finding out what they were thinking or having a meaningful conversation with them.

Pick up a copy of *Difficult Questions Kids Ask and Are Too Afraid to Ask About Divorce,* by Meg F. Schneider and Joan Offerman-Zuckerberg (Fireside). We recommend this title if you want advice on how to tell your children the truth without frightening them, how to strengthen your relationship with them, and how to keep and build their trust.

For insight into children's thoughts about divorce, read *My Parents Are Getting Divorced: A Handbook for Kids,* published by the American Bar Association's Family Law Section. After you read it, pass it on to your child. To order, call 800-285-2221. Single copies are $9.50.

Chapter 8
Taking Care of Your Emotional Self

. . . .

In This Chapter
▶ Preparing yourself for the emotional ups and downs
▶ Recognizing the stages of grief
▶ Controlling your feelings
▶ Anticipating the response of friends and family

. . . .

*F*or better or worse, your marriage is an important part of your life. So, if you're like most people, ending it isn't easy — whether you initiate the divorce, it's a mutual decision, or your spouse is the one who calls it quits.

As the reality of your divorce sinks in, clear and rational thinking may become difficult, if not impossible. While one part of your brain may know that divorce is for the best (or at least inevitable), the other part may be a jumbled and confused mess of emotions — sorrow for your failed marriage, anger at your spouse, self-recrimination over what you could have done to save your relationship, and fear for the future.

Focusing on your day-to-day activities and getting a good night's sleep may become increasingly hard to do. You may find yourself distracted by questions such as: Will I have enough money to survive? Where will I live? How will the children be affected? Will I ever marry again?

This chapter helps you understand the emotions you are likely to feel and provides you with suggestions for how to keep them under control.

If you did not initiate your divorce, and especially if your spouse's desire to split up took you totally by surprise, you will probably experience more intense emotions than your spouse will. Therefore, this chapter is definitely one for you to read. On the other hand, if you initiated your divorce or if you're anxious to be single again, don't assume that you can skip over this chapter. Unless you are made of stone, at some point during your divorce you will no doubt feel some strong emotions, too.

Readying Yourself for the Emotional Ups and Downs

Getting divorced can be like an emotional roller coaster ride. One day you feel angry, sad, depressed, and guilty, and the next you feel hopeful and confident. Your feelings may even change from morning to afternoon, or hour to hour. They will probably be most intense at first, and gradually ease up over time. You may also experience the same sorts of emotions when you separate.

Little things may trigger your mood swings: You hear a song you and your spouse used to enjoy; you go to a party by yourself and feel awkward trying to make conversation; you run across some photos of happier times; or your child asks you a question that you find especially painful.

Because divorce is a highly personal experience, there is no way to predict exactly how you will respond to it. Nevertheless, you'll likely find that you're experiencing at least a couple of the following emotions:

- ✔ Sadness or grief over the loss of your relationship
- ✔ Anger toward your spouse for past slights and oversights
- ✔ Embarrassment that your marriage is ending, especially if you've always tried to portray yours as the perfect marriage
- ✔ A sense of failure and disappointment that you couldn't make your marriage work
- ✔ Fear of the effect your divorce may have on your children and yourself (especially if it's been many years since you were single or if you've never lived on your own)
- ✔ Guilt if you initiated the divorce
- ✔ A sense of rejection or abandonment if your spouse initiated the divorce, especially if he or she left you for someone else
- ✔ Depression

Even if you no longer want to be married to your spouse, you still experience some amount of loss. That loss may include a part of your extended family, some of your friends, possibly your home, or your economic status. The more you understand your feelings, the better you'll be able to put your emotional response in perspective, handle it in a positive way, and prevent your emotions from derailing your divorce.

Understanding the Stages of Grief

Elisabeth Kubler-Ross, M.D., wrote an important book about grief and loss called *On Death and Dying* (Macmillan Publishing Co., Inc.). In it, she explains that when someone loses a close loved one, that person must progress through a series of stages in order to get over the loss and heal emotionally. Those stages, which follow, have been found to apply to the loss of anything that is especially important in life, including the loss of a marriage.

- ✔ Shock and denial
- ✔ Anger
- ✔ Depression
- ✔ Bargaining
- ✔ Sorrow
- ✔ Understanding and acceptance

Understanding each of the stages you must pass through in order to recover from a divorce won't make your pain go away. In fact, as you experience some of the earlier stages of grief, you may feel like you are going crazy or that life will never be normal again. However, knowing what to expect, realizing that what you are feeling is normal, and finding out that countless other people in your situation have gone on to find happiness in life can be very reassuring.

Because your judgment may be somewhat impaired during the early stages of the healing process, avoid making important decisions related to your divorce until you have reached the understanding and acceptance stage. If important decisions must be made, seek some objective input from a trusted friend or family member.

How long it takes to get through the grieving process is different for everyone. For some it takes just a few months; for others it takes a year or more. Furthermore, even after you think you have stopped grieving, something can happen to trigger your emotions all over again. Receiving your final divorce papers, seeing your former spouse with someone new, or the advent of a special holiday can dredge up feelings you thought you'd put behind you.

Shock and denial

Even if you knew that your marriage had problems and that your spouse was unhappy, the news that he or she wants a divorce can be gut-wrenching. *Divorce?* That's something that happens to other people, not to you! If the decision to divorce is a mutual one, you may still find it difficult to comprehend the idea that your marriage is actually ending.

During this stage, you may vacillate between thinking that it's all just a silly misunderstanding and that you and your spouse can work things out. You may also find yourself questioning your judgment (were you too naïve?) and the assumptions you made about your marriage and your spouse (were you too trusting?). You may also feel anxious about all the changes about to take place in your life and unprepared to deal with them.

Anger

Anger commonly follows shock (although not with everyone). Anger is a normal response to the demise of your marriage, especially if your spouse initiates the divorce. In addition to being angry at your spouse, you may be angry with yourself for the things you could have done but didn't do during your marriage.

Expressing your anger is actually a healthy response that can help to relieve some of the pressure you feel. Keeping that anger all bottled up can lead to depression. Of course, you can get *too* angry. If you let your anger get the best of you, you may find yourself lashing out at your children, experiencing problems at work, and in general making your divorce far more difficult and ugly than it needs to be.

If you get angry every time you talk with your spouse, try to figure out why. Figuring it out may take professional help. What "buttons" does he or she push for you, and vice versa? The sooner you can answer that question the quicker you can get off the emotional roller coaster you're riding on.

When you are feeling angry, talk to a close friend. Find one who is happy just to listen and won't tell you how to think, argue with you, or play devil's advocate by taking your spouse's side. You need someone who will let you blow off steam. Avoid friends who reinforce your anger. They may convince you that feeling angry all the time is okay and discourage you from moving beyond it. Feeling some anger for a little while is okay; but harboring too much anger for too long is dangerous and destructive.

When you can't seem to shake your anger, and especially if you become confrontational or violent, seek the help of a mental health professional immediately. It is imperative that you confide in someone who can help you put your feelings in perspective.

Depression

Depression is another perfectly normal response to a difficult life situation. However, if your depression won't go away or grows worse, if you begin drinking too much or doing drugs to numb your feelings, or if you're having thoughts of suicide, seek immediate help from a mental health professional. You may need some ongoing therapy sessions or medication to help you get through the tough times and out of your depression.

If you're are crying a lot, having difficulty sleeping or sleeping too much, gaining or losing weight, or ignoring your physical appearance, you may benefit from antidepressant medication. If your doctor prescribes an antidepressant (in combination with therapy, if necessary) it doesn't mean that you're crazy; it simply means that you need some help to get through the trauma of your divorce in the safest way possible.

A correlation exists between divorce and suicide. In fact, some studies indicate that the rate of suicide among divorcing couples is three times higher than among married couples!

Bargaining

At times during the healing process, you may respond to your divorce by trying to strike bargains with your spouse. In desperation, you promise to do just about anything to keep your marriage together and to make the pain go away.

Avoid making such deals. If your spouse accepts your offer and you stop your divorce proceedings, you're only postponing the inevitable. The promises you make may be impossible for you to keep, and you may find that you are more miserable than ever in your marriage. If you are tempted to promise your spouse the world in order to save your marriage, talk to a trusted friend or therapist first to get an objective outsider's viewpoint.

Sorrow

Feeling sad is yet another normal response to the end of your marriage. You may cry over what your relationship used to be or over the realization that all the dreams and hopes you had for your marriage won't be realized. You may mourn the loss of your role as a spouse and greatly miss the life-style you enjoyed as a married person.

You may also feel remorse over what your divorce may do to your children. Your kids may have to move into a smaller house or apartment, leaving behind their neighborhood, best friends, and favorite teachers. If your children will be living with your spouse, you won't be as much a part of their lives, and that aspect of your divorce can be very difficult for your kids to deal with.

Feelings of sorrow can also be triggered by the realization that you are losing the wife or husband role that you greatly value. You may feel sad about the coming life-style changes — living apart from your children, moving into a smaller home, living in a less comfortable neighborhood, or giving up club memberships or hobbies that you can no longer afford.

If you're feeling sad about what divorce is taking from your life, it's important to realize that no situation lasts forever. In the future, you may experience a more loving and more successful relationship, make more money, and even have more children. Try to use what you learned in this last relationship to make your married life better the next time around.

Understanding and acceptance

Eventually, if you're like most people, you will begin to accept the fact of your divorce. Ideally, you should reach this stage before you begin negotiating your divorce agreement with your spouse, but many people cannot resolve their emotional conflict until after their divorce is over. But, when you do reach this stage, you will finally begin to experience some peace in your life.

Although you may continue to feel some anger toward your spouse or depression over the changes that have occurred in your life, those emotions will gradually dissipate. Your energy level will climb and your enthusiasm for life will return. Laughter comes easier to you, you're ready to begin dating again, and you feel ready to take on new challenges.

 If you begin dating, keep it casual. Studies show that rebound marriages — marriages that occur just a short time after a couple's divorce is final — have a high failure rate. Divorced spouses need time to gain a perspective on why their marriages failed and how to increase their chance of marital success the next time around.

Preventing Your Emotions from Taking Over

How you handle your emotions can mean the difference between creating a fulfilling life for yourself as a single person and remaining stuck in the past. It can also mean the difference between helping your children cope with the situation and jeopardizing your children's happiness now and in the future.

You can end up bitter, angry, and defeated, or you can emerge from your divorce a stronger and more self-confident person.

How your emotions can affect you

It's important to recognize the possible negative effects of not dealing with the emotions you're feeling. Letting your emotions go unchecked can

- ✔ Impede your ability to make sound decisions.
- ✔ Sap your energy at the time you need it most.
- ✔ Prevent you from recognizing and acknowledging how you may have contributed to the demise of your marriage.
- ✔ Make you more apt to acquiesce when it comes to your divorce negotiations, especially if you feel wracked with guilt and remorse.
- ✔ Drive away your friends and family.

Techniques for getting through the tough times

You can take some steps to help yourself move through the emotional healing process as quickly as possible.

- ✔ **Give yourself permission to cry.** Crying is not a sign of weakness. A good cry can be a great way to release emotion. Plus, crying releases natural antidepressant chemicals in your brain.
- ✔ **Reach out to close friends and family members.**
- ✔ **If you are not comfortable talking with friends and family you may want to join a divorce support group.**
- ✔ **Keep a journal.** Sometimes, just the process of recording your thoughts and feelings can have a calming effect and help you gain a new perspective about your life.
- ✔ **Begin an exercise program, or start exercising more.** Exercise makes you feel better about yourself, something you may really need if your spouse initiated your divorce. Also, science has shown that exercise helps release those wonderful endorphins, which help lift your spirits naturally.
- ✔ **Be kind to yourself and enjoy focusing on your own needs instead of on your spouse or on your marriage problems.** Renew your interest in a sport you used to enjoy, pick up a new book by your favorite author, or take up a new hobby.

✔ **Enroll in a class, just for the fun of it, or with an eye toward future employment or a new career.** You can explore and develop new talents while making new friends.

✔ **Volunteer.** Getting involved in a cause that you care about can boost your self-esteem and take your mind off your own problems. If you are having trouble getting motivated to do anything other than sleep and eat, the more you can structure your life the better. Volunteer work is one way to do that.

✔ **Get reacquainted with friends you lost touch with after your marriage began failing.**

✔ **Refocus on your career.** But don't let your work consume your entire life. Withdrawing into your job won't make the unpleasantness of your life disappear.

✔ **Spend more time with your children.** Making your children an even more important part of your life than they already are helps reassure them that your divorce in no way diminishes your love for them and that you will continue to be a part of their lives, no matter what.

✔ **Appreciate nature.** The beauty of nature can help heal a wounded spirit. Go for walks in the park or along a waterfront; pause to take in the sunrise and sunset; listen to the birds; smell the air after a hard rain.

✔ **Make a point of taking a break from your troubles.** Go for a bike ride or a drive in the country, take in a movie, enroll in a class, or take a short vacation if you can afford it and if the time away doesn't interfere with your divorce proceedings.

✔ **Explore your spirituality.** Become more involved in your church, temple, or synagogue. Begin mediating or studying yoga.

✔ **Seek out the friends and family members who have a positive influence on your life.** Doing things together and sharing your thoughts with people you like and trust can take your mind off your troubles and help you gain a healthy perspective about your life changes.

✔ **Schedule time with your religious advisor or a mental health professional.** Counseling can help you to put your marriage in perspective and assess what went wrong. Then you can think more clearly about what the future many hold.

If you've tried the suggestions we just listed and you're still feeling blue, figure out what's missing in your life and identify safe and healthy ways to fulfill those needs. For example, if you miss the physical contact you had with your spouse, a massage or hugs from your friends may help you feel better. If you enjoy restaurant meals, ask a friend to split a two-for-one meal coupon.

Use your creativity. You may discover inexpensive activities that are just as enjoyable — and maybe even more enjoyable — than some of your more costly pre-divorce pastimes.

Women tend to be better than men at building emotional support systems and admitting when they need help. Men have a tendency to try to "tough it out" by repressing their emotions instead of confronting what is bothering them.

Dealing with the Response of Friends and Family

No doubt most of you will share the news that you are getting divorced with your friends and family soon after you've made your decision. You may even discuss the pros and cons of divorce with your very closest friends and family members before you decide to end your marriage.

Your decision to divorce shouldn't effect your close personal relationships; your true friends will remain friendly no matter what your marital status may be. But be ready for those friends and family members who may view the divorced you a little differently than the married you.

If your friends give you the brush off

Almost inevitably, some of the friends and acquaintances you and your spouse shared as a couple will stop calling you after your divorce becomes common knowledge. Others may act aloof and distant when you cross paths. That sort of behavior can be very hurtful, especially if you are already feeling rejected.

Some friends behave as they do because, for whatever reason, they decided to side with your spouse. Some may have business or social reasons for doing so, or they feel some loyalty because they knew your spouse before they knew you. Try not to dwell on their behavior. Some of those friends will come around over time, but others never will.

Some friends who act uncomfortable around you may do so because your situation reminds them of their own marital troubles. Others may feel awkward because they're uncertain how to behave around you. They may be wondering if they should tell you that they're sorry about your divorce or ignore the subject until you bring it up.

If certain friends are important to you, consider making the first move —
invite them over for coffee, ask them if they want to play tennis or go
shopping, or invite their children to come play with yours.

If your family disapproves of your divorce

You may also notice that your relationship with some of your family members has chilled now that you are getting a divorce. They may disapprove of
your divorce plans, perhaps because your divorce is your family's first, your
family's religion frowns on divorce, or because they are fond of your spouse.

Your family (and your in-laws, if you were close) may begin to resent that
you're relying on them for help with child care more now than you did
before. Maybe they're uncomfortable with your asking to borrow money
from them, or have grown tired of complaints about your ex-spouse.

Although you should expect your family to support you through tough
times, don't take their support or patience for granted. If they help you out,
let them know that you appreciate their generosity and stay alert for ways
that you can return their favors. Also, try to be sensitive to just how much
you can lean on them — everyone has his or her limits — and avoid cross-
ing that line.

Part III
Decisions, Decisions

The 5th Wave   By Rich Tennant

In this part . . .

The decisions you need to make during your divorce will be some of the most difficult of your entire life. You'll have to divide up your marital property (and debt), give consideration to alimony payments, work out a child custody arrangement that's in your children's best interests, and plan for your children's financial support. This part of the book provides guidance for making all of those decisions, with one important caveat — you still need the advice of your own attorney.

Chapter 9

Yours, Mine, or Ours? Dividing Up What You Own

. . . .

In This Chapter

▶ Figuring out what belongs to you alone and what you own together

▶ Valuing and dividing up marital property

▶ Commingling property and its results

▶ Deciding what to do with your home

▶ Dealing with retirement benefits

▶ Handling your marital debts

. . . .

*I*f your marriage has been a relatively lengthy one and if you've enjoyed a reasonably comfortable standard of living, you may be surprised when you realize just how much stuff you've managed to collect over the years and just how much it's all worth. Dividing up your property requires thought and deliberation, and possibly the advice and assistance of outside experts, because what you divvy up during your divorce and how you decide to divide it has both short-term and long-term financial implications for both of you.

This chapter focuses on how to handle the big stuff — your home, the retirement benefits you earned during your marriage, your financial investments — as well as some of the smaller items. We also give you some suggestions for dealing with your marital debts.

Getting Some Terminology Out of the Way

During your marriage you may have bought a home, furniture, vehicles, computer equipment, or maybe even fine art. You no doubt own other, less valuable items, too — kitchen equipment, bedding, a television set, VCR, books, and bikes, for example. And, don't forget that pile of wedding gifts you've had stashed in the attic for years! Now that you are getting divorced, something has to be done with that stuff, too.

The less-valuable stuff you own can be divvied up rather informally. It's usually a matter of making sure that each of you gets your fair share of what you need to set up new households and, also, that you get to take at least some of the items that may have special meaning to you. Chapter 13, which covers some of the divorce matters you can handle without the help of professionals, suggests some ways of accomplishing this division.

Distinguishing between tangible property and intangible property

In addition to the goods you own (such as vehicles and furniture), you must also take into account your *intangible property,* such as retirement benefits, stocks, and bonds, when you are dividing up your property. (An intangible asset is an asset that has no intrinsic or marketable value in and of itself but instead represents or has evidence of value.) Your car or your home, on the other hand, is *tangible property* that has value in and of itself.

Identifying separate property versus marital property

Before you can divide up the value of your property, you and your spouse must first determine what property has to be divided and what is yours to keep. In other words, you must figure out what is and isn't *marital property.* Marital property consists of those assets you and your spouse own together. (A closely held business or business interest may also be included among your marital property.)

You are each legally entitled to a share of the value of the marital property that you own together. If you haven't already done so, inventory and categorize your assets. (Chapter 6 gives you some advice on how best to do that.)

Any property that is not marital property is *separate property.* Separate property belongs to either you or your spouse, but not both of you. You do not have to share it with one another in your divorce.

The property laws of your state ordinarily determine which assets are marital assets and which are not (you can find more on this subject in Chapter 2). However, if you and your spouse signed a valid prenuptial or post-nuptial agreement, you may have already decided how you intend to divide up your property in the event of a split. (See Chapter 20 for more information on prenuptial and postnuptial agreements.)

We know of one Indiana couple whose split was so rancorous they argued over the division of just about everything they owned. But their biggest quarrel was over who would get custody of their much-beloved pet iguana. Unable to work out a joint lizard custody arrangement, they finally came to an agreement that seemed like a fair deal — one of them got the iguana and the other got the new car.

Valuing Your Assets

After you determine what out of everything you own constitutes marital property, you need to assign a dollar value to each marital asset. Ordinarily, that dollar figure is the item's *fair market value,* or what you could reasonably expect to sell the item for, assuming that you didn't *have* to sell it and that you have a willing buyer.

Although you can probably value many of your marital assets yourselves, you may need the help of outside experts, such as appraisers and CPAs, to determine the worth of particularly valuable or complex assets, such as real estate, certain types of retirement benefits, fine antiques, a closely held business, and so on. The services of an outside expert can also be helpful if you and your spouse can't agree on how to value an important asset.

After you value your marital assets, you have to divide up the value of those assets, either by applying the property law concepts and guidelines a judge in your state would use if your divorce went to trial, or by applying some other criteria that you and your spouse both agree to.

In deciding which property to take from your marriage, keep in mind your personal goals for your life after divorce, the separate property you already own, and your post-divorce financial needs.

According to newspaper reports, when former late-night TV host Johnny Carson divorced his third wife, Joanna Carson, in 1983 after ten years of marriage, she got their mansion, three (yes, count 'em, *three*) Manhattan apartments, a Picasso, their Rolls Royce, a Mercedes, and half of their jointly owned stocks and bank accounts, *plus* $35,000 a month in alimony. (It's safe to say that Johnny still had plenty left over.)

Following the Legal Guidelines

If you involve attorneys in your property division negotiations, or if you look to a judge to decide who gets what, your state's property laws and property division guidelines take center stage. The judge's prejudices and preferences, and the persuasiveness of your attorneys, can also be big factors.

Although property division guidelines vary from state to state, they generally take the following factors into consideration:

- **How much you and your spouse each earn now and can be expected to earn in the future.** Often, a judge awards a relatively larger share of marital property to the spouse who earns less money and who has the lower earnings potential. In evaluating your earnings potential, the judge may consider your education level, physical and mental health, and other factors that may have a bearing on your ability to earn a good living.

- **Your current standard of living.** A judge tries to allocate the value of your marital property between you and your spouse so that neither of you suffers a dramatic reversal in your lifestyle after you are divorced. In reality however, your lifestyle may change (probably for the worse).

- **The value of the separate property that each of you may own.** If one of you has considerably more separate property than the other, the wealthier spouse may end up with less marital property.

- **Your individual contributions to your marriage.** These days, most states recognize that paying the family's bills is only one way that a spouse can contribute to a marriage. In recent years, the courts have begun recognizing that being a full-time parent, helping your spouse advance his or her career, and making other contributions to the marriage all have financial value.

  If you worked so that your spouse could obtain a college degree or professional license, your state may view that degree or license as a marital asset and you may be entitled to a share of its value. In other states, you may be reimbursed for your contribution to your spouse's education.

- **How long you were married.** The longer you were married, the more likely it is that the court will view you as equal partners. At the very least, a long marriage often entitles the spouse with less separate property or the lower earnings potential to a greater share of the marital property.

- **Your age and health.** Older spouses and spouses who are in poor health often receive a greater share of their marital property than younger or healthier spouses.

- **Whether either of you squandered marital property.** If one of you wasted your joint funds by gambling or repeatedly making bad business investments or risky personal loans, for example, that spouse may end up with less marital property.

- **Other factors,** such as whether either of you is carrying a lot of debt from a previous marriage, is likely to come into a significant inheritance, or helped increase the value of the other's separate property during your marriage, and so on.

In states that consider fault when deciding how to divide up a couple's marital property and debts, fault can be the single most important factor in the eyes of the courts.

According to 1996 data from the Social Science Research Council in New York City, a year after divorce, a woman's standard of living declines an average of 30 percent, whereas a man's rises 10 percent! Men usually earn more than women, so they tend to be able to afford better lawyers and have more financial resources to fall back on after their divorce. Plus, women tend to get custody of the children and although they may be receiving child support, in most divorces the amount of that support does not allow the average woman to maintain her pre-divorce lifestyle.

A 1995 Nobel Prize winner agreed to give half of his million-dollar prize to his wife in their divorce (by the way, he won the prize for economics).

State guidelines to keep in mind if you divvy it up yourselves

If you do your own dividing, your individual judgments about what is and isn't fair and your ability to compromise will certainly influence how you end up allocating the value of your marital property.

Bear in mind that should you and your spouse end up in court because one of you wants your property division agreement overturned, the judge will assess the fairness of your agreement in light of your state's property laws and property division guidelines. Therefore, even when you do the dividing yourself, keep your state's laws and guidelines in mind:

✔ If you live in an *equitable distribution* state, you are entitled to your *fair share* of the marital property you and your spouse own. Your "fair share" is whatever the judge decides you are entitled to based on the guidelines your state uses to divide up marital property or whatever your lawyer negotiates for you.

✔ If you live in a *community property* state, the general presumption is that you and your spouse are each entitled to half of the value of your marital property. But, in reality, your state probably allows a judge to divide up your marital property on an equitable basis, rather than a strict 50/50 split. The judge will take into consideration many of the criteria that a judge in an equitable distribution state would use. Only three states — California, Louisiana, and New Mexico — adhere to a strict 50/50 split.

Commingling and the Confusion It Can Create

In the course of your marriage, you and your spouse may have mixed together your separate property or you may have mixed your separate property with marital property. For example, you may have used some of your separate property to improve the rental property that you and your spouse own, or the both of you may have deposited your separate money into a joint account. Blending together different kinds of property is called *commingling*.

Commingling will probably not be a problem for you unless you decide to divorce. Unless both of you have kept detailed records of exactly what you did with your assets, you will have a difficult, if not impossible, time distinguishing between marital property and separate property.

If you and your spouse try to decide which portion of your commingled assets should be treated as separate property and who owns that separate property, your decisions will probably be based on your "best guess." However, if a judge decides, the standard he will apply depends on your state.

You can use accountants to "trace" the commingled assets, but that can cost you more than what your attorneys may charge!

If you want to avoid commingling assets in your next marriage, follow these suggestions:

- ✔ Keep your spouse's name off any deeds or other ownership documents that relate to your separate property.
- ✔ Do not add your spouse to your separate accounts.
- ✔ Do not deposit your separate property in a joint account.
- ✔ Do not use your separate money to purchase marital property or to pay for marital expenses.
- ✔ Use a prenuptial or postnuptial agreement to define what is and isn't separate and marital property.
- ✔ Consult with an attorney familiar with the property laws of your state if you are concerned that a financial transaction you are considering may have the effect of changing your separate property into marital property.

Interest earned on separate property assets during your marriage can become marital property. For example, if you have a separate bank account and you roll over the interest income into your joint account each month, that income may be considered marital property. Therefore, you will be commingling separate property with marital property.

Getting Up-Front Advice Is Advisable

If you and your spouse are going to handle your own property division negotiations, and especially if the total value of what you own together is substantial, you should consult with a qualified CPA or financial planner before you start dividing up what you own.

By using computer models, financial services professionals can help you test various scenarios for dividing up what you own and what you owe together so that you can make strategically wise decisions. In essence, they can do a cost-benefit analysis of different property division schemes.

Some CPAs and financial advisers specialize in providing pre-divorce money management advice. They can help analyze the best way to deal with not only the division of property but also child support and alimony.

Placing a value on the vehicles you own

Determining the value of the vehicles you and your spouse own together is relatively easy and inexpensive. You can:

✔ Use their "Blue Book" value. Your local library should have a copy of a Blue Book, which is formally known as the *Official Used Car Guide* published by the National Association of Used Car Dealers. You can also head for the Kelly Blue Book Web site at www.kbb.com.

✔ Ask local car dealers what they would give you for your vehicles. Because used car dealers tend to make low-ball offers, you and your spouse may want to upward adjust the offers somewhat.

✔ Read the auto ads in the classified section of your local paper for vehicles comparable to yours.

Deciding What to Do with Your Home

When everything around you is changing, you may be tempted to hold on to your home at all costs. You feel comfortable there. Perhaps you spent a great deal of time and energy decorating your home and gardening in the yard. If you have young children and you're going to be their primary caregiver after your divorce, you may want to stay in your own home to bolster their emotional security.

When it comes to your home, you should try to put your emotions aside and approach the decision from a purely financial perspective. You may decide that keeping your home after you divorce is not wise or financially realistic, or with some savvy financial planning you may find a way to keep your house. The bottom line is this: Whatever you do about your home should be a financial decision and not an emotional one. If you let your emotions rule, you may eventually end up losing your home because you cannot afford to keep up with the payments, the property taxes, or with the cost of maintaining the home.

Finding out how much it's worth

The least-expensive way to determine the value of your home is to ask a real estate agent for some recent selling prices of comparable houses in your neighborhood and how much you may be able to get for your house. However, whatever figure the agent gives you represents an approximation of your home's value.

A better method, albeit more expensive, is to hire a real estate appraiser to value your home. (If your divorce goes to trial, you and your spouse would each have to obtain an independent appraisal by a real estate appraiser anyway.)

Real estate appraisals tend to be imprecise. As a result, if you and your spouse both get your own appraisals, the results can be quite different. And, *don't* value your home based on its tax appraisal. Tax appraisals are always considerably less than your home's actual value.

Evaluating your options

Most divorcing couples resolve the problem of "what to do about the house" in one of the following ways:

Sell it

When your home is the only marital asset of real value that you own, you may have to sell it so that you can both leave your marriage with some money in your pockets. You may also decide to sell because it holds too many unhappy memories for both of you, it's too big for you to live in and maintain by yourself, or because you can't afford to keep it.

If you decide to sell, remember that the selling price probably won't represent the actual amount of money you and your spouse are able to split between you. Most likely, you'll have a mortgage to pay off, selling costs, and possibly property taxes to deduct. If you use a real estate broker to sell your home, you will have to pay the broker a percentage of your home's gross sales price (that is, a *broker's fee*). After all is said and done, when those costs are subtracted from your home's anticipated sales price, selling your house may not appear to be a very attractive option but may nevertheless be the best one.

Keep it

Taking the house in your property settlement may be an option if you have enough other marital property that your spouse can take another asset of comparable value. However, this is not an option for many couples and instead they may work out a buy-sell agreement in which one spouse buys out the other's interest over time. We describe this option in the next section of this chapter, "Retain an interest in it."

If your spouse gives you his or her interest in the home you owned together, you will receive a special warranty deed from your spouse. In turn, you will give your spouse a deed of trust to secure your assumption of the mortgage loan.

If you want to take the house, you will also get the mortgage that goes with it. Therefore, review the household budget you have projected for your life after divorce so you can be sure that you can really afford to take over the monthly mortgage payments as well as the upkeep on your home. If you don't, you may have to sell the home eventually or you may even lose it in a foreclosure. If you haven't already developed a household budget for yourself, Chapter 2 tells you how.

To understand the tax implications of selling your home, call your local IRS office for a copy of its publication *Tax Information on Selling Your Home,* Number 523, or call 800-829-1040. You may want to pick up a copy of *House Selling For Dummies* by Eric Tyson and Ray Brown from the publishers of this book (IDG Books Worldwide, Inc.).

If your spouse keeps the home, takes over the mortgage, and then defaults on the loan, the mortgage holder can look to you for payment no matter what your divorce agreement may say. Therefore, consider adding a *hold harmless provision* to the agreement giving you the right to sue your former spouse for the money you may end up paying. However, you have to go to court to enforce it and, even if you get a judgment against your spouse, you have no guarantee that you can actually collect what you are owed.

A *deed of trust to secure assumption* gives you the right (in the event your spouse defaults on the mortgage after your divorce) to dispossess him or her, put a tenant in the house, or sell the house in order to eliminate your financial and legal exposure on the home. However, to accomplish that, you have to stay up-to-date on the status of your former spouse's mortgage payments, which may not be easy to do.

Retain an interest in it

You and your spouse may want to sell your home, but for practical reasons decide to delay the sale. For example, you may want your children to be able to live in your home until they complete high school. In this case, the spouse with primary responsibility for raising the children stays in the home with the kids. Your property agreement would then give each of you an interest in that property.

If you opt for this sort of arrangement, be sure that your agreement addresses the following questions:

- ✔ How much of an interest do each of you have in the home?
- ✔ At what point must your house be put up for sale?
- ✔ Who will put the house up for sale?
- ✔ How will the asking price be determined?
- ✔ How will you pay all sale-related expenses?
- ✔ How you will divide up the sale proceeds?

If you want to give one another the option of buying out the other spouse's interest in your home, the terms of the *buy-out* should also be clearly defined in your divorce settlement agreement.

If you will still owe money on the mortgage, your agreement should also address the following questions:

- ✔ How will the mortgage be paid each month?
- ✔ How will you pay the homeowner's insurance and property taxes?
- ✔ Who will be responsible for the cost of minor repairs and major ones, such as a new roof?

Specifying the regular upkeep your home requires in order to protect your investment in the property is a good idea. You should also specify who is responsible for doing the maintenance and how often. Enforcing this provision, however, may be tough.

Dividing Up Your Retirement Benefits

In most states, the retirement benefits you or your spouse may have earned during your marriage are treated as marital assets and should be included among the assets you have to divide up. Such benefits may include defined contribution plans such as 401(k)s, Individual Retirement Accounts (IRAs), stock option plans, profit sharing plans, Keoghs, SEPs, and old-fashioned pensions, also known as defined benefit retirement plans. Most people earn their retirement benefits by working for an employer who either makes a retirement plan available to them as an optional benefit or provides it to them as an automatic perk of their job.

If you have worked for several employers during your professional career, you may have earned a retirement benefit from each. Be sure that your asset inventory reflects all of those benefits.

Good news about capital gains tax

Congress and President Clinton did homeowners a big favor in 1997 by changing the rules that apply to capital gains on the sale of their primary residence. Now, single people get a capital gains tax exclusion of up to $250,000, which means that they will not be taxed on the first $250,000 of gain or profit they may realize from the sale of their home. Married couples who file a joint tax return will get an exclusion of $500,000. Married or single however, you must have lived in your home for at least two of the five years prior to its sale to qualify for the exclusion.

If you move a great deal, you will be pleased to know that the capital gains tax exclusion is no longer a one-time thing. You can use it every two years for an unlimited number of times.

In addition, the *rollover* provision (which required that for you to benefit from the exclusion you had to purchase a new home of equal or greater value than the home you sold) has been eliminated. This is good news for spouses who get the family home in their divorces but who may end up selling it because they cannot afford the mortgage payments or the upkeep.

If you make more than $250,000 (if you're single) or $500,000 (as a couple) from the sale of your home, your gain will be taxed at the rate of 20 percent. The tax rate will be somewhere between 10 percent and 15 percent for people in lower tax brackets. In 2001, the tax rate will be reduced to 18 percent or 8 percent, depending on your income.

Defined benefit or defined contribution: Which is which?

Retirement benefits fall into one of two categories: defined benefit plans or defined contribution plans.

The *defined benefit plan* is the traditional type of retirement plan that you imagine receiving along with a gold watch after 50 years of loyal service to an employer. Because they are expensive for employers, defined benefit plans are not as widely available as they used to be. More and more, they are available only to people in the highest levels of management.

A defined benefit plan comes as an automatic job benefit — you don't choose whether or not to participate in it. Also, your employer promises that when you retire you will receive either a predetermined amount of income each month or a monthly income to be determined through a formula. The formula takes into account how long you worked for your employer, your salary, your age, and other factors.

Ordinarily, you will not have access to the money in your defined benefit plan until you have retired. Therefore, if your spouse wants

to share in your retirement benefits, he or she has to wait for that money, just like you.

A *defined contribution plan* is the type of retirement benefit most employees are offered these days. Participation in a defined contribution plan is not automatic; if your employer offers one and you want to participate, you have to enroll in it. If you do enroll, you, your employer, or both of you, contribute money to your plan.

Your employer will not offer any guarantees as to how much income your defined contribution plan will provide you when you retire. That amount depends on how much is contributed to your plan and how much the value of the assets in the plan appreciates over time.

You can take money out of this kind of retirement plan before you retire, although you have to pay an early withdrawal penalty and you may have to treat the withdrawal as taxable income. When you are ready to retire, you can receive all of your retirement dollars in a lump sum or you can receive payments over time.

Vesting and your rights

Depending on the type of retirement plan you participate in, you may have to be *vested* in the plan in order to be entitled to the money that your employer contributed to the plan if you leave your job. You are entitled at any time to receive the money *you* have contributed, whether you are vested or not. To be vested, you have to work for your employer a certain number of years.

Depending on your state, if you are not vested in your employer's retirement plan when you get divorced, then the money in your retirement plan may not be considered marital property. Even if you are vested, if your marriage did not last for at least a year, your spouse is *not* entitled to any of your retirement benefits.

For more information on pensions in general and the pension rights of spouses and former spouses in particular, contact the Federal Department of Labor's Pension and Welfare Benefits Administration at (202) 219-8233 or the non-profit Pension Rights Center at (202) 296-3776.

The U.S. Department of Labor brochure "What You Should Know About Your Pension Rights" (Department of Labor, Pension and Welfare Benefits Administration, 1995) offers extremely useful information on many aspects of employer-sponsored pension plans. It can help make a complicated subject more understandable. To order a free copy, call 1-800-998-7542. Or you can read an online version of the brochure at the following Web site:

```
www.dol.gov/dol/pwba/public/pubs/youknow/knowtoc.htm
```

Valuing a defined contribution plan

Assessing the value of a *defined contribution plan* is fairly easy (see the previous sidebar "Defined benefit or defined contribution: Which is which?" for a definition of this type of plan). In most cases, it is simply the amount of money that is in the plan at any given time.

To find out how much is in your defined contribution plan, contact the plan administrator or review the plan's most recent summary statement. The federal Employment Retirement Security Act (ERISA) says that any private-sector employer who offers a retirement plan to its employees must also provide a summary annual report that tells employees the value of their plan.

If your participation in the plan predates your marriage, all of your retirement dollars are not marital property. By reviewing the plan reports you have received over the years and doing some careful calculation, you should be able to figure out for yourself what portion is marital property. If numbers intimidate you or if the total value of your plan is substantial, you may want to hire a CPA or pension consultant to do the figuring for you.

If you are participating in a stock ownership plan, the value of the plan is equivalent to the number of shares you own, multiplied by the current dollar value of a share. If the company you work for is *closely held* (one whose stock is not publicly traded), the company can tell you how much a share of its stock is worth. If the stock is publicly traded, you can find the current per-share value by going to the financial pages of your local newspaper. Or, you can ask your stockbroker or financial adviser for that information.

Valuing a defined benefit plan

Valuing a defined benefit plan and determining how much of that value is marital property can be a rather complicated process. (See the previous sidebar "Defined benefit or defined contribution: Which is which?" for a definition of this type of plan.) Therefore, if you want it done right, you should hire an actuary. Ask your accountant to recommend one.

Do not assume that the value shown on your plan summary statement is the actual worth of your defined benefit plan. It may not be.

Parceling out those dollars

This section presents three alternatives for dealing with retirement benefits. When you are considering which alternative may be best for you, you must take into account the following:

- ✔ The value of the benefits
- ✔ The value of your share of the benefits
- ✔ The value of your other marital assets
- ✔ The value of your separate property
- ✔ How much money you need now, not later
- ✔ How close you are to retirement age
- ✔ The likely tax impact of each option

If you need help analyzing your options in light of these factors, talk with a qualified CPA, your financial adviser, or family law attorney.

- ✔ **Let whichever spouse is earning the retirement benefits retain all rights to them.** The other spouse takes an appropriate amount of other marital assets. This is usually the cheapest way to deal with retirement benefits, and also tends to be the way most judges prefer to deal with these benefits. For this option to work for you and your spouse, you need other marital property comparable in value to the value of the retirement benefits.

- ✔ **Share the benefits.** This option provides each of you with regular income once the spouse who is earning the retirement benefits is eligible to begin receiving them. If you choose this option, you will probably need a Qualified Domestic Relations Order, or QDRO to make it work. (See the following sidebar " A crash course on QDROs.")

According to the 1994 U.S. Census, 68 percent of women with private sector jobs and 59 percent of those with public sector jobs do not have their own pensions! Therefore, sharing in your husband's pension may mean the difference between living in poverty and living in comfort during your golden years.

✔ **Give the spouse who is not earning the benefits a lump-sum payment now as his or her share.** Use this option in lieu of sharing the retirement benefits later. If you go this route, make sure to transfer the money to the spouse who is receiving the lump sum so that the other spouse does not have to claim the transfer as taxable income. This option will not work for every type of retirement benefit. In addition, talk with a qualified CPA before you agree to a lump sum payment so that you understand the tax consequences. Otherwise, you may face a sizable tax liability.

If you take your share of the retirement benefits in a lump sum, the amount you receive is based on the present cash value of the plan, not its future value. Therefore, you may receive more or less than what you would have received if you waited.

A crash course on QDROs

A *Qualified Domestic Relations Order (QDRO)* is a special type of court order that directs a retirement plan administrator to disperse benefits directly to you and your spouse after you are divorced in accordance with the terms of your divorce agreement or in accordance with a judge's decision. You need a separate QDRO for every retirement plan you share.

If you are sharing military or government retirement benefits (such as U.S. Civil Service Retirement benefits or state retirement benefits) with your ex-spouse, you will need to use a different kind of court order for these types of benefits to accomplish what a QDRO does.

QDROs are complicated legal documents, so don't try to cut corners by drafting one on your own. Hire a qualified attorney to do the job for you.

A poorly executed QDRO can not only jeopardize the tax-deferred status of the benefits but can also result in the plan administrator not dispersing the funds in the plan according to your divorce agreement.

Preparing a QDRO for a defined contribution plan is almost always cheaper than preparing one for a defined benefit plan.

Social Security benefits you're owed as a former spouse

Based on your former spouse's work history, if you meet certain criteria when you reach a certain age, you may be entitled to collect Social Security benefits, including retirement and survivor benefits. Whether you're entitled to these benefits is a matter that's between you and the Social Security Administration, not between you and your former spouse. Your benefits do not depend on what your divorce agreement says.

You may be entitled to retirement benefits if

- ✔ Your former spouse paid into the Social Security Trust Fund.

- ✔ You and your ex-spouse were married for at least ten years and you've been divorced for at least two years.

- ✔ You are at least 62 years old.

- ✔ You are not married when you apply for benefits.

- ✔ You are not already receiving Social Security spousal or survivor benefits based on someone else's employment history.

If you meet these criteria, you can either collect the Social Security benefits you have earned in your own name, or you can collect dependents' benefits. The benefits equal one-half of the benefits your former spouse is entitled to, even if your spouse has not yet begun collecting Social Security.

If you collect benefits based on your former spouse's work history, the amount of benefits that your spouse can collect is not affected.

To establish your eligibility for benefits, visit the Social Security office closest to you at least three months before you turn 62. Bring proof of

- ✔ Your identity
- ✔ Your age and the age of your former spouse
- ✔ Your marriage
- ✔ Your divorce

If you cannot find all of the information you need, go the Social Security Administration office anyway. The staff there can help you locate what you are missing.

Social Security survivor benefits

If your former spouse dies and you were married to him or her for at least ten years, you may also be eligible to receive Social Security survivor benefits, assuming that your former spouse would have been eligible to collect Social Security benefits at retirement age or was already doing so.

By and large, the eligibility criteria for Social Security survivor benefits mirror the criteria for retirement benefits except that you can begin receiving reduced survivor benefits when you turn 60, or full survivor benefits when you turn 65. If you are caring for a child who is under the age of 16 or disabled, and eligible to receive benefits based on the work history of your deceased spouse, you may be able to begin collecting survivor benefits when you reach the age of 50.

If you remarry before you turn 60, you are not eligible for survivor benefits; if your new marriage occurs after your 60th birthday your eligibility is unaffected. However, your new marriage cannot take place within two years of your former spouse's death.

If you want to receive an estimate of your survivor benefits, call the Social Security Administration at 800-772-1213 and ask for a "Request for Earnings and Benefits Estimate Statement."

The eligibility rules and benefit amounts for Social Security benefits are always subject to change especially as Congress tries to figure out how to accommodate retiring Baby Boomers.

Getting Down to Business: What to Do with Your Joint Enterprise

If either of you owns a closely held business or has a share in one, or if you and your spouse own a business together, some portion of its value is ordinarily considered marital property unless you agreed to a different arrangement through a legally valid prenuptial or postnuptial agreement. (Chapter 20 explains how those agreements work.)

If you and your spouse have both been actively involved in your business, deciding what to do with it can be especially difficult. The idea that you may have to leave the business, shut it down, or sell it can be tough to accept when your marriage is ending. On the other hand, making plans for a new career may be just what you need to get over the loss of your marriage.

Your options, in a nutshell

To help you deal with the difficult decision of what to do with the business you and your spouse own, we offer you a number of options that have worked for other couples:

✔ **One spouse keeps the business and the other gets marital assets equal in value to his or her interest in the business.** Usually, the spouse who takes the business is the one who has been most actively involved in it or whose skills and knowledge are most essential to its continued success. For financial reasons or because sufficient other marital property may not exist, the spouse who keeps the business may buy out the interest of the other spouse over time. You need to formalize the buyout in a written agreement. Also, to help secure your spouse's payments to you, placing a lien on his or her real estate, on the assets of the business, or on some other assets, if there are any, is a good idea.

When you let your spouse buy you out over time, you assume certain risks because your ex may be slow to pay you, stop paying you at all, or bankrupt the business. Unfortunately, you may not be able to avoid assuming these risks despite the steps you may take to secure his or her payments to you.

✔ **You divide up the business and each of you takes a part of it.** This arrangement is practical only if you can logically divide up your business and if the division can be done without jeopardizing the financial integrity of each part.

An Austin, Texas, couple owned a chain of hamburger joints called Dan's Hamburgers. When they divorced, one spouse took the South Austin locations and the other the restaurants located in North Austin. He continued to call his business Dan's Hamburgers. Hers became Fran's Hamburgers!

✔ **You sell the business and split the proceeds.** This may be your only option if all of your marital assets are tied up in your business. However, if the continued success of the business depends on your skills and know-how, the business may not have much worth on the open market unless it includes significant assets that would be of value to a new owner.

✔ **Liquidate the business.** If neither of you is interested in continuing the business and you cannot sell the business as a going concern, liquidating it is a reasonable alternative. However, to take advantage of this alternative your business's assets must have market value. *Marketable assets* can include machinery, equipment, real estate, or accounts receivable. Depending on the type and value of the assets you are selling, you may want to sell the assets yourself, hire a liquidator to sell them for you (you'll have to pay the liquidator a piece of the proceeds), or have the assets auctioned off.

✔ **Keep operating your business together.** For obvious reasons, only a relatively small number of divorcing spouses who are also business partners choose this option. Most divorced spouses do not want to continue such an important and mutually dependent relationship. In fact, doing so may actually be harmful to the business.

If you worked in your spouse's separate-property business without compensation, your contribution to the business may be a factor in your property settlement.

Assigning a market value to the business

To implement any of the options just described (except for liquidation), you have to assign a fair market value to the business. You'll need the following if you want to make that determination yourself:

✔ Profit and loss statements for the past three years

✔ Balance sheets for the past three years

✔ Records of accounts receivable

✔ Records of accounts payable

✔ Tax returns for the past three years

✔ Checking account records for the past three years

✔ Contracts for future business

✔ Recent good-faith offers to buy the business, if any exist

✔ Information about the purchase price of businesses comparable to yours

When you are valuing your joint business, don't overlook its *goodwill value.* Goodwill consists of your business's reputation, name recognition, track record in pleasing its customers, role in the local community, and other factors that make it a respected enterprise.

If you are going to leave the business you have shared with your spouse, be sure to take an active role in valuing it, or hire an independent CPA or business valuation expert to value it for you. As much as you may trust your spouse, it is in his or her best interest to value the business for as little as possible. That way, either your spouse has to pay you less if he or she buys you out over time, or you end up entitled to less of the other marital property.

The National Association of Certified Valuation Analysts is a resource for trained, certified business valuation experts. The organization's toll-free number is 800-677-2009.

If you can afford to do so, you and your spouse can each hire outside experts to value your business and then you can average their estimates. Getting the help of an outside expert who is familiar with your particular type of business is advisable if your business is especially large, valuable, or complex. However, the help of such experts does not come cheap.

The Web site Divorceinfo Resources offers excellent how-to information on valuing your business. You can find this site at:

www.divorceinfo.com/businessvalue.htm.

When you began your business, you and your co-owners may have decided how your share of the business would be valued if one of you decided to exit the business or sell it. Therefore, that agreement determines what your share of the enterprise is worth, and it isn't a decision you and your spouse can make on your own.

Last but Not Least: Dealing with Your Debts

In our credit-oriented society, if you owe more than you own, you are like countless other divorcing couples. Unfortunately, your divorce may be more about dividing up your debts than about what to do with your assets. Although you can leave your marriage behind, you can't do the same with your debts. Divorced or not, the debts must be paid and you and your spouse must decide how to do that.

Some of that debt may be *secured debt,* such as your mortgage or car loan. Secured debt is debt that you have collateralized with an asset. If you don't pay the debt, the creditor can take the asset that you put up as loan collateral. You probably also have *unsecured debt,* such as credit card debt, for example. For some of you, all your debt may be unsecured.

Unsecured debt has the potential to create a great deal of discord in a divorce because, unlike a secured debt, it is usually not associated with an asset of any significant value. In many divorces, if you agree to assume responsibility for a secured debt, you also get the asset that the debt is financing. But unsecured debts typically include the purchase of things like restaurant meals, gas for your car, clothing, vacations, groceries, and so on.

Tips for avoiding trouble

Here, we offer some suggestions for dealing with what is certainly an unpleasant task — figuring what to do with your debts:

- **Pay off all your marital debt as part of your divorce.** This is usually the best way to deal with marital debt, assuming that you and your spouse have enough ready cash or sufficient assets that you can liquidate easily. That means that you both get to begin your post-divorce lives unencumbered by financial obligations from your marriage. Paying off your debts also means that neither of you has to worry about how you will be affected if your ex-spouse doesn't pay the debts he or she agreed to pay. Remember, creditors can look to you for payment on any debts that you and your spouse incurred together, no matter what your divorce agreement may say.

- **Trade debt for assets.** If you can't wipe out all of your marital debt, one of you may agree to take more than your share in exchange for getting more of the marital assets — the financial equivalent of taking a spoon-ful of sugar to make the medicine go down — because you can afford to pay more of the debts than your spouse can.

- **Take your fair share.** If you and your spouse own little, if anything, of real value, dividing up your debts may simply mean that each of you takes your fair share of the debt. For example, you may agree to pay off the balance on a credit card that was in both of your names but which you, not your spouse, used regularly.

- **Pay off your debts together after your divorce.** Avoid this arrange-ment. It requires too much cooperation and communication between you and your former spouse. However, if this arrangement is your best or only option, securing your spouse's obligation to pay his or her share of your unsecured debt (your credit card debt, for example) by placing a lien on one or more of your spouse's separate assets is highly recommended.

If you separate before you are divorced, just who is legally responsible for the debts you or your spouse may incur depends on your state. Most states presume that you have joint debts unless you or your spouse can prove otherwise. However, some states treat such debt as individual debt whereas others consider what the debt financed. If it helped pay for essentials, such as food, clothing, and shelter, it may be treated as joint debt.

Where the law stands on your debts

When you are deciding the best way to deal with the money you owe, bear in mind that a judge considers the same property laws and guidelines that he or she would apply to the division of your assets. (For an in-depth discussion of those laws and guidelines, turn to Chapter 2.)

✔ Any money you owed before you got married is treated as your individual debt.

✔ Your joint debts are "equitably" divided up if you live in an equitable distribution state.

✔ You and your spouse may be equally liable for the debts you acquired during your marriage or there may be only a presumption of equal liability if you live in a community property state. If you live in a community property state, when dividing up your debts, a judge considers your individual abilities to pay on the debts and what the debts financed, among other things.

Usually, if you secured or collateralized a debt with your separate property during your marriage, it will be regarded as your individual debt.

Uncle Sam wants his piece, too

Ordinarily, you will not have to pay taxes when a *capital asset* (such as a home, other real estate, retirement benefits, and so forth) are transferred to you in a divorce. However, if you sell a capital asset later, you may have to pay taxes on its appreciated value. Also, depending on how you transfer a *tax-deferred asset*, you may incur penalties. (A tax-deferred asset is an asset that allows you to defer or delay paying taxes on the income it generates until you sell it or begin collecting the income on it.) IRAs, 401(k) plans, and Simplified Employee Pension Plans (SEPs) are all examples of tax-deferred assets.

When you and your spouse are deciding how to divide up your marital property, your tax minimization strategies may depend on the types of assets you're dividing up, the value of those assets, and your individual financial situations. Without appropriate planning, the taxes and penalties you end up paying have the effect of reducing the amount of marital property you both end up with.

Talk with your CPA or a trusted financial adviser about how to minimize taxes and penalties in your property settlement.

Chapter 10

Alimony: Determining When and How It's Paid

. . . .

In This Chapter

▶ Examining the law's stand on alimony

▶ Understanding the pros and cons of lump-sum alimony

▶ Knowing when an increase or decrease in alimony may be justified

▶ Protecting yourself against the sudden loss of alimony

▶ Complying with tax laws

. . . .

*E*ven if you and your spouse concur that alimony (also known as *spousal support*) should figure into your divorce, you may have a tough time agreeing on the basic terms — how much alimony should be paid and for how long.

If you want a divorce and your husband doesn't, he may bristle at the suggestion that he pay you alimony, no matter how reasonable your request may be considering your ability to earn a living right away. Or, maybe you're angry and hurt because your wife who's a successful business owner wants a divorce and you don't. You may retaliate by demanding alimony, and a lot of it! You think it is the least that your spouse can do, given what she is doing to your life.

To deal with this issue as dispassionately as possible and make decisions that are fair to both of you, this chapter provides you with basic information about alimony and the part it plays in divorce.

If you want to know what you can do to minimize the damage that a divorce can do to your money situation, see Chapter 2 for practical advice on managing your household finances and Chapter 6 for information on financial preparations for divorce.

The Way It Used to Be with Alimony

Alimony, stated simply, is the payment of money by one spouse to the other after a couple is divorced. If a couple separates before their divorce is final, a spouse may also have to pay *temporary alimony.*

In generations past, unless a man paid his ex-wife alimony, she had no way to pay her bills. Few well-paying jobs were available for women, and most women had neither the job skills nor the confidence to compete successfully in a "man's world." Because most ex-wives ended up with the kids, a couple's children would also suffer if a former husband did not provide adequate financial support.

Assuming that he could afford it, an ex-husband paid his ex-wife *permanent alimony,* usually by sending her a monthly check for a set amount of money. In reality, however, permanent alimony did not really last forever because usually a couple's divorce agreement provided that the checks would stop coming if the woman remarried or if the ex-husband died.

Since the 1970s, permanent alimony has pretty much gone the way of the typewriter, eight-track tape, and rotary-dial telephone. However, it continues to be a part of some divorces — most often divorces that involve wealthy couples and older couples who are ending lengthy marriages.

Today, many agreements for permanent alimony provide that the alimony checks will stop coming if the ex-spouse begins a serious live-in relationship and shares living expenses with a new love interest.

It's a Little Different Now

Attitudes toward alimony have changed as the roles of men and women in our culture have changed. Whereas alimony used to be a standard part of most divorces, today only a small percentage of divorce agreements provide for it. Furthermore, the laws in all states are now gender-neutral when it comes to alimony. In the eyes of the law, men and women are now equally entitled to alimony (in actual practice, however, few men receive it).

If you receive any alimony at all these days, it will probably be *rehabilitative alimony,* not permanent alimony. Just as the term implies, rehabilatative alimony is intended to help you "get on your feet" and lasts for a relatively short period of time. Stay-at-home moms and dads and full-time homemakers most often receive rehabilitative alimony.

The amount and duration of rehabilitative alimony payments depend on a number of factors including

- ✔ Your financial needs and resources
- ✔ Your spouse's financial needs and resources
- ✔ The value of the marital property you receive in your property settlement
- ✔ Your education and your spouse's education level
- ✔ Your work experience and your spouse's experience
- ✔ The duration of your marriage
- ✔ Your health and your spouse's health — both physical and emotional
- ✔ The number of children in your household and their physical and emotional health
- ✔ Any other factors you may want to consider if you are working out the terms of your divorce together, or other factors that a judge feels are relevant if your divorce goes to trial

This new breed of alimony is premised on the assumption that most ex-spouses can and should earn their own livings after a divorce. However, it also recognizes that a woman (or a man, for that matter) may have put her own career on the back burner to raise the children or support the other spouse's career. Therefore, the stay-at-home spouse needs some time to become self-supporting after she is divorced. For example, she may need to develop new job skills and professional connections. Rehabilitative alimony is intended to help her do that.

In many situations, however, the amount and duration of the alimony checks are inadequate given a woman's needs. This is particularly true when the divorced woman is middle-aged or older and has never worked outside the home or not done so in many years. These women often have a very hard time finding good employment.

If your alimony payments help your former spouse get the education needed to earn a good living, you may eventually be able to get a reduction in the amount of your child support payments.

Stay-at-home moms who view raising their children as a full-time job face a difficult dilemma. If they begin preparing themselves for the possibility of divorce by getting the education and training they need to be employable should their marriage end, they not only take time away from their primary job (child rearing) but they get less alimony when they do divorce. On the other hand, if they don't prepare themselves for the job market while they're still married, they receive more alimony but won't be as prepared to support themselves when the alimony ends (which it usually does).

Out of pride or a desire to be 100-percent free of your spouse, don't summarily dismiss the idea of asking for alimony. If you believe that you will need time to become competitive in today's fast changing and skill-oriented job market, your wisest course of action may be to swallow your pride and ask your spouse for fiancial help.

What the Law (And Judges) Say about Alimony

If you are wondering whether alimony is appropriate in your divorce, you won't have much legal precedent to go by. Alimony-related decisions tend to be relatively subjective and are decided on a case-by-case basis for two main reasons:

- ✔ Divorced spouses have no legal obligation to support one another. Therefore, alimony is not as much of a given as is child support in divorces that involve minor children.

- ✔ Most states do not have strict guidelines for determining the minimum amount of alimony a former spouse is entitled to. This contrasts sharply with the way child support payments are determined.

 Alimony, more than any other aspect of divorce, is determined by individual state law and lacks clear federal or even state standards. For example, until 1995, Texas had *no* provision for alimony other than temporary spousal support that would end when the divorce was granted. Even now, although Texas law provides for alimony, the terms under which a court will order alimony are very limited — for example, only in situations of severe need, and then for up to a maximum of three years.

 In some states, if your ex-spouse isn't living up to the alimony obligations, you can try to enforce that obligation by asking the court to hold your spouse in *contempt*. Your ex-spouse may then be sent to jail. In other states, contempt is not available and therefore you're stuck in the same position as any other creditor your former spouse fails to pay. In such situations, whether you can collect the alimony you are owed depends on the debtor protection laws of your state, which may make all or most of your ex-spouse's property exempt from the debt collection process. If that is the case, your alimony is uncollectable.

Factors a judge would consider

Unless your divorce is litigated, you and your spouse must decide about alimony, possibly with the help of your attorneys. To help guide you in your decision, the following is a list of factors a judge would consider when ruling on alimony. The greater the number of factors that apply to your marriage, the stronger your argument for alimony.

- You have been married for a long time. You won't find a legal definition of "long time" when it comes to marriage. However, if your marriage is less than ten years old, a judge probably won't treat it as a long-term marriage — although it may feel like an eternity to you!

- Your spouse makes significantly more money than you do and can be expected to continue doing so, at least for the immediate future.

- Your age or health status make earning a good living nearly impossible.

- You have made significant contributions to your marriage or to your spouse's career. For example, you gave up your career to be a stay-at-home parent, you continued to work throughout your marriage and let your career take a back seat to your spouse's so that you could help him or her advance professionally, or you helped build your spouse's business.

- Your educational background or employment history puts you at a disadvantage in the job marketplace.

- You will be your children's primary caregiver, making the pursuit of a career immediately after your divorce a difficult task.

- You do not have other sources of regular income, such as income from trusts, real estate, or investments.

- You are exiting your marriage with relatively little marital property.

- Your spouse can't afford to pay alimony. If he earns very little income, the court won't expect him to pay you much.

- You will have sole custody of your children and one or more of them has special needs — perhaps due to serious physical or emotional disabilities or health problems — that preclude your working or that allow you to work only on a part-time basis.

Ideally, judges would like to see the lifestyle you enjoyed when you were married continue after your divorce, but in reality they know that most ex-spouses do not make enough money to support two households equally well, not even for a short period of time.

States that allow fault divorces may allow a judge to take the issue of fault into consideration when making a decision about alimony. When a judge does consider fault, the spouse who is at fault will be punished for his or her behavior (adultery, physical abuse, so forth). The judge may order the spouse at fault to pay more than the usual amount of alimony or may award that spouse less alimony than what he or she may have otherwise received.

Watch out for unfair arrangements

If your spouse wants to make the amount of the alimony or its duration contingent upon your doing or not doing certain things, do not agree unless you feel completely comfortable with the offer. Some people will go to almost any length to continue to control their spouses, even after divorce. For example, one spouse may try to make alimony payments contingent on the other spouse not dating a particular person, or require that the children be sent to a particular school as a condition of alimony. You may need to consult with a family law attorney to be assured that your spouse's alimony offer is fair to you.

At the same time, however, there is no 100-percent guarantee that you'll actually see the alimony your spouse is supposed to pay you. Depending on the state you live in, you may have little legal recourse if your former spouse does not pay up. So, figuring out the best way to structure your alimony arrangement can be a bit of a gamble.

Be wary of agreeing to take more marital property in exchange for less spousal support. Unless the property can provide you with a regular flow of income, you may end up on the short end of the financial stick.

When it comes to dollars and cents, divorce is still harder on women than men despite the large numbers of women who work outside the home. Most women, even those who receive permanent alimony, experience a drop in their standard of living after their marriage ends. However, some divorced men experience the same financial consequences.

Opting for Lump-Sum Alimony

Some divorced spouses receive their alimony in a lump sum instead of taking it as a series of payments over time. The *lump sum alimony* arrangement can be particularly attractive if you don't trust your ex-spouse to live up to an agreement that provides for payments over time or if you are concerned that his or her financial situation may deteriorate after your divorce.

Be sure that the lump sum your spouse offers you is adequate. Don't assume that just because it sounds like a lot of money that it is a fair amount for you to receive, especially if your spouse wants you to take the lump sum in lieu of marital property. Talk with a family law attorney or possibly a CPA as well before you sign any paperwork.

Consider the tax consequences of taking a lump-sum alimony payment and what you can do to mitigate those consequences before you agree to accept a lump-sum payment. You may be able to shelter some of the lump-sum alimony by using trusts. This is a subject to discuss with your attorney or CPA.

If you take a lump-sum payment, and then put the full amount in your checking account, you may end up spending it all at once. The larger the sum, the more important it is that you have an investment plan that maximizes the interest you can earn on the money and gives you ready access to at least a portion of it.

If you are giving your spouse a lump-sum alimony payment, get the help of an attorney or CPA. Your alimony agreement should be worded so that the IRS does in fact view your payment as alimony — which you can claim as a tax deduction — and not a property settlement, which you can't deduct.

If you receive alimony, you must claim the alimony as income on your tax return and your former spouse can claim it as a deduction when filing his or her tax return. (You can find out more about taxes and alimony in the section "Some Important Advice about Taxes" later in this chapter.)

Seeking a Change in Alimony

The amount of alimony you receive may be increased or decreased after your divorce is final, under certain circumstances.

- ✔ The amount can change if you and your former spouse both agree to the change.
- ✔ Depending on your state, the amount of alimony you receive can also change if the court orders it.

For the court to order a change in alimony, you or your ex-spouse will have to provide a good reason. A judge is unlikely to view your desire to share in the hefty salary increase your former spouse just received as a good reason, nor your wish to benefit from his or her sweepstakes windfall.

A judge will likely be more sympathetic if you ask for more alimony because you were seriously injured in a car accident, or if your former spouse asks for a reduction in alimony payments because he lost his job and can prove to the court that paying the same amount will quickly land him in the poorhouse. However, in both scenarios, the adjustments would probably be temporary.

In some states, a court loses its ability to change alimony arrangements as soon as a couple's divorce decree is finalized.

Preparing for When Alimony Payments Cease

If your spouse dies, your alimony payments stop and you do not have a legal right to be paid by his estate unless he or she provided otherwise. Obviously, if those payments are an important source of income for you and you have no way of compensating for that loss, the death of your ex-spouse may be financially devastating for you.

Although death can come unexpectedly to people of any age, this issue is of particular concern to individuals who are ending marriages to spouses who are elderly or in poor health. This issue can be addressed by requiring, as a term of your divorce, that your spouse purchase a life insurance policy and name you as beneficiary.

Other options that can provide greater financial flexibility (and take into account the gradually declining total amount of alimony) include an annuity or whole life plan. Your attorney or CPA can advise you about the best option.

The premium payments your ex-spouse makes are tax deductible as alimony. If he or she dies and you begin receiving benefits, you will have to claim the benefits as taxable income.

Some Important Advice about Taxes

Perhaps one of the few benefits of paying alimony is that you can declare the payments as deductions on your federal tax return. However, like everything else to do with the IRS, to qualify for the deductions the agency requires you to comply with certain rules.

✔ Your alimony arrangements must be formalized in a divorce decree or in a separate written agreement.

✔ You must make your payments with a check or a money order. Ordinarily, property or services in lieu of cash do not qualify as tax deductible alimony.

✔ When you are making alimony payments, you cannot be living under the same roof with your former spouse. That means no living on separate floors of the same home or in different parts of your home.

✔ You cannot tie your alimony payments to circumstances or milestones in the lives of your children. For example, your agreement cannot provide that when your child turns a certain age you will reduce the amount that you pay your ex-spouse or stop your payments entirely. If the IRS learns that you have done so, it may rule to reclassify the payments you have made as child support. Because child support payments are not tax-deductible, you may end up owing extra taxes to Uncle Sam.

✔ On a related note, you cannot stop paying alimony or change the amount that you have been paying your ex-spouse six months before or after the date that one of your children becomes a legal adult — age 18 in most states. Again, if the IRS finds out that you've stopped paying alimony prematurely, it may reclassify some of the alimony you paid as child support, which could have tax implications for you.

✔ You must file your federal taxes using IRS Form 1040, not Form 1040A or Form 1040EZ.

Do not make your alimony payments in cash. If you do, you won't have a record of your payments. If any question arises concerning how much you may have paid your former spouse, or exactly when you made a particular alimony payment, you'll lack the documentation you need.

Finally, a word about front loading your alimony payments. Don't do it. *Front loading* involves paying your ex-spouse excess money during the first two years that you are making alimony payments. If you are audited, the IRS views the excess money you paid as a property settlement, not alimony. As a result, you may have to include the excess in your gross income, which could mean that you have to pay additional taxes. Front loading may apply only if you paid out more than $15,000 in alimony during each of the first two years that you're making alimony payments and if you claimed the full amount of those payments as tax deductions.

For help in determining what the IRS may view as excessive alimony payments in your divorce, head to www.divorceinfo.com/excessalimony.htm.

If an attorney or a CPA helps you work out the terms of your alimony agreement, you can deduct his or her fees on your taxes. Also, if you pay the medical insurance, college tuition, mortgage, or rent payments of your former spouse as part of your alimony agreement, you may be able to claim them as tax deductions, too.

 If you earn considerably more than your spouse and you intend to pay him or her more than your state's minimum in child support, you may want to pay that additional money as alimony. Although that move increases your tax deductions, it may also increase your ex-spouse's tax liability.

Chapter 11

Custody: Deciding in Your Children's Best Interests

. . . .

In This Chapter

▶ Avoiding courtroom custody decisions

▶ Distinguishing between legal custody and physical custody

▶ Understanding your options for sharing custody

▶ Considering split custody

▶ Using primary custody and its drawbacks

▶ Using a "parenting plan"

▶ Deciding on visitation arrangements

. . . .

*G*rappling with custody decisions can consume every ounce of your patience and resolve. In fact, it may represent your biggest challenge yet as a parent. If negotiating your own custody arrangement seems about as likely as winning the lottery, we offer some encouraging statistics. Estimates show that only 5 percent of all divorcing parents ask a judge to decide child custody for them, which means that 95 percent of all divorcing parents negotiate their own custody arrangements — either by themselves, with the help of a mediator, or with legal help — and chances are you will, too.

This chapter prepares you to make your own custody decisions by informing you of your options (and their pros and cons) and suggesting ways you can make your custody arrangement work to benefit everyone, your kids especially. We also cover issues regarding visitation, including each spouse's rights and limitations. If it turns out that you and your spouse can't come to an agreement on your own, this chapter also explains what a court may do if you ask a judge to decide on the custody matters in your divorce.

Avoiding the Courts by Deciding on Custody Yourselves

If you and your spouse can decide one thing and one thing only in your divorce, decide how you will handle the custody of your children. Here we offer you just a few of the reasons why *you,* and not a judge, should decide on custody for your children. (More information on negotiating your own divorce terms without the aid of a court of law is provided in Chapter 13.)

✔ If you go to court, you have no guarantee that you will get the custody arrangement you want, even if it is available under your state's laws. The judge makes the final decision.

✔ No matter how well-intentioned they may be, because of their caseloads most family court judges can devote only a very small amount of time to making custody decisions. Your kids deserve more attention than that, don't they?

✔ Most judges rely on the input of outside experts such as social workers and psychologists to help them make custody decisions. Therefore, a bunch of strangers may end up having a great deal of say over your future roles as parents.

✔ A court custody battle can be extremely costly and time-consuming. One reason for the great amount of money and time involved is the testimony of experts (who may include your children's teachers, the director of your children's day-care center, the personnel at your pediatrician's office, and so on) who will probably be asked to provide testimony. You will be expected to pay for their time.

✔ Your "dirty laundry" will be aired for all to see and hear because courtroom proceedings are open to the public.

✔ Members of your extended family, friends, associates, people in your children's lives, and others may be dragged into your divorce. Your children may even have to testify.

✔ After the court has made its custody decision, you and your spouse may not be able to put your differences aside for the sake of the kids. In a worst-case scenario, your battle may continue long after your divorce is final, taking a long-lasting emotional toll on your children and adding stress and strife to your own lives.

Of the estimated 95 percent of divorcing couples who come to a negotiated agreement about their custody arrangement (rather than having the custody arrangement determined by a judge), nearly 50 percent of them would actually *prefer* to wage a custody battle. But they lack either the financial resources to do so or deliberately avoid such a battle for fear of the emotional harm a trial would have on their children.

Want to talk to other divorcing parents who are dealing with the same custody questions you are? Share ideas and concerns with one another at this interactive child custody forum on the Web:

www.divorcesource.com/cgi-bin/divorce/netforum/custody/a/1

Legal Custody versus Physical Custody

Every custody arrangement requires your making two basic and interrelated decisions — how you and your spouse will share the legal custody of your children and how you will share their physical custody. *Legal custody* refers to a parent's right and obligation to make decisions on behalf of his or her children after a divorce — including decisions concerning the children's education, medical care, choice of religion, and other important matters. *Physical custody* refers to the amount of time the children live with each parent after divorce.

In most cases, the children will spend time with each parent in proportion to how involved each parent was in their lives before the divorce — that is, to whatever degree each parent has functioned as the children's caregiver, life planner, and source of emotional support. In addition, each parent is given decision-making authority in proportion to the amount of time the children live with that parent.

Typically, the parent who has been most involved in his or her children's lives before the divorce will spend the greatest amount of time with them after divorce and will assume more decision-making responsibilities. That parent is said to have *primary custody* (we talk more about this type of custody in the section "Primary Custody" later in this chapter).

Parents who have been equally involved in their children's lives before divorce will normally get nearly equal, if not completely equal, decision-making authority and time with the children after divorce. Those parents are said to have a *joint* (or *shared*) *custody* arrangement. (You can find more on this type of custody in the section "Shared Custody" later in this chapter.)

In recent years, social changes have introduced changes in custody decisions. An increasing number of fathers are playing active roles in the day-to-day care and nurturing of their children, and many couples are sharing both the legal and the physical custody of their children. Among the reasons for this relatively new trend in custody arrangements is that more women work outside the home, whether due to choice or financial necessity.

Custody decisions and their tax implications

Depending on the custody arrangement you negotiate, you may lose your eligibility for certain child-related tax benefits. The following items provide a brief explanation of how your eligibility may be affected:

✔ **Filing as head of the household.** If your children live with you more than half the time, you can file your taxes as *head of the household,* but if you and your spouse share physical custody 50/50, neither of you can file as head of the household. To get around this, you and your spouse can agree to divide up your kids for tax purposes. For example, if you have two children, one of you can claim that during the tax year one of the children lived at least

51 percent of the time with you, and your former spouse can make the same claim for the other child.

✔ **Child care tax credit.** This tax credit is only available to an employed custodial parent raising a child who is younger than age 13. Incidentally, the greater the custodial parent's income, the lower the dollar value of the tax credit.

✔ **Deductions for medical expenses.** You and your spouse can each deduct your out-of-pocket child-related medical expenses, assuming the total amount of those expenses exceeds a certain percentage of your adjusted gross income.

The laws in most states assume that each parent has an equal legal right to custody of his or her children. In reality, when the court gets involved, the mother usually ends up with primary custody of the kids. That decision is based on the fact that in most families the woman is the primary caregiver for her children and the parent who is most involved in their lives (despite the increased care-giving role that many fathers have assumed). However, if the father is the primary caregiver the courts are more apt to award him primary custody of the children. This is especially true if the couple lives in an urban area where the judges tend to be more progressive and more precedent-setting rulings are made.

Shared Custody

When parents share custody of their children (another term for *shared custody* arrangement is *joint custody*), they are both responsible for all or some aspects of their children's lives. Shared custody encourages both parents to be full participants in their children's lives after their marriage has ended and gives both parents equal responsibility for the emotional and physical well-being of their children. It also helps facilitate a continuation of the relationship that the parents and children enjoyed prior to the divorce.

Generally, when divorcing spouses agree to share physical custody of their children, they are more apt to share the financial support of their children than if only one spouse has primary physical custody. However, child support arrangements are always decided on a case-by-case basis and depend on a variety of factors. (For the full scoop on child support, turn to Chapter 12.)

Nearly all states recognize joint (or shared) custody as an option and some treat it as the presumed or preferred arrangement. In these states a judge can even order joint custody. Other states permit joint custody by agreement only.

Options for sharing custody

You and your spouse can structure a shared custody arrangement in any of several ways:

✔ One option is for your children to live with both of you on a 50/50 basis, or a 60/40 basis, or an 80/20 basis — whatever seems best for you and your former spouse to share decision-making about your kids. If you opt for this type of joint custody arrangement, you will probably parent your children much the same way you did during your marriage. The only difference is that now you and your spouse are living under two separate roofs, not one.

✔ Another joint custody option gives one of you sole or primary physical custody of the kids, the other parent liberal visitation rights, and lets both of you share responsibility for making the important decisions in your children's lives. This arrangement has its advantages when one parent frequently travels out of town for work, is regularly on call or works a night shift, or when other similar demands take one parent away from the home for periods of time.

If you choose this custody option, you may want to consider adding a provision to your custody agreement that the parent with legal custody must involve the other parent in all important decisions about the kids' welfare, but when you and your spouse cannot agree, the parent with legal custody has tie-breaking rights.

If you decide to share decision-making authority about some things but not others, avoid conflict and misunderstanding after your divorce by clearly spelling out the areas of shared decision-making in your custody agreement. For example, you may agree that you will both decide on your children's nonemergency medical or dental treatment only when the treatment involves invasive procedures, or you will both decide about any psychiatric and psychological treatment, or will share decision making when it comes to consenting to your children marrying or enlisting in the military.

Your state's laws with regard to child custody may specify certain rights and duties that you and your spouse must share at all times after your divorce, the rights and duties that you can share as you want, and the rights and duties that each of you retains whenever your children are in your care. Your attorney can fill you in on your state's law in this regard.

Whatever custody arrangement you decide on, be sure that you and your spouse are happy with it before it becomes a formal part of your divorce agreement. Although you can change the custody arrangement later, if you and your ex don't see eye-to-eye on the change, it will be up to a judge to decide if it's merited. Most judges are reluctant to alter a custody arrangement unless it is obviously in the children's best interests.

Shared custody pitfalls

The benefits of sharing physical and legal custody of your children with your former spouse are obvious: Your children get to maintain their relationships with both of you, and you both remain actively involved in your children's lives. Nevertheless, joint physical and legal custody is not without some potentially serious drawbacks, including the following:

- ✔ Shared custody is relatively expensive. You and your former spouse both need to provide your children with a place to sleep and a place to store their clothes and other belongings when they are at each of your homes (unless you want them living out of suitcases and boxes). Plus, you each have to provide your children with separate sets of clothing, toys, and other items that they use regularly.

  By the time your children reach adolescence, they may not want to switch back and forth between homes and instead may prefer to live with one of you most of the time. Living in one place gives your kids ready access to all of their belongings and so their friends will always know where to find them.

- ✔ You and your spouse must communicate and cooperate with one another much more than you would with other custody arrangements.

- ✔ Shuffling back and forth between your home and your ex-spouse's home can be hard on some children, particularly very young children, because they may feel constantly unsettled.

When children live with each parent part-time, their education can suffer unless both parents have the same attitude about homework, getting to school on time, school behavior, and doing well in their studies.

Taking into account your kids' preferences

If your children are old enough and mature enough to know their own minds, and especially if you are considering joint custody, you may want to consider their preferences for where they want to live and how much time they want to spend with each of you. They may have already let you know their desires, directly or indirectly, but if they haven't and you want to find out what they are thinking, sit down and have a talk with them. Decide whether to talk with them together with your ex-spouse or separately. Make it a casual chat and do not pressure your children to decide one way or the other.

Making joint custody work

To have a successful joint (or shared) custody arrangement, you and your spouse must do something you may have had a hard time doing while you were married — get along with each other! To determine if you and your spouse have what it takes to manage a joint custody arrangement, read the following rules of joint custody:

✔ **Avoid post-divorce warfare.** Arguing over your children can be emotionally devastating for both you and the kids. When you do have disagreements about your children, talk things out. Don't shout them out, especially when your children are within earshot.

Don't use your children to try to get back at your former spouse. Your marriage is over — it's time to move on. If you can't forgive and forget, you have no business sharing custody.

✔ **Respect one another's parenting abilities and styles.** You may not like the way that your ex-spouse parents your children but unless your ex endangers the kids or unless you have good reason to believe that he or she is harming their emotional, scholastic, or sexual development, how your ex parents is really none of your business. Plus, if you critique the parenting abilities of your ex-spouse, you can expect your ex to do the same to you.

✔ **Support one another's efforts to learn new parenting skills.** Even if you were both active, involved parents, each of you probably had primary responsibility for certain things — one of you may have gotten the kids dressed in the morning and prepared their lunches while the other helped with their school projects and got them ready for bed. Now, you may have to learn new skills so that you can do all of those things you both used to share.

✔ **Agree on a schedule for when the children will live with each of you and stick to it.** Children depend on predictability. At the same time, don't be inflexible.

✔ **Mind your own business when your children are with their other parent.** Don't check up to find out what time your ex-spouse got the kids to bed, what they ate for dinner, or to tell your ex what the kids should wear to school the next day. Your ex-spouse is in charge of your kids when they are at his or her home.

✔ **Support one another as parents.** Don't let your children play one of you against the other in order to get what they want, and don't criticize your ex-spouse in front of your children.

To learn more about joint custody and how to make it work, order an information kit from the Joint Custody Association (310-475-5352).

Make certain that your children aren't basing their living arrangement preferences on the fact that one of you may be a lax disciplinarian or a more indulgent parent, or that one of you has an emotional need to live with them. Also be sure that your children's preferences are not the product of revenge. For example, if you're leaving your ex for someone else and your kids know about it, they may want to stay with your ex out of loyalty to him or her and out of frustration with you.

Avoid bribing your children into spending more time with you by making glorious promises about what their lives will be like if they do, and avoid "guilting" your kids by telling them how sad and lonely you'll be if they don't choose to be with you more often.

Your children very much want your approval, which means you may not be able to take their "preferences" at face value. Your children may be apt to tell you what they *think* you want to hear, not what they really feel. For that same reason, they may tell your spouse the exact opposite of what they tell you. Avoid discussing your children's preferences until they are old enough and mature enough to honestly assess what they really want and feel comfortable communicating that information to you.

More than half the states have laws authorizing the courts to consider a child's preferences if the child is of a certain age (typically 10 or older). A few other states require that the court abide by the wishes of children who are at least in their teens.

Split Custody

Split custody is another option, although few parents elect to use it. With split custody, some or all of your children live with each of you for a part of the year, or some of your children live with one of you all of the time and the rest of your children live with your former spouse all of the time. You may opt for a split custody arrangement because, among other reasons,

- ✔ One of your children has special educational or medical needs.
- ✔ One or more of your children refuses to spend time with you or with your spouse.
- ✔ You have other special problems or limitations, such as one parent's limited finances.

A split custody arrangement is seldom in the best interests of your children. For most kids, not living with both parents in the same house after a divorce is hard enough, but separating siblings from each other can be downright cruel.

Nevertheless, separating your children can make sense in certain situations — for example, if one of your older children was involved in gangs, abusing drugs or alcohol, or exhibiting other antisocial behavior, you would have a legitimate concern about his or her influence on your younger children. If you or your ex will spend less time with your children after you are divorced because of work, travel, or education demands, you may be especially concerned that a delinquent older child may have more opportunity to influence the younger ones.

Primary Custody

If you receive *primary custody* of your children, they will probably live with you *most* of the time after you are divorced. More than likely, you will have day-to-day responsibility for your children as well as the legal right and obligation to make all major life decisions on their behalf. However, you and your spouse may decide that a somewhat different primary custody arrangement better suits your personal needs. Exactly how you structure your primary custody arrangement is up to you.

Surprise: Child support payments are not tax deductible (but alimony payments are). If you will have primary custody of your children, you may want to consider working out a win-win arrangement with your spouse that gives you more child support in exchange for him or her taking the child-related tax exemptions and deductions.

Deciding on a visitation schedule

Ordinarily, when you have primary custody, your former spouse — the *noncustodial parent* — has visitation rights, or the right to spend time with your kids according to a predetermined, fixed schedule. Also, in most primary custody arrangements, the noncustodial spouse pays child support and health insurance.

Visitation for most noncustodial parents usually means that they have the children every other weekend, one day midweek each week (the kids may or may not stay overnight), on certain holidays, birthdays, and maybe during part of their summer vacations. However, if you and your spouse work out your own visitation schedule, you can agree to anything you want.

Primary custody drawbacks

Having the children live with you all or most of the time and being responsible for making all of the decisions about their lives makes sense if your spouse does not want to be or cannot be actively involved with your children after you are divorced. But be aware that a primary custody arrangement can be fraught with problems, especially if your spouse ends up with very limited visitation rights but would have preferred to be a more involved parent after your divorce.

- ✔ In primary custody arrangements, noncustodial parents often feel excluded from their children's lives.

- ✔ Many noncustodial parents slowly drift away from their children, especially if they remarry and start new families. When that happens, the divorced couple's children no longer have the benefit of a relationship with two biological parents.

- ✔ Studies show that noncustodial parents who fail to spend an adequate amount of time with their children are less apt to meet their child support obligations.

Then again, the custodial parent's situation isn't always a bed of roses. Consider the following:

- ✔ As most single parents can tell you, shouldering all or most of the day-to-day responsibilities of raising children can be a tremendous burden, physically and emotionally, particularly if you are working full time or even going to school as well. Juggling child care, work, and school, not to mention housekeeping and yard work, all on your own, can leave you feeling completely spent at the end of each day.

- ✔ You may have little quality time to give your kids, much less any time for yourself.

- ✔ Your children may spend more time in day care, after-school care, or at home by themselves than they did when you were married and your spouse was around to help out. In such situations, children of divorce frequently end up doing more of the cooking and housework while playing parent to their younger siblings.

Most states have expanded the limited legal rights of noncustodial parents by allowing them to make emergency medical decisions for their children and by giving them access to their children's medical and educational records. For example, most noncustodial parents can request that their children's school send them copies of their kids' report cards.

If your ex-spouse has primary custody of your children, he or she can move the children to another state unless your state law forbids such a move or your custody agreement restricts your children's residence to a specific geographical area.

The Single Parents Association (SPA) brings together single parents so that they can improve their parenting skills, share experiences, support one another, and have good times together with their kids. To find out if there is a SPA group in your area, call 800-704-2102. (If you live in Arizona, call 602-788-5511.) Parents Without Partners is another group you may want to check out by calling 800-637-7874.

Noncustodial mothers

Although they are in the minority, some mothers do not seek custody of their children. Some make the decision for personal, professional, or economic reasons. Other noncustodial mothers want custody but end up on the losing end of a custody battle because they lack the financial resources to hire a competent attorney and put up a good fight.

Sadly, many noncustodial mothers are stigmatized by our society. They tend to be viewed as uncaring, selfish, or even unfit parents. Men who choose not to seek custody usually don't suffer the same criticism.

MOM-LAC (Moms Living Apart From Their Children) is a growing support group for mothers without custody of their children. The group has chapters in New Hampshire and metropolitan Dallas and Atlanta. If you don't live in any of these areas, but are caught up in a custody battle with your spouse or do not have custody of your children, this Web site can still be of interest. It links you to other sites for Moms without custody, to articles about the issue of child custody, and to other resources of interest. You can find it at

```
www.dhc.net/~lavietes/momlac.htm
```

Making primary custody work

Primary custody can be hard on everyone, but sometimes it *is* the best option. Yet, study after study shows that kids do best when they have the affection and attention of both parents. In addition, they may suffer long-lasting emotional, developmental, and personal damage if their parents continue to act out their negative feelings toward one another after they are divorced.

Kids require positive male and female role models in order to develop into well-adjusted adults. Therefore, if you are the parent with primary custody, for your children's benefit, do what you can to help ensure that your children have an opportunity to maintain a strong relationship with their other parent, even if you dislike or distrust your ex. Terrible spouses can still make great parents.

The following offers some suggestions for how to maintain a relationship between your kids and your ex:

- Don't try to shut your ex-spouse out of your children's lives by placing needless restrictions on their time together. Agree on a visitation schedule that's as generous as possible. Also, let your children have some control over when they spend time with their other parent.

- Encourage your children to call their other parent, but let them have some say in when and how often they do it. Your kids should call their other parent to share their good news and their concerns, to get that parent's advice, or to get help with homework. Calling should not become a chore or a duty.

- Share report cards, homework assignments, or school art projects with your former spouse.

- Encourage your former spouse to attend parent-teacher conferences.

- When you take photos of your children, get extra copies made for your ex-spouse.

- Let your ex-spouse know the dates and times of your children's recitals, school plays, and athletic events.

- Invite your ex to your children's birthday parties, to go trick-or-treating at Halloween, and to share other important dates with you and your kids.

- Let your ex-spouse know well ahead of time when you will be taking the kids out of town.

- Keep your ex-spouse informed of your children's medical problems.

- Consult your former spouse about the important decisions in your children's lives. However, in a nice way, be clear with your spouse that you are not legally obligated to act on his or her wishes or even consider them.

- Don't forbid your children to spend time with your ex's new girlfriend, boyfriend, or spouse. If you do, you will force your ex to do things without your children, which could add to the stress they may already be feeling.

Going the Extra Mile with a "Parenting Plan"

A growing number of divorcing parents are writing *parenting plans* in addition to traditional custody agreements. A parenting plan is a highly detailed, written description of how both parents will be involved in the lives of their children after their divorce. Parenting plans tend to be more detailed than traditional custody agreements. In this way, parenting plans can help reduce the potential for post-divorce conflict and power struggles, or the need for mediation or litigation.

States differ dramatically in the comprehensiveness and level of detail of their custody provisions. In those states where the provisions are very general, parents can help minimize future problems by negotiating parenting plans. Some states, in fact, require that a parenting plan be included as an integral part of a custody agreement or a judge's custody order.

What to put in the plan

Parenting plans spell out in great detail how each parent will be involved in his or her children's lives after a divorce. The plan can state, among other things, the following:

- ✔ Exactly how you will share the routine day-to-day care of your children — that is, who will be responsible for what

- ✔ How you will share your children's time on holidays, vacations, and birthdays

- ✔ Who will take off work to care for a sick child

- ✔ Who will care for the children when one parent is out of town overnight for business or pleasure

- ✔ Exactly how you will share decision-making about your children's religious upbringing, medical care and treatment, education, and day care

- ✔ How you will deal with issues related to an older child's dating, curfews, sexuality, or what to do if that child develops a substance abuse problem

How parenting plans can improve your custody arrangement

Although parenting plans are most often used by couples who are going to share custody, these plans can help make any custody arrangement work better by

- ✔ Helping both of you to be more realistic about the amount of time and energy you need to care for your children on a day-to-day basis as single parents.

- ✔ Encouraging you to get all your post-divorce parenting issues out on the table. (Acknowledging those issues and resolving them together, before your divorce is final, is better than doing so after you have a custody agreement in place.)

- ✔ Minimizing the potential for post-divorce strife by helping you antici-pate and resolve potential areas of conflict before they develop and by spelling out on paper, before you are divorced, every detail that may make or break your custody agreement.

- ✔ Letting you establish mutually agreed upon procedures for resolving any post-divorce conflicts that develop related to your kids.

- ✔ Allowing you and your ex-spouse to express your long-term goals for your children in qualitative terms. For example, your parenting plan can state the following goals: "It is our goal to support our children to the fullest extent possible in their scholastic and extracurricular activities" or "It is our goal to limit the amount of time our children spend watching TV and playing computer games, and to encourage outdoor activities, reading, and conversation to the fullest extent possible."

Making the plan flexible

If you and your spouse negotiate a parenting plan, avoid making your plan so rigid and inflexible that it cannot bend and change to meet the develop-mental needs of your children. Remember that what your children need from each of you changes over time, depending on their personalities and their ages.

Your plan should also be flexible enough to respond to the changing circum-stances in your own lives. That flexibility may include changing when or how often your children spend the night at your home and assuming more of or giving up some of your decision-making responsibilities. These and other plan adjustments could be necessitated by changes in your professional lives, a serious illness or accident, changes in your living situation or finances, or changes in your children's needs.

When You and Your Spouse Can't Come to a Decision

It's understandable if you and your spouse are at loggerheads over the custody of your children. After all, your decision making may be complicated by any number of things going on in your head:

- ✔ Fear that you may be squeezed out of your children's lives if you do not participate equally in all ways on decisions regarding your kids

- ✔ Guilt over how your divorce will affect your children

- ✔ Anger at your spouse

- ✔ Concern that if you don't see your children every day, your influence in their lives may diminish or they won't be well-cared-for

- ✔ Worry that over the coming years you'll miss out on the special moments in your children's lives

- ✔ Fear that if a new man or a new woman comes into your spouse's life, that person will try to take your place when you're not around

- ✔ Worry that the political, religious, socioeconomic, or cultural views of your spouse or your spouse's family may have a serious impact on your children's personal development after your divorce

If you and your spouse can't agree on the best way to handle custody, putting the issue in the hands of a judge is not your only alternative. You can also talk with your religious adviser, meet with a mental health professional, or try mediation. In fact, if you take your case to court, the court may require that you try to work things out through a mediation program before it even gives you a court date. (Chapter 16 explains how mediation works.)

To encourage an out-of-court settlement, some courts require couples who cannot agree on custody to view special educational videos.

Questions you can expect a judge to ask

Like it or not, if you take your custody battle to court, the judge who hears your case will probably consider most, if not all, of the answers to the following questions before deciding on a custody arrangement that's in your children's best interests:

✔ Where are your children living now?

✔ During your marriage, how did you and your spouse share parenting responsibilities?

Were both of you actively involved in your children's lives — bathing and dressing them, feeding them, helping them with their homework, playing with them, talking with them and helping them resolve their personal problems, addressing their emotional needs, taking them to and from day care or school, attending parent-teacher conferences, taking them to their doctor and dentist appointments, handling their emergencies, and so on?

The judge may also want to know which one of you takes care of your children during the day and who arranges for them to play with their friends, who shops for the children, who organizes their birthday parties, who arranges for baby-sitters, who stays home with your children when one of them is sick or on vacation from school, and how you and your spouse each discipline your children.

✔ Do any of your children have special educational or health care needs? How do you and your spouse deal with them now?

✔ What kind of relationship do your children have with each of you? To whom do they turn for emotional support or help when they have problems?

✔ What hours do you work and does your work require that you travel? Do you expect that your work and travel schedule will remain the same after your divorce?

✔ What do you and your ex-spouse want in the way of custody, and can you be expected to cooperate with one another on behalf of your children after your divorce?

✔ Where will you be living after your divorce and what kind of home life can you offer your children?

✔ How stable are your finances?

✔ What are your personal habits? Do you abuse alcohol or do drugs, stay up late partying, or engage in sexually promiscuous behavior?

✔ How solid is your moral character and what are your religious beliefs?

✔ Have you ever attempted suicide or been hospitalized for an emotional or psychiatric disorder?

✔ Do your children have an especially close relationship with either or both sets of grandparents?

The judge also takes into consideration the age and gender of your children, your physical health, and if either of you has a criminal history.

Homosexual parents and the courts

Although society's attitude toward gay parents has been evolving over the past few decades, the laws are slow to address those changes. Some states even allow the courts to deny custody or visitation rights to a divorced parent just because that parent is a homosexual.

The role that sexual orientation plays in a custody decision usually reflects how the general community in the court's geographic area views homosexuality. For example, the laws in some states (Alaska, California, New Mexico, and Pennsylvania) say that sexual orientation *cannot* play a role in a court's custody decision.

Nevertheless, a judge has considerable discretion in deciding custody cases. Sexual orientation often influences the decision, although the judge may not indicate that it was taken into account when deciding custody.

Before you go to court, compare yourself as a parent with your state's custody criteria. How do you measure up? If you fall short, think twice (and maybe three or four times) about whether a court battle is *really* worth the expense and the stress it will create for you and your children. Maybe it's time to settle out of court.

Some states have begun requiring divorcing parents to attend parenting classes in order to learn how to help their children adjust to divorce and to become familiar with some of the more common issues divorced parents face. Ask your attorney or a mental health professional if a nonprofit organization in your area offers a similar class that you could attend.

Arming yourself for a custody battle

For many reasons — both good and bad — some parents want to limit the time their former spouses can spend with their children after a divorce. Others attempt to strip the other parent of the right to make decisions about their children or seek custody rights unjustified by the roles they've played in the lives of their children so far, possibly to reduce the amount of child support they will be paying.

If you are concerned that your spouse may try to limit your right to continue playing a meaningful role in your children's lives after you are divorced, or if you want to limit your spouse's involvement in your kids' lives after your marriage has ended, you may be headed for a custody battle. If that seems likely, you can take action now to improve your legal standing:

✔ **Become aware of the general guidelines that judges in your state use to make custody decisions.** See how your situation stacks up against those guidelines. You should be able to get a copy of the guidelines by calling the state family court in your area or a local family law attorney if you are not already working with one. (You can find names of family law attorneys in your local yellow pages.)

If an attorney asks you to pay for the guidelines, the price should be nominal — little more than the cost to copy them. Another way to learn about your state's custody guidelines, especially if you would like an opportunity to discuss them, is to buy an hour of a family law attorney's time.

✔ **Stay involved in all aspects of your children's lives.** That includes participating in parent-teacher conferences, taking your kids to the doctor, dropping them off or picking them up from day care, being home at night to feed and bathe them and get them to bed, and helping them with their homework.

When child custody becomes an issue in a divorce, most judges look to see which parent has been the children's *primary caregiver,* the parent who has been most involved in their day-to-day lives. One of the best ways to prove that you are integrally involved in your children's lives is to bring objective witnesses into the courtroom who can testify that you were there for your children in the years prior to your divorce and that you appeared to enjoy an ongoing and meaningful relationship with them.

✔ **Be there for your children so that they view you as a "go-to" parent.** They need someone they can count on for emotional, physical, and psychological support and for general care giving.

The tips we just listed may sound somewhat cold and calculating, but close custody battles can be won by presenting this kind of evidence. This advice should serve as a wake-up call for those of you who have been spending too much time at the office, or have been using up all your free time dating or honing your golf or tennis games, and devoting too little time to your kids. Now may be the time to get your priorities straight.

The late 20th century has produced some bizarre custody battles! Take the couple who waged a heated custody fight over which of them should get the frozen fertilized eggs they had stored away during happier times. In this case of "petri dish parenting," we wonder, who got visitation rights?

Neither of you may get the kids

Although this happens in only a very small number of custody cases, if both spouses have a history of child neglect or child abuse, substance abuse, emotional problems, or other negative behaviors, the judge may very likely decide that neither of the parents should have custody. However, a judge will not consider making such a decision unless a third party raises the issue or unless it is undeniably obvious to the judge that neither spouse is fit to parent his or her children.

In cases such as this, the judge appoints a *guardian ad litem* (someone with master's degree–level training or the equivalent in psychology, counseling, or social work) to represent the children in court and to help the court determine where the children should live. Often, a grandparent or another adult relative assumes temporary custody of the children under a court-ordered guardianship until a permanent living arrangement can be established.

Your Kids Come First: Agreeing on Visitation Arrangements

Ordinarily, if you have primary custody of your children, your spouse has *visitation rights* — that is, the right to spend time with the children. When you and your spouse negotiate your custody agreement, you can decide on those visitation terms — when your spouse will have the children, how long the kids will stay with your ex, and other stated arrangements.

WARNING!

Worse than a bad dream: The kidnapping parent

Although not a frequent occurrence (and we're glad of that), parental "child-napping" does, on occasion, happen. Some parents kidnap their children because they're afraid that they'll be denied custody (or because they already have been denied custody). Others abduct their children to exact revenge on their ex-spouse or force a reconciliation with their ex, or to keep their children away from what they regard as a dangerous parent. Abducting spouses may flee with their children to another state or, worse yet, to another country.

According to the U.S. Department of Justice, 60 percent of child-napping cases involve the violation of written custody orders. All states and the federal government uphold laws to prevent child-napping. Parents convicted of child-napping may be subject to civil or criminal penalties including imprisonment. (For more information about the laws that apply to child-napping and some of the organizations that can help you if your ex-spouse disappears with the children, see Chapter 19.)

If you are separated, and your spouse takes off with the kids and you have no idea where they are (and neither of you has a temporary court order for custody), immediately call a family law attorney. The attorney can initiate the appropriate legal actions to get you temporary legal custody of your missing children so that your children can be returned to you.

Knowing when visitation becomes an issue for the courts

When bad feelings between ex-spouses run deep, visitation can become a hotly contested issue, even if the court clearly stated the rules of visitation. For example, to get back at an ex-spouse, the noncustodial spouse may deliberately return the children to the custodial parent later than scheduled, pick them up late, cancel plans to spend time with the kids, or withhold child support. Or the custodial parent may refuse to allow the other parent to see the children, or place unreasonable restrictions on visitation. Often the only way this emotionally charged duel can end is if one parent takes the other to court.

In cases of one parent having primary custody, a judge may order either "reasonable visitation" or "generous visitation" rights for the noncustodial parent and let you and your spouse work out what that means. Or the judge may spell things out for you more specifically.

To help protect the best interests of the children, as well as protect the visitation rights of the noncustodial parent, most states have established guidelines for a minimum amount of time that a noncustodial parent can spend with the children.

Burying the hatchet for your kids' sake

When you and your spouse use visitation as a vehicle for expressing your negative feelings for each another, you're inflicting emotional damage on your children. Children hate to see their parents fighting and, more important, tend to blame themselves for the discord. Those feelings can create many problems for your children, including a loss of self-esteem, emotional distress, and even marital troubles of their own down the road.

Avoid this scenario at all costs! Your children deserve the opportunity to have both of you in their lives. Remember, a bad spouse does not necessarily equal a bad parent. Using your children to get back at your ex-spouse is a form of punishment for your children. You and your spouse must act like mature adults and put your children, not your hurt and angry feelings, first. If you don't, you may do some serious emotional damage to your children.

No law requires the parent with visitation rights to use those rights. In other words, a noncustodial parent cannot be forced to spend time with his or her children.

A top-ten reason to stay put

A mother and her son eating pizza at a restaurant near the *Late Show With David Letterman* studio were invited into the studio to appear in a sketch. Unbeknownst to Letterman, the woman had been on the lam with her son for more than four years in order to deprive her ex-husband of his visitation rights, and was reported to have moved 14 times during those years. Ironically, when the boy mentioned that he and his mom had moved to California and then to New York City, Letterman responded, "Wow! Sounds like a kidnapping!"

How right he was! What the mother didn't know was that her ex-husband was watching Letterman that night. The woman and her son disappeared again soon after their television appearance.

Visiting with restrictions

When there is a good reason to believe that the noncustodial parent will harm or endanger the children, the visitation rights of a parent *should* be restricted, or even prohibited. Examples of this include situations in which the noncustodial parent has a history of

- ✔ Mental, physical, or sexual child abuse.
- ✔ Child neglect.
- ✔ Criminal activities.
- ✔ Mental or emotional instability.
- ✔ Alcohol or drug abuse.
- ✔ Exhibiting explicit sexual behavior in front of children.

Ordinarily, when a parent's visitation rights are restricted, a designated adult must be present whenever that parent spends time with the children.

If you're a custodial spouse and you think the visitation rights of your ex-spouse should be restricted, you have no legal right to take the law into your own hands. You must ask the court to limit those rights.

Some parents cruelly and maliciously use unwarranted accusations of child abuse or molestation by their spouses as a way to try to deny that parent access to their children. If you are unfairly accused, get legal help from an attorney. You can also get emotional support from the organization Victims of Child Abuse Laws at 612-521-9741.

If allegations of abuse surface in a divorce, the court usually appoints a guardian *ad litem* or attorney *ad litem* to represent the children. This individual conducts an investigation into the allegations and prepares a report that a judge uses to rule on custody, visitation, and what to do about the alleged abuse.

Grandparents have visitation rights, too

All states have laws giving grandparents the legal right to spend time with their grandchildren. In most states, if grandparents are not allowed to spend time with their grandchildren after a divorce, or if they are fearful that the custodial parent will try to exclude them from their grandchildren's lives, they can ask to be given formal visitation rights. As with other issues related to children and divorce, the court will determine whether spending time with their grandparents is in the children's "best interest."

Some grandparents go one step further and seek custody of their grandchildren. Usually this happens when a grandparent thinks that both parents are unfit to raise the children or when the grandparents have been acting as *de facto* parents.

Usually, if your custodial rights have been terminated, your parents (your children's grandparents) cannot request access to your children, nor can they request to be given custody of your children.

If you suspect your ex-spouse of child abuse

If you think that your ex-spouse is abusing your children, talk to an attorney immediately. The attorney can advise you of the appropriate steps to take, which may include any of the following:

✔ Contacting the police

✔ Filing a criminal lawsuit against your former spouse, and stopping all communication with your ex

✔ Asking the court to prohibit your ex-spouse from having any future contact with your child until your allegations are investigated

✔ Having your child examined by a doctor

✔ Having your spouse undergo evaluation and treatment for chemical dependency, alcohol abuse, psychiatric problems, or anger management

✔ Taking photos of any unusual marks, bruises, or cuts on your children that you believe are evidence of the abuse or molestation

Your ex-spouse should also be reported to your local Child Protection Services office immediately. In fact, you may be held criminally liable if you *don't* report your spouse.

Chapter 12

Child Support: Providing Your Kids with the Necessities

. . . .

In This Chapter

▶ Determining who pays child support

▶ Figuring out the appropriate amount of child support

▶ Negotiating your own child support agreement

▶ Ensuring that you receive the child support that you're due

▶ Dealing with child support on your federal tax return

. . . .

*A*s a parent, you have a moral and legal responsibility to support your minor children so that they have a roof over their heads, clothes to wear, enough food to eat, and an education — the basics, in other words. Divorce does not change this obligation whether your children live with you or with your former spouse after your marriage ends. If you have minor children (younger than age 18 in most states), deciding how you will share the cost of raising your kids is a key issue in your divorce.

In this chapter, we explain which parent usually pays child support to the other and how state child support guidelines are used to determine a minimum level of support. We also help prepare you to negotiate your own child support agreement and explain what a judge may decide if you and your spouse can't work things out yourselves. We also cover other child-related expenses beyond the basics that you and your spouse may want to include in your divorce agreement or that a judge may order you to pay.

What Is Child Support and Who Pays It?

Child support is a fixed amount of money that one parent pays to another parent after the couple is divorced to help cover the cost of raising their dependent child or children.

If you receive child support, the payments are not intended to enhance your lifestyle — child support is intended for the benefit of your child or children *only*.

In primary custody arrangements

Ordinarily, if one parent has primary custody of the children, the other parent (the *noncustodial* parent) is obligated to pay child support. (The parent with primary custody is usually considered to be meeting his or her child support obligation by raising the children. In fact, that parent typically spends as much as three times the amount of money as the noncustodial parent on their children's necessities.)

Although some states deduct *reasonable living expenses* from a parent's income before determining child support, in primary custody arrangements especially, most states are using the noncustodial parent's gross income to calculate child support.

In 50-50 shared custody arrangements

If parents share custody on a 50-50 basis, depending on their income and assets, neither parent may pay child support to the other. Instead, each parent pays for the day-to-day care of a child at the time the child is living with that parent.

On the other hand, depending on each parent's individual circumstances and the needs of the children, one parent may pay the other child support. (This is the more common arrangement.) For example, if one of the custodial parents in a 50-50 custody arrangement earns much more than the other custodial parent, the higher-earning spouse may have to pay child support, although the amount of the support is probably less than if the parents did not have a shared 50-50 custody arrangement.

Under these circumstances, if you and your spouse negotiate your own child support arrangement, one option for determining how much each of you should pay is to calculate the percentage of each of your individual incomes relative to your combined income; then apply that percentage to the total cost of your children's day-to-day care. You may also want to factor in how much time your children will be spending with each of you.

In other types of shared custody arrangements

In some joint custody situations, each parent's financial contribution to child support is a function of each parent's individual income relative to the combined total income of both, and a function of how much time the children will be spending with each parent. But that's not the only way to determine how much money both parents will contribute to the care of their children and your attorney may suggest a different arrangement.

If you decide to share custody but agree that one of you will stay at home to care for your children until they have reached a certain age, you still need to negotiate child support just as you would if you agreed to a sole custody arrangement. However, make sure that this aspect of your custody and support agreement is clearly spelled out. That way, if a conflict arises later between you and your former spouse about what you agreed to exactly, the judge hearing the matter knows what both of you were intending at the time of your divorce.

Figuring Out the Size of the Check

In the late 1980s, Congress passed a law requiring all states to establish guidelines (formulas really) that family court judges must use to calculate the appropriate amount of child support in a divorce. One of the reasons behind Congress's decision was the desire for a more consistent level of child support from state to state.

Taking into account state guidelines

In most states, guideline amounts are expressed as a percentage of a parent's income. Usually, the more dependent children a couple has, the larger the percentage of that income.

Considerable variation exists among state child support guidelines:

- ✔ Some states consider the income of the noncustodial parent only, whereas other states take the incomes of both parents into account.
- ✔ Some guideline amounts are based on a parent's gross income, and other guidelines use net income.

✔ Some states also cap the total amount of income that a guideline percentage applies to, or apply a different percentage to income over a certain amount.

✔ State guidelines even differ in their definitions of *income* — either wages only, or *all* sources of a parent's income, including wages, investment income, trust income, government benefits, and other income sources.

To find out about your state's child support guidelines, ask your attorney to spell them out for you or call the attorney general's child support division for your state. In addition, the family law court in your area may be able to provide you with a child support worksheet to calculate just how much support you're likely to receive or may have to pay.

If you have custody of your children and you move to another state where the cost of living is higher than where you used to live, you can ask the court that issued the original order for child support to increase the amount of support your former spouse must pay you.

One example: Calculating support in California

To help you understand how state child support guidelines are used to calculate child support payments, assume for a moment that you are getting divorced in the state of California and that you have asked the court to decide how much child support you or your spouse should pay.

The judge considers the amount of time your children will be living with each of you after you are divorced as well as the net income of you and your spouse. *Net income* is broadly defined to include wages, unemployment income, self-employment income, Social Security payments, disability and worker's compensation payments, less federal and state income taxes, Social Security taxes, the cost of health insurance, and the cost of state disability expenses. Mandatory union dues or retirement contributions, unusually high health-care expenses, or the cost of raising children from other relationships may also be deducted.

According to the California guidelines, if you have one dependent child, you and your

spouse are each expected to contribute 25 percent of your net income to the support of that child. If you have two children, the percentage increases to 40 percent of your individual net incomes. (These percentages are adjusted based on how much time each of you will be spending with your children.)

The judge may also require one or both of you to provide your children with medical insurance if it is available to you at no cost or at a reasonable cost through your job or through a group plan.

At the time this book was researched, the California guidelines did not take into account the cost of "extras" such as child care, out-of-pocket medical expenses, special education needs, travel, extracurricular activities, and other expenditures. Unless you specifically ask the judge to include those costs in the child support court order, you and your spouse will be expected to share the cost of those extras 50/50.

Allowing for more than one child

If you and your spouse have more than one child, the judge may order the noncustodial parent to pay his or her child support in one of several ways. Those options include ordering the parent to pay a per-child amount of child support, make a lump sum payment of child support, purchase an annuity calculated to cover the financial needs of all your children, set aside specific property to be administered for the benefit of the children, or some combination of all of these options. However, the lump sum option is usually frowned upon because judges realize that many people may have trouble managing a large chunk of money paid out all at once.

Special circumstances a judge may consider

In most states, family law judges have the flexibility to order more or less child support than guideline amounts would dictate if certain conditions exist. Those conditions can include the following:

- The custodial parent earns considerably more than the other parent or has considerably greater assets.

- The total value of the noncustodial parent's financial assets is very small or very significant.

- The couple's children have emotional, physical, educational, or other special needs.

- During the couple's marriage their children enjoyed a standard of living that is higher than what the guideline amount would provide.

- The noncustodial parent has the ability to pay much more than the guideline amount or makes too little to pay the guideline amount.

- One of the parents must incur substantial child care expenses in order to maintain gainful employment.

- One parent assumed a lot of debt during the couple's divorce.

- One parent is experiencing a significant amount of positive or negative cash flow from real or personal property.

- The noncustodial parent is not earning to his or her full potential.

  In this case, the judge may decide to order an amount of support based on how much that parent *could* earn, not on how much money the parent *is* earning. For example, if a former corporate executive trades his high-stress job (and with it his six-figure salary) for less-lucrative, but more-relaxing employment as a woodworker, the judge may order that parent to pay child support more in line with his corporate executive income.

✔ The noncustodial spouse becomes unemployed.

The judge may order the noncustodial spouse to pay less support, or none at all, until that parent finds a job. However, if the court has reason to believe that the parent's unemployment is little more than a ruse to avoid paying child support, the judge's order may require that, by a certain time, the parent must begin paying an amount of support equal to what he or she would pay if that parent were working at full earning capacity. Even if the judge doesn't think that the unemployment is a ruse, he or she may order the unemployed parent to pay what should have been paid if that parent had a job, or pay up after that parent lands a job.

✔ The children will be living full time with the noncustodial parent during the summer months.

In this case, the judge may allow the noncustodial parent to pay less child support during those months.

In the eyes of the law, child support is more important than alimony. Therefore, if both are at issue in your divorce and you look to the court to decide on both, the judge will not order a spouse to pay an amount of alimony that may limit how much child support that spouse can afford to pay.

Unless the judge orders otherwise, a noncustodial spouse with child support obligations must pay support year-round, not just when the custodial parent has the children.

Additional Child-Support Expenses You May Have to Pay

Child support is not the only expense that a judge may order you, your spouse, or the both of you to pay for the benefit of your minor children, nor is it the only expense you and your spouse may decide to absorb if you negotiate your own support agreement.

In some states, a judge can order the noncustodial parent to contribute to the cost of his or her children's college or trade school education (assuming that the parent can afford to do so) and to provide health insurance for the children unless the parents have worked out another arrangement that is acceptable to the court. The following sections cover other expenses a judge may order.

Purchasing life insurance for the benefit of your minor children

If you die while your children are still minors and dependent on your financial support, the policy proceeds help provide for their care. You may also be ordered to provide your ex-spouse with proof every year that your life insurance policy continues to be in force. If you and your spouse decide to share the cost of raising your children, you should both purchase life insurance policies.

If you purchase life insurance, you must designate a trustee — an adult who would mange the policy proceeds on behalf of your children should you die. Your children's other parent is a logical choice assuming that he or she can be trusted to manage the money responsibly. However, the trustee can be another financially responsible adult.

Your state's laws may require that you redesignate your life insurance beneficiaries after you divorce. Failure to do so could mean that the law would void your current beneficiaries. (Your attorney can tell you if this is an issue in your state.)

Providing your children with medical coverage

Usually, the parent with employer-sponsored insurance maintains the children on his or her policy. However, if either of you can provide your children with comparable coverage at a lower price through a different insurance policy, the court will probably accept that alternative.

Health insurance may not cover all medical expenses — dental or orthodontia expenses and eyeglasses, for example, may be excluded — nor does it pay 100 percent of covered medical expenses. Therefore, you and your spouse or the judge have to decide how those costs will be shared. If you are the custodial parent, do not overlook uncovered medical expenses, because unless they are specifically dealt with during your divorce negotiations or trial, you may end up having to cover those expenses.

If you are the custodial spouse and as part of your child support agreement your spouse will provide your children with health coverage, be sure to become very familiar with the details of your spouse's health plan before you come to a final agreement about child support.

These days, some health plans cover all medical expenses if you pay a little more each month than the standard premium, or provide a lower level of medical expense reimbursement if you use doctors "outside the plan," something that may be important to you if your children are currently being treated by doctors who are not on the list of preferred providers issued under an employer's insurance plan. You and your spouse, or a judge, should decide how to deal with these and other possible issues related to the scope and cost of your spouse's medical coverage.

Purchasing disability insurance

Disability insurance provides a working parent with a percentage of his or her income if that parent becomes unable to work due to illness or injury. Carrying disability insurance is a common requirement when the parent paying child support is self-employed.

Disability insurance is especially important if a parent's business is a sole proprietorship, a partnership, or a small, closely held corporation. In such businesses, the active involvement of the business owner is critical to the business's financial success. If the owner becomes incapacitated due to illness or an accident, he or she will have little or no income and would probably be unable to meet his or her child support obligation after a period of time.

Even if your children are very young, do not overlook the issue of how you will fund their college education — you can't start saving too soon for this major expense. It's projected that by the year 2010 the cost of a four-year education at a public college will average $103,240, and four years at a private college will cost an average of $217,854! (The projections assume a return on investment of 8% and an inflation rate of 7%. They also assume that the current cost of a public college education averages $9,649 a year and the current cost of a private college education averages $20,361 a year.)

Providing Child Support "Extras"

Gifts, trips, clothes, and anything else that you give a child because you *want* to (and not because you *have* to) do *not* necessarily count as child support when you have a court order for the support, Therefore, you can usually assume that if you are paying child support, you *cannot* deduct the value of those gifts from the total amount of support you are obligated to pay. To be certain, however, check with your attorney.

If you do *not* have a court order for child support, gifts, trips, outings, and so forth are considered in-kind child support that may be applied to your child support obligation.

For tax purposes you can agree to treat any extra money you or your spouse may contribute to help cover the cost of extras as alimony — not child support — because alimony payments are tax deductible for the payer but child support payments are not. However, the parent who receives alimony must count it as income on his or her tax return which may increase that parent's tax liability. (If taxes are an issue for you or your spouse, consult with a CPA.)

If you initiated your divorce and feel guilty about its likely effect on your children, don't try to ease your guilt by agreeing to pay more support than you can really afford. If you have a tough time coming up with the payments after your divorce, you could find yourself in legal trouble if your former spouse takes you to court to enforce the terms of your child support agreement.

Calculating your share of those child support "extras"

Under state guidelines, child support is essentially an average dollar amount that is presumed to provide adequate support for a child. But that amount may not cover the "extras" you want your children to have — private school, special classes, summer camp, sports uniforms, or tutoring, for example. If a judge is deciding child support in your divorce and you want certain extras to be included in the court order, you must ask the judge to consider those special expenditures in the child support amount.

Even if you agree that each of you will be responsible for paying the basic day-to-day costs of your children's care depending on where your children are staying, you still have to decide on which extras to fund and how to split the cost of any big-ticket extras you both feel your kids need.

It's a good idea to first calculate how you will split the cost of special activities and other extras for your kids. One easy way to calculate the split is for each of you to pay a percentage of the cost of the extras based on your individual incomes relative to your total combined income.

For example, assume that the total annual cost of the extras you want to fund is $10,000. Also assume that you earn $40,000 a year and your spouse earns $45,000 a year, for a total combined annual income of $85,000. In this case, your income would represent 47% of the total, and your spouse's income represents 53% of the total. If you applied these percentages to the $10,000 total cost of the extras, in order to pay for them you would contribute $4,700 a year, and your spouse's share would be $5,300.

Realistically speaking, given the cost of maintaining two households, you may not have enough money left over to give your children all the extras they've become used to — or paying for them will require some cutbacks in your post-divorce budgets.

Budgeting for Child Support

If your spouse will be paying you child support and you believe that you need more support than your state's guidelines provide for, prepare a post-divorce budget for your children that clearly demonstrates just how much you need to care for them.

When you're preparing this budget, include expenses such as your mortgage or rent payment, your car payment, phone service, cable, and other similar expenses as well as expenses that are directly associated with your children — clothing, day care, and so on. Be sure to figure in your income, too.

To make preparing your children's budget as painless as possible, try using the budget worksheet found at the following Web page:

www.divorcehelp.com/WR/W40Budget.html

If you pay your child support by check, note exactly what the payment is for on the bottom of each check. A canceled check provides proof of payment in the event that some question arises in the future about whether you paid or not.

Realizing the Benefits of Negotiating Your Own Child Support Agreement

Like most everything else to do with divorce that you can accomplish without the help of a court, negotiating your own child support agreement has its advantages:

- ✔ The negotiation process encourages both of you to assume equal responsibility for deciding how you will take care of the financial needs of your children. (Mothers often end up being their children's financial advocates in a divorce. Sometimes it can appear to their spouses that these women are really arguing on their own behalf, not for their kids.)

- ✔ Negotiating together reinforces the fact that although your marital relationship is changing, you have a relationship as parents and you are both legally responsible for your children's welfare.

- ✔ Working things out together also helps increase the likelihood that once you are divorced, the parent who is obligated to pay child support will actually do so.

Your child support agreement should clearly spell out how child support will be paid, how often it will be paid, the amount of each payment, and the date by which it must be paid. Preparing a child support agreement that will pass muster with a court requires legal help. Judges look for a tightly crafted agreement that leaves little open to question.

Increases in the *inflation rate* will ultimately decrease the value of the child support you receive. A practical way of dealing with this potential problem is to build into your agreement nominal increases in the amount of child support your ex must pay you. If those increases do not keep pace with the inflation rate, you and your former spouse can agree to a different amount of child support. (Be sure to get a new court order reflecting that amount.) Or, you can ask a judge to order an increase in your child support.

Helping to ensure that support will be paid

Don't underestimate the importance of using a negotiated agreement to help ensure that your ex-spouse pays child support as promised or as ordered. Just consider the following facts:

- According to the 1992 U.S. census, of the estimated 5.3 million divorced parents due to receive child support payments, only half were actually receiving the full amount of their payments.

- An estimated *one million* custodial parents have never received a penny in child support despite court orders for support.

- As of 1995, parents legally responsible for making child support payments owed a total $34 billion to 17 million children.

- In 1995, the federal government estimated that 800,000 women and children were on welfare due to lack of child support.

Allowing you to change the agreement as your lives change

Another advantage to negotiating your own child support agreement is that you and your spouse can craft one that readily allows you to anticipate and accommodate changes in your lives and in the lives of your children over the years. For example, you can spell out how you will deal with future possible expenses related to your children — such as orthodontia, sports, extracurricular school activities, clubs, the cost of the prom, an opportunity to study abroad — or deal with salary increases or decreases either of you may experience.

Obstacles to getting a fair child support agreement

Despite the benefits of negotiating your child support agreement yourselves, getting to closure may be easier said than done if your emotions get in the way of rational thinking.

Following are some examples of common stumbling blocks that get in the way of clear-headed negotiations:

✔ The spouse who will be paying child support may view it as nothing more than alimony in disguise. Therefore, he or she may argue for as little child support as possible and against any extras.

✔ The spouse who will be receiving the child support may demand an unreasonable amount of support as revenge for having to get divorced, to "protect" the children, or out of fear for the future.

✔ Looking forward to being single again, some spouses begin dreaming about the exciting new lifestyles they'll enjoy. Because living that kind of life takes money, and because money is usually in short supply after a divorce, the noncustodial parent wants to pay as little as possible and the custodial parent wants as much as possible.

Having all of this worked out ahead of time will save time and money. Otherwise, every time you want to change something related to your child support agreement, you will have to petition the court for a modification, show good cause why you ought to get more child support, and get a new court order, assuming that the judge approves your request.

State courts are not bound to honor provisions you may include in a prenuptial or postnuptial agreement concerning the custody or support of your children.

Making Sure the Support Gets Paid

You have no way of knowing what the future will bring, and the truth is that being single again sometimes changes the priorities of a previously devoted parent. As a result, that parent may begin to take his or her child support obligations less seriously. Or, if you and your former spouse have a falling out, your ex may decide to withhold child support as a way to get back at you. Other developments that can affect your former spouse's commitment to your child support agreement include

✔ A new marriage

✔ Another child

- ✔ Excessive debt
- ✔ A failing business
- ✔ Substance abuse problems

Having your spouse secure the obligation

If your spouse is self-employed, a good way to help ensure that the child support checks keep coming is to ask the court to order your spouse to post a bond to secure the child support. Another option is to ask the court to order your spouse to secure that obligation with a liquid asset such as a checking or savings account, a profit sharing plan, or other resource. Then, if the child support checks stop coming, you can begin drawing the money you need from the collateralized asset until the payments resume.

If your spouse has a history of writing bad checks, agreeing to accept your child support in the form of a personal check is a bad idea. However, you can ask that the payments be made in the form of cashier's check or money order.

Getting a court order

If you negotiate your own child support agreement, submit it to the court for approval so that you have a court-ordered agreement. This precaution is an important one even if you believe that your spouse is totally trustworthy and you are certain that your spouse will live up to your agreement.

Without a court order for child support, you will not have the full force of the law behind you should your former spouse stop making regular child support payments, begin paying less than he or she is supposed to, or fail to make any payments at all. (Chapter 19 has additional information on what you can do if you begin having trouble collecting your child support.)

Using automatic wage withholding

To help custodial parents collect their child support, all new child support court orders and all modified court orders written after December 31, 1993, must include a provision for an *automatic deduction* of child support from the wages of the parent legally obligated to pay that support. (Legal limits do exist on how much can be deducted from each paycheck.)

The parent's employer is served with a court order for the deduction and if that employer fails to comply with the court order, the *employer* is violating federal law. The automatic wage deduction does not help you collect if your former spouse is self-employed. States can also withhold for child support from other sources of income.

If your former spouse has a stable work history, the automatic wage deduction is an excellent way to ensure that you get the child support you need. But, it will not be as effective if your ex regularly changes jobs — you have to be sure that each new employer is served with a new automatic wage deduction court order — and it is particularly difficult to enforce if you don't know about the job changes.

You and your spouse can agree to waive the automatic wage deduction; however, your attorney should structure your court order so that if your former spouse gets behind on his or her support payments, after a period of time the automatic wage withholding will be activated without your having to go back to court.

To help deal with these potential problems, your divorce decree should order your former spouse to let you know whenever your ex changes jobs. Also, the court order for automatic wage deduction requires your former spouse's employers to inform you and the court of any change in your ex's employment status. Despite these safeguards, it is possible that you won't receive notification of any changes in your former spouse's job situation or the notification may not come on a timely basis.

Initially, your spouse may resist the idea of having child support payments automatically deducted from his or her paychecks (the automatic deductions may seem like an invasion of privacy or your ex may think the automatic deductions make him or her look like a deadbeat). However, it's likely that your former spouse will come to appreciate this setup because it makes paying child support somewhat hassle free. Plus, your spouse may find it easier to manage his or her money if the child support is already taken care of and the rest of the paycheck can be spent as needed.

When Do Child Support Obligations Cease?

Ordinarily, a parent's child support obligation ends when a child becomes a legal adult. However, depending on your state, that obligation can continue while your child is a full-time college student or is attending a trade school. But, diploma or no diploma, your responsibility to provide child support typically ends once the child reaches his or her early 20s.

Your obligation to help support a child may end before your minor child becomes a legal adult if he or she

✔ Becomes an *emancipated minor*. Emancipated minors are children who become legal adults before they have turned age 18 or 21. They must initiate a legal process to become emancipated.

✔ Enters the military.

✔ Takes a full-time permanent job.

✔ Gets married.

✔ Dies.

If an unmarried dependent child becomes a parent, that unmarried child's noncustodial parent still has to help support that child. However, the noncustodial parent is *not* legally obligated to support his or her grandchild.

If you are paying child support and the minor child you are supporting moves in with you on a full-time, permanent basis, ask the court for a court order canceling your child support obligation. If you do not, your legal obligation to pay child support to your former spouse continues.

Child Support and the IRS

As far as adjustments to taxable income go, if you are paying child support, you *cannot* claim your payments as a tax deduction. If you are receiving child support, you do not have to claim it as income.

Although the IRS assumes that the custodial parent will claim his or her dependent children as tax deductions, as part of your divorce negotiations you and your spouse can agree to split up that deduction. For example, each of you can claim them in alternate years, one of you can claim one child and the other can claim another child, and so on.

Generally, the parent with the higher income realizes the greatest benefit from claiming his or her children as tax deductions.

By agreement, a custodial parent can transfer his or her dependent child exemption to the noncustodial parent by completing IRS form 8332, something that can be financially beneficial to both parents. You can use this transfer as a bargaining chip in your negotiations — possibly creating a win-win situation for both of you — if you give your spouse the deduction in exchange for getting more support. (The court cannot order this transfer because taking the tax deduction for children is a privilege granted by the federal government.)

Part IV
Working Out the Terms of Your Divorce Agreement

The 5th Wave   By Rich Tennant

"You get an allowance? Is that like child support?"

In this part . . .

*I*f you and your spouse hope to negotiate as much of your divorce as possible on your own, this part of the book should prove helpful. It provides a framework for negotiating, tells you when negotiating on your own may not be such a great idea, and when you should get legal help.

We also explain the important role that mediation can play in helping couples avoid the expense and emotional trauma of a divorce trial. We offer tips on finding the best attorney for your situation, and tell you how to build a mutually cooperative partnership with your lawyer.

If, in the end, you fail to negotiate a divorce settlement with your spouse, the last chapter in this part gives you a taste of the divorce trial process. At that point, the big decisions are left up to the judge.

Chapter 13

Doing (Some of) the Negotiating Yourself

*N*egotiating your own divorce agreement (or at least some of it) can definitely save you some money on attorney's fees and court costs. But it does require that you work side-by-side in a cooperative way with your soon-to-be ex-spouse, which can be a challenge. No mediator will be in the room with the two of you to keep your meetings civilized and productive, nor will you have an attorney do the negotiating for you. Making it work is all up to you. Nevertheless, negotiating your own divorce terms doesn't have to degenerate into a scene from *The War of the Roses.*

Although we don't tell you *what* to decide (that's up to you), we do try to prepare you to make good decisions by suggesting how to plan and organize your negotiation sessions and by offering some basic negotiating advice. In this chapter, we also provide a primer on the basic issues that you may have to resolve before you and your spouse can make your divorce legal.

Note: This chapter touches on topics including alimony, child support, custody issues, and division of property that are covered in more depth in other parts of this book. For more specific information on these topics and how the law addresses them, see the related chapters in Part III.

First, a Word of Caution

When you read this chapter, keep in mind that the plan of action we describe is an ideal scenario to shoot for. Realistically, you may not have the desire or inclination to do *everything* this chapter recommends, which is okay. Just accomplish what you can — you can still save yourself some time and money.

We should warn you that negotiating on your own is not for every couple, and can be downright dangerous for some. You may end up with a number of problems: a divorce agreement that gives you less than you're legally entitled to, a custody arrangement that could be emotionally harmful to your children, or an agreement that is completely unenforceable.

What you say to your spouse during your negotiations can be used against you if you end up in court, unless you and your spouse have a written agreement that guarantees that whatever you say during your one-on-one negotiations remains confidential. If you don't have such a written agreement, what you say to your spouse may come back to haunt you.

Rule Number One: Be on Your Best Behavior

Successful negotiation takes hard work, a commitment to the negotiation process, and a willingness to act like mature adults. That can be a tall order for many happily married couples, let alone those who are splitting up. You and your spouse have to sit down together, one-on-one, talk honestly, figure out how to solve your problems in a rational manner, and be willing to give, as well as take.

You have to treat one another fairly and politely during your negotiations — the last thing you may really feel like doing. If you don't, your negotiations are apt to become little more than a painful and harsh reminder of why you are getting divorced in the first place.

Negotiating your own divorce means that both of you must

- Let reason, not emotions rule.
- Avoid using your negotiations as an excuse to replay old, angry, and hurtful accusations.

- ✔ Listen without interrupting one another. Waiting to have your say can be tough to do, especially if you don't like what you're hearing.

- ✔ Resist forming a response to what your spouse is saying while he or she is still talking.

- ✔ Allow your spouse to express his or her opinions and respect what your spouse has to say. Ridiculing your spouse's choice of words is one way to put your spouse on the defensive and shut down two-way communications entirely.

- ✔ Be open to compromise. Neither of you will get everything you want from your divorce, so be ready to make some trade-offs.

- ✔ Stay cool. If something your spouse says or does during a negotiating session upsets you, just bite your tongue. Try not to respond in the heat of the moment.

- ✔ Avoid using intimidation and threats to get what you want. Tactics like that will backfire on you.

- ✔ Be honest and polite with your spouse.

When you and your spouse are negotiating, stay seated. If you stand or walk around and talk to your spouse at the same time, you are less apt to hear what your spouse is saying and more apt to get overly emotional.

Starting Off Right with a Few Preliminaries

If you and your spouse want to get your negotiations over with as quickly as possible, it isn't surprising. But taking the time to plan how you will negotiate can mean the difference between progress and frustration. Ideally, before you actually begin your formal negotiations, you and your spouse should decide the following:

- ✔ When and where to negotiate.

- ✔ What issue(s) you plan to address at each negotiation session.

  Unless your divorce is very simple — with little to divide up, no minor children, and no spousal support — you will probably need more than one session to negotiate your divorce.

- ✔ How you will structure your negotiation sessions.

- ✔ What information and documentation you need and what kind of record-keeping system you're going to use to record your progress.

Working out seemingly simple things such as when and where to meet for your negotiations can easily lead to a fight. To avoid having that happen, you may want to work out the preliminaries in a public place such a coffee shop or restaurant. If you meet in a public place, your discussion will be less likely to degenerate into a name-calling session. (Wherever you meet, make sure your conversation can't be overheard.)

Because a deadlock is always possible no matter how hard you try to come to a meeting of the minds, you should also decide ahead of time what to do if your decision-making reaches an impasse. Your options include mediation, arbitration, and hiring attorneys to do your negotiating. You should also decide ahead of time where you will go to get information or clarification when a matter of law arises that you don't understand.

If you and your spouse negotiated a prenuptial agreement prior to your marriage or a postnuptial agreement after you were married, you will have less to negotiate. (For an explanation of how these agreements work turn to Chapter 20.)

Divorce à la diskette: Form-preparation software

If your divorce is extremely simple and you have very little to negotiate (you have few marital assets or debts of significant value, no minor children to consider, and neither of you is asking for alimony), getting divorced is mostly a matter of filling out some paperwork. In which case, you may want to prepare your divorce documents by using a divorce agreement software program. (You can find these programs at most software retail outlets.)

When you go shopping for divorce agreement software, keep the following tips in mind:

✔ Make sure that the program is specific to your state and not generic. The software package should provide that information.

✔ Look for software that provides more than just forms. For example, some software provides an overview of the divorce laws in your state, a list of issues you need to consider, and step-by-step instructions for completing the forms.

We recommend checking out the following products (prices are as of this writing and subject to change):

✔ *Divorce* (E-Z Legal Software, $19.95)

✔ *Personal Law Library* (Pro One Software, $44.95)

✔ *Smart Family Law* (American Institute for Financial Research Inc., $29)

After you have completed the forms in your software kit, ask a family law attorney to review them so that you can be sure you are not botching anything up.

It should take no more than an hour of the attorney's time to review your agreement and most attorneys should be willing to do it for a flat fee. The amount of that fee will vary from attorney to attorney.

Planning a Method of Negotiation

There's no one right way to negotiate. A method that works for one couple may not be appropriate for another. However, prior to starting your negotiations, you and your spouse should come to at least a general agreement about how you will structure your negotiation sessions to make them as efficient and effective as possible. The following steps outline one plan of action that may work for your situation:

1. **Prior to tackling a major new issue in your divorce — child custody, child or spousal support, or the division of your property — share your goals and priorities with one another and discuss any special concerns you may have.**

   Try to speak in terms of your realistic needs, or your children's realistic needs. Then identify where you agree or disagree and where your shared interests lie.

2. **Develop a list of possible options for settling the issue, keeping in mind your individual goals and priorities, and your areas of agreement and disagreement.**

   When you are identifying your options, be creative and try not to censor or prejudge any ideas. A seemingly silly idea may inspire a new, more practical one that works for both of you. You may each want to develop your own list of options and then share both lists with one another.

3. **Eliminate all of the ideas on your list that you both dislike or both agree are unrealistic.**

4. **Using the options that still remain, develop written proposals for resolving whatever issue you are negotiating.**

   You can each develop your own proposal for the issue, present it to one another, and respond with counterproposals, or you can write a proposal together. After you have settled on a decision, put it in writing. Each time you concur on a specific issue, you are that much closer to a final divorce agreement.

The negotiating process you use doesn't have to be as formal as the one just described. Find a method that you both feel comfortable with and that facilitates a fair resolution of each issue in your divorce.

Choosing the Right Setting

When deciding on a place for your negotiation sessions, pick a quiet, comfortable (but not too comfortable) location that is relatively free of distractions. That probably rules out negotiating in front of the television set or any time at home when your children are up and about. Wait until they have gone to sleep or, better yet, do your negotiating away from home in a neutral location — in a corner of your local library, at a coffeehouse, or in a park, for example.

When you negotiate in a public place, you are more apt to be on your best behavior, which means that you are less likely to yell at each other, burst into tears, or stomp away in a huff.

Scheduling the Time

Negotiating your divorce agreement will probably take a couple of sessions, depending on what you have to resolve and how quickly you and your spouse can come to a consensus on things. Therefore, schedule your sessions ahead of time and make them a priority in your life. They should be every bit as important as business meetings, doctor's appointments, parent-teacher conferences, and your kids' birthdays.

Set a time to begin and end each session. Generally speaking, your sessions shouldn't run for more than two hours. Longer sessions will probably become unproductive.

Do not back out of a scheduled session without a very good reason. (Incidentally, wanting to play golf, having dinner with friends, or "just not feeling like it" are not good reasons.) However, the unexpected does come up. So, if one of you has a legitimate reason for rescheduling, try to provide the other with at least a few days' notice.

Chill out before you storm off

Keeping your cool can be tough to do no matter how hard you try. Old hurts and insecurities may resurface during your negotiations, especially if your spouse exhibits an uncanny knack for pushing your emotional hot buttons and either deliberately or unwittingly hurts your feelings. Rather than letting your emotions get the best of you and maybe even derail the negotiations, try these alternatives instead:

✔ Take a short "time out." Walk around the block, fix a snack, listen to calming music, or read a magazine. Then resume your negotiating.

✔ If you need more than a quick break, tell your spouse you can't continue negotiating and reschedule for another time.

✔ Acknowledge that you need third-party help.

Don't rush your negotiations. Take all the time that you need — you're making important decisions that will affect your life and the lives of your children for years to come.

Deciding on the Order of Business

Develop written agendas for your negotiating sessions and determine ahead of time who will prepare them. You can take turns writing the agendas, or one of you can agree to prepare them all. Whatever you decide, make sure that both of you have a copy of the agenda well in advance of the next negotiating session.

Plan on taking up the major issues in your divorce in the following order:

- **Child custody and support.** Your number-one responsibility in your divorce is your children's well-being.

- **Alimony,** assuming that any money is left after you decide how you will meet your children's financial needs.

- **Division of your marital property,** including any outstanding debts you may have.

Using written agendas may sound like needless work but, in fact, preparing them ahead of time means that you

- Will know what sort of "homework" you should do before your next session.

- Can get down to business at the start of each session instead of trying to decide what you will discuss.

- Are more apt to stay on track during a negotiating session because you have a written reminder of what you are supposed to be talking about.

When you can't resolve an issue the first time out, agree to return to it later or get outside help. An issue that initially seems unresolvable may be easier to address the next time you tackle it, especially after you and your spouse have a few successful resolutions under your belts.

Educate yourself about your divorce-related legal rights and responsibilities before you begin negotiating. You can do that by scheduling a meeting with an attorney and by reading divorce-related literature (such as this book).

TIP

Making your negotiations as painless as possible

Obviously, negotiating the end of your marriage isn't going to be a barrel of laughs. But consider your options: staying married or turning your entire divorce over to someone else. So buck up and get busy. We offer some suggestions that may make things easier:

🖊 Start your negotiations off with some easy stuff — something both of you can probably agree on. Early success is a confidence builder and helps create momentum for continued progress.

🖊 Don't lose sight of your goals: a less-expensive divorce, an agreement that satisfies both of you, and a mutual commitment to making your agreement work after your divorce is official.

🖊 Avoid over-reaching or posturing to gain control.

🖊 When your spouse makes a concession that benefits you, acknowledge it. (Go on, swallow your pride and do it!) You will help encourage your spouse to make yet more concessions and compromises. But don't forget, in order to keep the concessions and compromises coming, you must make some of your own.

🖊 Be sure that your spouse does not mistake your willingness to concede a few points as a desire to get back together, unless that is definitely what you want.

🖊 Hard as it may be, try not to make important decisions "in the heat of the moment" or when you are feeling especially depressed or guilty about your divorce. You are more apt to make decisions that you will regret later.

Acquiring Expert Advice (And How to Pay for It)

Before your negotiating gets underway, you and your spouse should determine what sort of information you need in order to make intelligent decisions and which of you will be responsible for getting that information. First, make a list of what you need, and then take turns choosing a research topic. Next, you may need to hire any or all of the following professionals:

🖊 A CPA to help you understand the possible tax implications of your financial decisions and how to plan for them

🖊 An appraiser to help you value your home, other real estate, collectibles, fine art, and so on

🖊 A financial planner to help you determine what to do with the assets you may get in your property settlement

If you are going to share the cost of outside experts, deciding whom to use and how you will pay their fees is something else you should work out ahead of time. Any of the following options may be feasible:

- ✔ Liquidate a marital asset. For example, sell one of your cars, sell some stocks or bonds, or dip into your savings.

- ✔ Suggest bartering (or trading) your professional services, skills, or labor in exchange for outside professional help.

- ✔ One of you pays all of the expenses involved in hiring professional help in exchange for getting an equivalently larger share of your marital property or taking on less of your marital debt.

- ✔ One of you pays all of the expenses. The other spouse then reimburses that spouse.

- ✔ You split the expenses 50/50, 60/40, 75/25 — whatever you both agree is fair.

- ✔ One of you pays the full cost of hiring one expert and the other pays for hiring another expert. However, for this to be fair, the cost of hiring each expert should be relative to your individual salaries.

 So that you have no doubt about the fairness of an outside expert's advice, choose experts who have no personal or business relationship with either one of you. Meet with the expert together (not separately) and make sure the expert understands that he or she is working for *both* of you.

Write it all down and save it

During your negotiations, keep an accurate record of what you agree on and what areas of disagreement remain.

Without a written record of your discussions, you won't know where each of you stands in the negotiating process, and writing a final divorce agreement will be difficult if not impossible.

Decide which of you will be in charge of record-keeping. If one of you agrees to be responsible, make sure that your records are always readily available to the other spouse.

If either of you has access to a word processing program, enter your records electronically. You can then make hard-copy printouts of the records and also copy them to a diskette (make an extra copy so that both of you has a disk and a set of printed pages). If one of you doesn't own a computer, have a friend or a computer service read the disk for you.

Bringing In an Attorney to Help with Your Agreement

If you're like most people, one of the key reasons you may want to negotiate your own divorce is so that you can keep your legal costs down. However, excluding attorneys entirely from your divorce can be penny-wise and pound-foolish. Lawyers have a valuable role to play in *all* divorces. (For more on how to shop wisely for legal counsel read Chapter 14.)

You should each hire your own attorneys. No ethical lawyer will accept both of you as clients. In fact, a code of ethics in most states prohibits attorneys from working with both spouses in a divorce.

Getting some basic information

Meet with your divorce attorney prior to starting your negotiations. Use this meeting to acquire an overview of the divorce laws and guidelines in your state, gain an understanding of what must be included in your divorce agreement, and determine the issues and trade-offs you may want to consider during your negotiations. Unless you read law books just for the fun of it or have been divorced a number of times, these are subjects that you probably know little about.

Be sure to get advice about any special concerns you may have related to the decisions ahead of you, and find out about potential legal pitfalls or problems. After talking with an attorney about the issues in your divorce, you may decide that your divorce is much too complicated for you to negotiate yourselves.

You may also want to hire an attorney to help you with specific tasks during the negotiating process — for example, to review financial documents, to provide you with feedback about a proposal your spouse has made, or to review the counteroffer you are considering.

If money is an issue, be up front about it. Tell the attorney you can only afford to purchase an hour or two of his or her time.

Having an attorney review and draft your final agreement

If you and your spouse are able to resolve all the issues in your divorce, or if you work out just some of them, before you sign anything, ask your attorneys to review what you have drafted. Having your attorneys review your draft agreement assures you that nothing important has been overlooked and that you have not created potential future problems between you and your spouse.

In addition, you and your spouse must decide which of your attorneys will draft your final agreement. You can make that decision with a coin toss or the spouse with greater financial assets can agree to hire an attorney to prepare your final agreement. If your attorney drafts the final agreement, your spouse's attorney should review it and vice versa.

The lawyer you hire can tell you whether the agreement you and your spouse negotiate by yourselves is equitable to both of you under the law. The agreement may sound like a great deal to you, but after reviewing it, the lawyer may tell you that you're actually entitled to more. Although you may decide that you are happy with what's in the draft agreement, at least you'll know what you're giving up after meeting with an attorney. An attorney can also make sure that your draft agreement does not overlook certain issues that may create problems (with taxes, for instance) down the road and that it is legally enforceable.

Attorneys are conditioned to assume that each case is a worst-case scenario and to provide legal advice to prevent or mitigate such a situation. So, if an attorney says something that alarms you or makes you question whether you should negotiate your divorce on your own, don't panic. The attorney is legally obligated to inform you of all possible outcomes. A scenario that you find alarming may have little chance of actually occuring.

Creating a Custody Arrangement That Works for Everyone

If you are like most divorcing parents, both of you want to be actively involved in your children's lives after your marriage has ended, and well you should. Plenty of research shows that kids do best when they have two parents actively involved in their lives.

Therefore, your custody negotiations will probably focus on deciding how both of you can continue to spend time with your children, how you can continue sharing parenting responsibilities with one another after you no longer live together, and how you can both assure your children of your continued love. (For more on the subject of custody, see Chapter 11.)

The custody arrangement you finally decide on may not be as good as having two parents under the same roof, but it can be the next best thing. And, if your marriage was tense and full of strife, parenting under two roofs may end up being better than one.

If you want to talk with other divorcing parents who are also deciding about custody, or with parents who are raising children alone, visit the following interactive forum on the Internet:

www.divorcesource.com/cgi-bin/divorce/netforum/custody/a/1.

As you and your spouse identify and eliminate possible custody options and prepare a written proposal (or proposals) for the custody of your children, you should be considering

- ✔ Your children's individual requirements, both practical and emotional.

   A good way to do this is by developing a written list of your children's day-to-day needs, activities, and so on. Although this may seem like a simplistic exercise, writing everything down can help both of you become more realistic about what is actually needed to meet your children's needs.

- ✔ Your individual strengths and weaknesses as parents.

- ✔ Your post-divorce lifestyles.

   Without a crystal ball, describing what your life will be like after your divorce takes some guesswork. But you probably have at least a general idea of what your life will entail. You may know, for example, that you'll probably be working at your current job for a while and that you will be traveling a great deal; that you won't be able to afford to quit the night shift for several more years; that you have to begin working outside the home after your divorce and will be juggling a job and child care; or, that you'll be returning to school so that you can upgrade your job skills and eventually make more money.

- ✔ How well you think you can cooperate with one another as divorced parents.

Most judges will approve whatever custody arrangement you and your spouse choose as long as it is consistent with whatever is in the best interests of your children.

Sometimes, seeing all your options on paper can make it apparent that the child custody option you were considering simply won't work. This can be especially valuable for your spouse if he or she has not been your children's primary caregiver. To help you ensure that you don't overlook anything when you are developing your lists, use the Child Care Tasks worksheet at www.divorcehelp.com/WR/W51kidtasks.htm.

Figuring Out Child Support

If you and your spouse share dependent children, your child support arrangement may be the most important item you negotiate.

Determining a reasonable standard of living

First, you must come to an agreement about the standard of living you want for your children after your divorce. Although you may both agree that you want the very best for your children, if you are like most couples, money was tight during your marriage and there will be even less of it to go around after you're divorced. Therefore, to provide your children with the extras that you want them to have, you and your spouse may have to agree to cut some items out of your own post-divorce budgets.

Another possibility, sad as it may be, is that after your marriage ends, you simply won't have enough money to maintain your children's current life-style, and you won't be able to provide them with all the extras that you hoped they could have. Deciding what to cut will probably be a tough decision to make.

When you are developing budgets for the cost of raising your children, be sure to include the cost of their share of household expenses, including the rent or mortgage, utilities, food, clothing, transportation, school lunches, child care, athletic activities, lessons, and so on. Also, don't forget to consider how you and your spouse will pay for other expenses, such as orthodontics, college, travel, health care, weddings, tutoring, and so on.

You and your spouse can decide how you will fund college when you draft your agreement, or, if your children are very young, you can include a clause providing that you will return to that issue as each child turns a certain age (10 years old perhaps) when you should have a clearer idea of his or her academic ability and potential interest in college.

Getting a court order, even if you're in agreement

Even if your divorce is amicable, if you will be receiving child support, or if you both have agreed to share the cost of supporting your children, get a court order to ensure the agreement is upheld. If your spouse doesn't live up to the agreement, the full force of the law can help you collect. In fact, your ex can even end up in jail!

Securing a court order is an important just-in-case step because without one your options for getting the agreement enforced are quite limited. Although you can get a court order for child support after the fact, the process takes time, and while you are waiting, you and your children may suffer financially. (Chapter 12 talks more about enforcing child support agreements.)

If the spouse who will be paying child support can afford to pay more than just the minimum according to your state's guidelines, your negotiations must also address how much that additional payment amount will be.

Don't forget to spell out in your agreement exactly how the child support will be paid — personal checks, direct deposits, automatic withdrawals, and so on. Before you sign a child support agreement, hire an attorney to review it so that you can be sure what you and your spouse agree to is legally enforceable and is fair to both of you.

Discussing the Subject of Alimony

If you feel that you need some financial support after your marriage has ended and can present solid reasons why your spouse should pay for it, then your divorce negotiations need to include discussions about alimony. (For more in-depth information on the subject of alimony, turn to Chapter 10.) Be aware that alimony can be a difficult issue to negotiate, so don't give up if you can't come to an agreement right away.

If you are the spouse who needs or wants alimony, in order to make your case, compare your post-divorce financial needs and resources with your spouse's. Note the contributions you made to your marriage or to your spouse's career. Steer clear of phrases such as "I must have," "I require," and "I deserve." (Those words won't get you the results you want.) Don't act resentful about the sacrifices you may have made in the interest of your spouse or marriage. At the time you made those choices, you likely did so because you believed they were for the best.

If possible, frame your arguments in terms of how your spouse, not just you, will benefit from any alimony he or she may pay out. For example, perhaps you need alimony so that you can develop good job skills and earn a better living. Depending on your circumstances, you may be able to argue that after you have a good job not only will your spouse be able to stop paying you alimony, but you may also be able to begin contributing more to the support of your children. In other words, your spouse may trade a short-term sacrifice for a long-term gain!

When you are preparing your projected post-divorce budget and are estimating your monthly income without alimony, do *not* include in your income figure any child support you will be receiving. Child support is for your children, not for you.

Dividing Up Your Property and Debts without a Court Battle

If you don't have any young children to support and you and your spouse both earn good money, the only decisions you may have to make may relate to the division of your marital property and debts. Before you can actually get down to deciding who gets what, you must come to an agreement about what is and isn't marital property and what percentage of the value of that property each of you is entitled to. Obviously, developing a comprehensive inventory of your marital assets and debts and assigning accurate values and amounts to each is critical. (See Chapter 6 for information on creating inventories for your personal and marital assets.)

 If you and your spouse own and operate a business together or if one of you owns a closely held business, do not try to negotiate what to do about the business without the help of attorneys. The financial issues are too complicated to work out on your own. They're vexing even for attorneys!

If you are divorcing after just a short marriage, you and your spouse may have few if any joint assets and debts to divide up and you may be able to accomplish that division in a single negotiating session. Usually, the longer your marriage, the more you will own and owe together, and the more time you will need to reach a property settlement agreement.

Split it down the middle or not?

Many divorcing couples decide to split up their property and their debts 50/50 for practicality's sake. Depending on the circumstances of your marriage, your assets, and your debts, this method may not be fair. (For more information on ways to divide property, turn to Chapter 9.)

The following are some of the factors that can suggest that a non-equal split is called for:

  ✔ One of you was significantly more responsible for the assets you acquired during your marriage or the debt that you ran up.

- One of you has a greater need than the other for more than half of the assets or less than half of the debts. For example, one of you makes much less money than the other or one of you has never worked outside the home and has little earning capacity.

- A significant disparity in your ages or your health is going to affect your ability to pay half of the debt or replace the assets you would give up.

- One of you has an important emotional investment in certain assets.

As a point of reference or a reality check, find out what criteria a family law judge in your state would use if it were up to him or her to decide how your marital property and debts should be divided. You can get this information if you meet with an attorney before you start your negotiations, or you can get it from an attorney later, after your negotiations have begun.

Regardless of what percentage split you use to divide up the value of your marital property and debts — 50/50, 60/40, 80/20, for example — both of you should be 100 percent clear about the rationale for that percentage and feel comfortable with it. Otherwise, a number of things may occur:

- One of you may feel cheated out of something or swindled in some way and head to court later to get the arrangement changed.

- The disgruntled spouse may refuse to pay off the joint debts as you both agreed to and the other spouse may get stuck paying those debts.

- The spouse who feels cheated may renege on child or spousal support obligations (it's illegal, but it happens all the time).

First divide the big assets, and then the miscellaneous ones

Dividing up your property in two stages — for significant assets and miscellaneous personal property — can make practical sense.

The first stage focuses on the division of your significant marital assets — your home, other real estate, bank accounts, pensions, investments, vehicles, and so on — and the debts that may go with them. Don't overlook the tax consequences of your decisions during this stage. Be open to selling assets if doing so will help create a win-win situation. (You are most apt to need the help of outside professionals during this phase.)

Dividing up the big stuff

When you divide up assets that secure loans — your home, vehicles, and so forth — look at both the debt associated with the asset and the asset itself. Value that asset according to the amount of equity you have in it, or its market value less the amount you owe on it.

Use the second phase to divide up your miscellaneous marital property — household stuff like your stereo system, furniture, CDs, computer equipment, kitchenware, linens, the lawnmower, power tools, and so on. You may not be able to assign specific values to these items — approximate values will probably do. During this stage you can also divide up credit card debts and other miscellaneous unsecured joint debts.

Don't overlook your family pets when you are dividing up your property. If you have children, you may want to let the pets live with whichever parent will have the children most of the time after your divorce is final. Having their pets around increases your children's sense of stability and security after your marriage has ended.

If you and your spouse are childless and you have multiple pets, you can use any one of the property division methods outlined in this chapter to decide who gets Fido, Spot, Fluffy, and Rover. Another possible option is a "shared custody" arrangement giving each of you the pets on specific days.

Dividing up smaller items

Deciding how you want to divide up your miscellaneous marital property can be as simple as

- ✔ Taking turns choosing, asset by asset, debt by debt, until each of you has an appropriate amount of assets and debts given the percentage splits you agreed to.

- ✔ Letting one spouse divide a pile of miscellaneous property in half, and giving first pick of either of the two piles to the other spouse (thus assuring that whoever does the dividing makes an even 50-50 split).

- ✔ Preparing separate lists of what each of you wants and comparing the two. When some of the same things are on both your lists, you will have to decide what's fair. (One option is described in the nearby sidebar, "When you both gotta have it: A negotiating secret.")

- ✔ Choosing comparable categories of assets and debts without strict regard to dollar amounts and percentages. For example, you take the dining room furniture and your spouse takes the furniture in the den; you take the car and your spouse gets the boat; you each take half of the bed linens; you take the Visa card debts and your spouse takes the MasterCard debts.

When you both gotta have it: A negotiating secret

You and your spouse may both want the same asset. If it's not significant enough to merit scheduling a mediation session or getting legal help to break your stalemate, try the following simple solution that's one of the best-kept secrets of high-priced legal help.

Ask a neutral third party to take two small pieces of paper, write the name of the asset on one of the pieces, fold up both pieces of paper and put them in a hat, box, or some other container. Then, you and your spouse should each pull one of the pieces of paper out of the container. The spouse who pulls out

the piece of paper with the name of the asset written on it gets the asset; the other spouse gets something else in exchange — another asset or less debt of equal value.

Another option is to collect all the items you both want and wait to deal with them after you have completed dividing up everything else. Then, put all of the remaining items into a box and alternate selecting items until there is nothing left.

Just think — some people pay top dollar for this kind of advice!

You can trade off debts for assets or vice versa. For example, you can agree to pay off more of your marital debt in exchange for getting a larger share of your marital assets; or you can agree to take less marital property so that you don't have to pay off as much of your debt.

If it's realistic or cost-effective, wipe out as much of your joint debt as you can by selling marital assets. Minimizing your post-divorce financial ties is almost always a good idea. You may also want to sell joint assets to provide both of you with the cash you may need to start your lives as single people. Be careful that in your quest for cash you don't sell items for less than their actual value.

Figuring Out What to Do with the House

If you are like most other couples, your home is probably the most valuable asset you own together. What you do with your home after a split can be tough on you emotionally as well as financially. Nevertheless, what happens to your house is a bottom-line issue that should be based on financial considerations only.

To help you make a smart decision, you should be asking yourself the following questions and talking over the answers to those questions with your spouse:

✔ How much does comparable housing cost?

✔ What emotional ties do each of you have to your home and to your neighborhood?

✔ How much can you sell the house for?

✔ Is it important for your children to continue living in the same neighborhood or school district?

✔ Are other houses in the same neighborhood or school district available that you and your children can move into?

✔ If you want to keep the home, can you afford to do so, taking into account your mortgage payment, insurance costs, taxes, upkeep, and maintenance? (Don't forget, mortgage interest is tax deductible.)

✔ What will your spouse get in return if you keep the house?

Don't Forget Your Taxes

Don't overlook income taxes when you are negotiating your divorce agreement. If you will still be married on December 31, you can file either a separate return or a joint return for that year.

Filing a joint return is usually the better option for the spouse with the bigger income, but it can work against the spouse who earns less. Ask your CPA to determine the most advantageous filing method.

Other tax-related issues you may need to consider include

✔ How you will share any tax refund you may have coming.

✔ How you will share responsibility for any taxes you may owe.

✔ How you will share liability for any interest, penalties, and back taxes you may owe if you are audited sometime in the future.

Getting to Closure

After you and your spouse think you are close to an agreement on all of the issues in your divorce, draft a final agreement that reflects your decisions so far. Even if a few issues remain unresolved, start drafting anyway, noting what stands between you and closure. When you see how close you are to a final agreement, you may be encouraged to get down to business and tie up those loose ends.

Chapter 14

Hiring a Divorce Attorney

. . . .

In This Chapter

▶ Knowing when you need an attorney

▶ Evaluating and hiring the best attorney for you

▶ Firing an attorney

▶ Seeking affordable legal help

. . . .

*R*egardless of your opinion about attorneys — that they're sage and savvy legal counselors or a necessary evil — you almost can't escape having to hire a lawyer when you are getting a divorce. In complicated and contentious divorces the help of an attorney is absolutely essential. In more straightforward and amicable breakups a lawyer's input and assistance is advisable, even if you and your spouse handle most of the divorce negotiations yourself.

Unless your divorce is extremely simple — for instance, if you and your spouse were married just a short period of time, you have few if any marital assets or debts, you have no minor children, and you're in total agreement with one another about how to end your marriage — *not* securing appropriate legal help is penny-wise but utterly pound-foolish.

After you read this chapter, you should feel a little less intimidated by attorneys and much more confident about hiring one. We show you what to look for in an attorney, how much they charge, and how to begin your search for a lawyer you can trust and afford. After reading this chapter, you'll be armed with a set of questions to ask the attorneys you meet with and will be aware of other issues to consider when hiring an attorney.

When to Hire an Attorney

Assuming that you are a law-abiding citizen and have never been sued or had to sue, you've likely never hired an attorney before. Therefore, the prospect of hiring and working with a lawyer may be downright intimidating, especially if you have always looked to your spouse to make the really important decisions in your household.

Most divorces aren't simple and therefore the active involvement of an attorney is critical. In any of the following situations, you should seriously think about hiring a divorce attorney:

- ✔ You and your spouse have young children.

- ✔ You have been a stay-at-home-spouse and do not have the job skills and contacts you need to begin earning a good living right away, or you are an older person who has never worked.

- ✔ Your marital property is substantial or complicated; you have capital gains taxes and other tax issues to consider; you commingled marital and separate property during your marriage; or other similar factors.

- ✔ One or both of you owns your own business, or you and your spouse are business partners.

- ✔ You and your spouse share a lot of debt.

- ✔ You do not feel comfortable dealing with financial issues.

- ✔ You are reluctant to speak up when you disagree with your spouse and tend to back down when your spouse disagrees with you.

- ✔ You don't trust your spouse to be honest, open, and fair.

- ✔ You think your spouse is hiding assets.

- ✔ You and your spouse are so estranged that civil discourse and compromise are no longer part of your discussions.

- ✔ Your spouse has become physically or emotionally abusive.

- ✔ Your spouse has hired an attorney.

- ✔ Your spouse has made threats such as: "I'll see you in court," "You're not getting what you want without a fight," or "I'm going to take every penny you have."

What to Look for in an Attorney

An attorney can be involved in your divorce from start to finish, or work with you on a very limited basis. (Generally, if you and your spouse both feel confident about your ability to draft your own divorce agreement, you may be able to limit your use of an attorney to initial advice and information and final evaluation and feedback.)

When you do hire a divorce attorney, it's more than a matter of running your fingers through the lawyer ads in the yellow pages until you spot the word "divorce" or simply hiring the lawyer who helped you negotiate your office lease or draw up your will.

✔ You need to hire an attorney experienced in family law.

In some states attorneys can be *board-certified* in family law. These lawyers specialize in divorce cases and other kinds of family law issues. To be certified, they must have significant trial experience and pass a rigorous test. To maintain their certification, they must receive substantial continuing education in family law each year, generally twice the amount of required continuing education of non-board certified family law attorneys. This type of family law attorney tends to charge more and demand higher retainers to begin a family law case than those who are not board-certified but are usually more experienced.

✔ The attorney you hire should talk to you in plain English, not legalese.

✔ The attorney should be someone you trust and feel comfortable with, because you may have to reveal highly personal information about yourself and your marriage.

✔ If you have young children, look for an attorney who makes it clear that during your divorce you must put your children's needs first and that he or she will not pursue unreasonable demands for child support or help you pursue indictive child custody and visitation arrangements.

✔ And last, but certainly not least, your lawyer should be affordable.

Appropriate skills and experience

An old adage states that "there are horses for courses." This saying is as true for an attorney as for any other professional. In other words, when you select a family law attorney, you want one with the legal skills and knowledge needed to get the job done for you:

✔ If you need help negotiating your divorce agreement, the ideal attorney is a problem solver, works well with people, is adept at compromise, and is comfortable in court. Although you and your spouse may have no intention of going to court, an attorney's trial record and history of success in court can have some bearing on his or her ability to negotiate a settlement with your spouse's attorney.

✔ If you know from the start that you're headed for a divorce trial, you want an attorney who has considerable courtroom experience. Not all lawyers do.

✔ It is also helpful if the attorney you choose is familiar with the family law judges in your jurisdiction. Knowing the courtroom style of the judge who's likely to hear your case and how the judge has ruled on previous cases similar to yours helps your attorney adapt his or her legal strategy and style to that particular judge.

Don't base your hiring decision on which attorney has the nicest office. A fancy office in an expensive building says nothing about the adequacy of a lawyer's legal skills. At the same time, don't assume that just because you pay a lot of money to an attorney that his or her legal representation is appropriate to your needs or is of high quality. Also, don't let a lawyer's physical appearance influence your hiring decision.

If your financial situation is complex, the lawyer you hire should either have a solid understanding of the issues and laws that pertain to your divorce or work closely with other lawyers or financial experts who have that knowledge, such as a CPA or appraiser. Remember, negotiating your divorce agreement is as much about financial matters as it is about ending your marriage.

Personal style

If you are relying on an attorney to do more than simply review your divorce paperwork, you must be prepared to share details about your personal life, marriage, and finances. Therefore, you must feel comfortable with whomever represents you.

In addition, your attorney should share and support your basic philosophy or attitude toward your divorce. For example, if you want to keep things as calm, cooperative, and nonadversarial as possible, then avoid attorneys who like to "go for the jugular."

Do not confuse your attorney with your therapist or religious advisor. Your attorney's clock is usually running regardless of whether you call with a legal question or to complain about your spouse.

Affordability

If you do not have much money to spend on legal help, you may have to hire a relatively inexperienced lawyer instead of a seasoned professional. New attorneys tend to cost less than lawyers who have been practicing law for years and already have solid reputations. However, working with an up-and-coming or novice attorney has a potential advantage. In order to build up a good reputation, the attorney may be willing to work a little harder for you than a more-seasoned lawyer would.

Most family law attorneys bill for their services on an *hourly basis*. Few agree to take a *flat fee* based on the total amount of time and labor they think your divorce requires. Estimating up-front just how much time is necessary to finalize your divorce is difficult, because no lawyer knows exactly how any divorce is going to play out.

You're more apt to find an attorney who'll take your case for a flat fee if your divorce is 100-percent amicable and if the tasks the attorney will perform are very well defined. You may be able to find an attorney willing to accept a flat fee if your legal needs are very specific and very limited — for example, you just need some paperwork filled out and filed.

Among other things, an attorney's hourly rate depends on your region of the country and whether your community is rural or urban. Those of you living on the East and West Coasts can expect to pay the most.

Depending on where you live, on average the services of a divorce attorney will cost you anywhere from $100 an hour to more than $600 an hour, *plus* expenses.

Finding the Right Attorney

Locating the right attorney takes time. To start your search, you can develop a list of potential attorneys by

- ✔ Asking friends and family members who have gone through a divorce and were happy with their attorneys.

- ✔ Asking attorneys you have worked with in the past. Before requesting the name of a divorce attorney, explain the nature of your divorce and the kind of legal help you think you need.

- ✔ Checking with your local, county, or state bar association. An association may be able to match your specific needs with the right attorney.

- ✔ Consulting the Martindale-Hubbell directory. It lists lawyers by state and city and rates them based on the evaluations of other attorneys and judges. Your public library should have a copy.

- ✔ Calling the American Academy of Matrimonial Lawyers (312-263-6477), which can provide you with a list of attorneys in your area who specialize in divorce and family law. To become a member of this association, 75 percent of an attorney's practice must be in matrimonial law, the attorney must have been practicing for at least ten years, pass a national exam, and submit to a stringent screening process. You can head for the academy's Web site at www.aaml.org.

- ✔ Looking under "Attorneys" in the phone book yellow pages.

- ✔ Asking your mental health counselor, religious advisor, or social worker.

✔ Surfing the Internet. Many divorce attorneys have Web sites and one of them may be located in or near your community. Some divorce-related Web sites also have links to divorce attorney Web sites.

✔ If you belong to a divorce support group, asking the other members for names.

If you would feel more comfortable being represented by a female attorney, contact the women's bar association in your area, if one exists, or other female lawyers in your community. If you want a male attorney to represent you, you may want to get in touch with a father's rights organization in your area.

Attorneys to Avoid

If you anticipate an especially rancorous divorce, you want an attorney who acts as your legal ally and your advocate, not one who is merely interested in collecting a fee. Steer clear, therefore, of attorneys who brag about themselves a great deal, act distracted when you speak, trivialize your questions by not answering them or telling you "not to worry about that," or who ignore your questions entirely.

Avoid attorneys who talk down to you, don't ask you any questions, or allow themselves to be constantly interrupted by phone calls or conversations with people who come into their office while you are meeting.

If any of the attorneys on your list ask you few, if any, questions about your marriage, your finances, or your divorce goals, cross that lawyer's name off your list.

Interviewing Potential Attorneys

After you compile a list of attorneys, schedule a get-acquainted meeting with each of them. Don't hire an attorney just because someone you know and respect gives the lawyer a glowing review. Make up your own mind after an in-person meeting.

During each in-person meeting, don't be afraid to ask questions. Also, find out about an attorney's credentials and talk about possible strategies and tactics for your divorce case. Make sure that you and the attorney you decide to work with are in agreement regarding the type of divorce you want to pursue and that he or she concurs with your divorce goals and priorities (unless the attorney can give you good reasons for revising them).

Request a free consultation

Many attorneys will give you a free 30-minute to one-hour initial consultation, but you will have to ask for it. Don't expect the attorney to offer the free meeting first. Attorneys who do not offer free consultations may charge a nominal sum — $25 to $50 — for an initial meeting or may charge their normal hourly rate. However, the amount of money attorneys charge for an initial meeting has no bearing on their skills in divorce law.

Prior to meeting with an attorney for the first time, write down questions to ask. Don't be afraid to let the attorneys know where you are emotionally. Although you don't want to use up your entire free consultation explaining how awful your spouse is or how angry you are, or by giving a blow-by-blow account of the demise of your marriage, a good attorney knows that your divorce case will be affected by your emotions. Therefore, the attorney will factor your emotional state into his or her assessment of your case and its likely cost. Some attorneys will even suggest resources such as counseling and support groups to help you deal with your emotions.

Questions to ask the attorney, and responses you need to hear

Bring a notebook with you to your meetings so that you can record how each attorney replies to your questions. Do not be shy about taking notes. Also, as soon as possible after each meeting has ended, write down your impressions of the attorney you've just met with.

To get you started on developing a list of questions, the following are some of the most important ones to ask. (These questions are most appropriate if you're hiring an attorney to help with your divorce negotiations or because you need to be represented in court.)

✔ **How long have you been practicing divorce law, how many cases have you handled, and how many trials have you been involved in?**

Look for an attorney who has been a divorce lawyer for at least three years. If you anticipate that your divorce may end up in court, make sure that the attorney has successfully represented other clients in divorce trials.

✔ **Do you take other kinds of cases as well? If so, what percentage of your law practice is represented by divorce cases?**

Fifty percent of the attorney's caseload should be divorce cases.

✔ **Have you ever had a case like mine? How did you handle it?**

Avoid an attorney who has never dealt with the particular issues in your divorce case. Lawyers can't give you specific details about another case, but they can tell you enough for you to determine whether they have sufficient experience to deal with a divorce such as yours.

✔ **Who will actually handle my case? You, another lawyer with your firm, or both of you?**

If another lawyer will be involved, ask about that lawyer's divorce-related experience.

Don't assume that you're receiving inferior legal care if a skilled paralegal under the supervision of an attorney works on your case. A paralegal can do a good job of handling certain aspects of a divorce for considerably less money than if your lawyer took care of those details.

✔ **What do you think about mediation?**

If you and your spouse reach a stalemate on some aspect of your divorce and you want to give mediation a try, select an attorney who believes in mediation and has used it successfully in divorces such as yours.

✔ **How do you charge, and how do you expect to be paid?**

Find out the lawyer's hourly rate and get an estimate of how much your divorce will cost. This estimate is a best-guess on the lawyer's part — the final cost depends on how smoothly your negotiations go, whether or not you end up in court, and other factors. If another lawyer or a paralegal will be working on your case, get his or her hourly rates, too. If you are worried about how to pay for the legal help you need, be up-front about your concerns.

✔ **Will I have to pay you a retainer and, if so, how much will it be?**

Most lawyers require a *retainer,* or down payment, on the cost of their services. The cost of the time the attorney actually spends on your case is then credited against the retainer.

✔ **If the cost of your services exceeds the amount of your retainer, how will I be expected to pay what I owe you? Monthly billings? A lump sum payment? Under what circumstances is the retainer refundable?**

Most attorneys do not consider a retainer to be refundable unless there is money left over after they have completed a client's divorce, or if you fire the lawyer and all of the retainer has not been spent.

✔ **How do you calculate your billable hours?**

Many attorneys round up fractions of hours, which increases their total cost. In other words, if the attorney spends five minutes talking with you on the phone, he or she may round it up to 15 minutes of billable time. Rounding up to quarter-hours can really add to your costs over time.

✔ **Will you provide me with an estimate of my expenses and an explanation of what those expenses may include?**

You may have to pay the cost of long-distance calls, facsimiles, copying, delivery fees, outside expert fees, court costs, and so on. Some lawyers may bill you for expenses not directly related to your divorce such as the cost of working dinners and cabs. If you object to paying certain expenses, ask for an explanation of why you should be billed for them. If the expenses are not essential to your case, tell the lawyer that you refuse to pay for them.

✔ **How often will I be billed for your expenses, and will I get an itemized bill?**

You should expect to receive an itemized monthly bill.

✔ **If I have questions about my case, can I call you? How quickly can I expect to have my calls returned?**

It is reasonable to expect to have your calls returned within 24 hours, unless you make it clear that you are calling with an emergency. Then, your call should be returned within an hour or two.

✔ **Based on what you know about my divorce, what is your game plan?**

The attorney should be able to provide you with an assessment of the strengths and the weaknesses of your case (and your spouse's case) and a clear explanation of how he or she intends to exploit your strengths and minimize your weaknesses in order to get you the best divorce possible. Steer clear of attorneys who emphasize "playing hardball" rather than negotiating and trying mediation. Hardball tactics cost big bucks.

✔ **If you can't negotiate a settlement and my divorce goes to trial, will you represent me in court or will you recommend another attorney?**

If you think your divorce may go to trial, you want an attorney who has trial experience and who can handle your divorce from start to finish. Switching to a trial attorney mid-stream will increase the cost of your divorce because that attorney will require a separate retainer to take your case. Your divorce will also take longer because the trial attorney needs time to get up to speed on your case.

✔ **What can I do to minimize my legal expenses?**

Some lawyers are more amenable than others to letting you handle certain aspects of your case yourself — picking up documents, copying, conducting simple research, and doing other tasks a layperson can handle.

Before you agree to take care of some of the simple, nonlegal tasks that are involved in a divorce case, be sure that you have the time to accomplish them on deadline. You don't want to be responsible for delaying the finalization of your divorce.

✔ **What do you expect from me?**

Any reputable attorney expects a client to provide full disclosure of all relevant facts, provide information on a timely basis, return phone calls promptly, be honest, pay bills on time, and obey the attorney's directives regarding what to do or not do in terms of the case.

Documents you need to produce

When you meet with prospective attorneys, be sure to bring along information regarding your family's finances, including the following:

✔ An inventory of your assets and debts

✔ Copies of your and your spouse's current will

✔ Recent tax returns

✔ Deeds to property

✔ A copy of any prenuptial or postnuptial agreements that you may have signed

✔ Any correspondence that you've received from your spouse or your spouse's attorney about the divorce

Chapter 6 provides a comprehensive list of the types of financial and other information you should have already prepared and assembled in preparation for divorce. After you hire an attorney, you'll probably have to provide additional background information and documentation.

The American Bar Association (ABA) Family Law section publishes *Your Divorce: A Guide Through the Legal Process.* This publication provides worksheets for recording information your attorney needs from you and also outlines and explains the various documents your attorney may want you to produce. As of this writing, single copies cost $9.50 plus $3.95 for shipping and handling. You can write to ABA Order Fulfillment, 750 North Lake Shore Drive, Chicago, IL 60611, and send a check for the exact amount made out to the American Bar Association.

What an attorney wants to know about you

Your initial meeting is a two-way street — you won't be the only one asking questions. Lawyers need to get some information from you before they can answer your questions. The questions lawyers ask help them decide whether they want to take you on as a client, and whether your goals for your divorce are reasonable and legitimate.

An attorney also wants to determine if you're using your divorce as revenge against your spouse. Some clients spell *trouble* and many attorneys steer clear of them unless they really need the work or figure that the money they'll earn from the case is worth the headache of dealing with a particular client.

Reputable attorneys also want to be assured that they won't have a conflict of interest if they represent you. A conflict exists, for example, if their law firm represents your spouse's business.

The following list gives you an idea of the types of questions you can expect an attorney to ask you:

- Why you are getting a divorce?
- Do you have any minor children from your marriage?
- Do you work outside the home?
- How long have you been married?
- Are you and your spouse still living together? If not, with whom are your children living (assuming you have children)?
- Do you and your spouse have a prenuptial or postnuptial agreement?
- What major assets do you and your spouse own, and what would you estimate each of those assets is worth?
- What are your marital debts?
- What kind of employment-related benefits do you and your spouse have?
- Do either of you have a drug- or alcohol-related substance abuse problem?
- Are you and your spouse retired or do either of you have plans to retire soon?
- What are your goals for your divorce in terms of spousal support, property settlement, child custody and visitation, and child support?
- What kind of relationship do you have with your young children and what role do you play in their day-to-day lives as a parent?
- Why do you think you deserve to have custody of your children?
- Has there been any violence or abuse in your relationship?
- Should I know anything else about you, your spouse, or your marriage?

Be prepared to provide honest answers to questions that may make you feel uncomfortable such as: "Are you having (or have you had) an affair?" and "Is your spouse aware of your affair?"

Getting the Hiring Agreement in Writing

After you decide on an attorney, ask for a contract, written agreement, or a letter of understanding before you pay any money, give the attorney a lien on any of your property in lieu of cash, or make any other kind of payment. The document should detail all of the specifics you and the attorney agreed to during any of your meetings, including financial arrangements, certain services the attorney will provide, payment arrangements, and so forth.

Do not hesitate to take a day or two to thoroughly reread the contract or agreement or before signing it. Ask the attorney about anything you do not understand and keep asking until all of your questions have been answered to your satisfaction. If you and the lawyer agree to add or delete anything, make certain that those changes are reflected in the document before you sign it. Keep a copy of the final signed contract or agreement for your files.

What If You Become Dissatisfied with Your Attorney?

The lawyer who helps you with your divorce is working for you. So, if you are unhappy with something your lawyer does or doesn't do, communicate that dissatisfaction to your attorney, but be reasonable about it. Avoid complaining about insignificant matters or constantly calling to gripe — it may impact your lawyer's commitment to your case.

If you feel that your lawyer is not doing a good job of representing you, you can fire him or her whenever you want. However, you do have to pay for any work the attorney has performed up to that point and for any and all expenses the attorney has incurred on your behalf.

Firing one attorney and hiring a new one slows the progress of your divorce and will probably increase your legal costs. Therefore, don't take that step without giving it some thought. Try to analyze objectively why you are unhappy with your current attorney. Is it because the attorney consistently seems unprepared, ignores your wishes, or never responds to your phone calls or letters? Is it because your attorney is giving you advice that you don't want to hear, or because you are letting your emotions get in the way of rational thinking?

The further you are into the divorce process, the greater the potential harm you may do to your case if you fire your attorney. Your case will grind to a halt until you find a new attorney; it will take your new attorney time to get up to speed; your divorce will cost more; and your new attorney may have a different strategy than your first attorney, which could take your divorce in a whole new direction.

Before you fire your attorney, consider getting a second opinion from another lawyer. Your attorney may be doing the very best job possible under the circumstances and you may not be any happier with a different attorney.

What If You Can't Afford Legal Help?

Not everyone can afford to pay the fees of even a relatively inexperienced attorney. If you've checked your wallet and come up short, some legal resources may be available to help you with your divorce.

Try a legal clinic

You may be able to use the services of a local, state, or federal legal clinic in your area. Not all of these clinics take divorce cases, however, and if they do, your household income must be very low (usually some percentage of the U.S. poverty level) to qualify for their services. Furthermore, if your divorce is complicated, you will need more help than a legal clinic can provide.

For-profit legal clinics are another source of low-cost help. These clinics tend to rely heavily on standardized legal forms and paralegals and usually charge set fees for certain types of cases — typically in the $200 to $500 range plus court costs. However, if your case is particularly time-consuming, the amount you actually pay may be more than the standard fee.

Although the price may be right, a for-profit legal clinic is not the place for you if your divorce is complicated. Its staff may not have the expertise or the time to give you the legal help you need.

Alternative ways to pay

You may have other means at your disposal to pay for legal help if you don't have sufficient cash:

- ✔ **Trade or barter:** If you have a special skill or talent that is worth a significant amount of money or of particular value to an attorney, you may be able to work out a trade — your expertise in exchange for legal services. This avenue may be a long shot, but it's worth a try.

- ✔ **Payment plan:** You may be able to find an attorney who allows you to pay for his or her services over time, depending on your future earnings potential.

- ✔ **Lien on your property:** If you own real property or other significant assets that are not marital property, an attorney may be willing to take a lien on that property. If you sell the property, the attorney is in line to receive all or some of what you owe him or her from the sale proceeds.

Your city or state bar association may have a program for affordable legal representation for low-income people.

Chapter 15

Helping Your Attorney to Get the Best Results Possible

*W*hen you hire an attorney to represent you in a divorce, you and your attorney become partners — you give and get, and your attorney gives and gets — and the progress and outcome of your divorce, not to mention its cost, depend in part on how well your partnership works.

To help make your attorney-client relationship productive and efficient, this chapter explains what you and your attorney should expect from one another and the type of information your attorney needs in order to represent you in the most effective (and economical) way possible.

Because the divorce process becomes much more formal when you hire an attorney, this chapter also explains how settlement conferences and draft proposals work. Finally, this chapter provides some information on the preparation of the final divorce agreement.

What to Expect from Your Attorney

You and your attorney should understand from the very outset what you need and expect from each other. At the very least you should expect that your attorney will do the following:

- Provide a written contract or agreement that states the terms and conditions of your attorney-client relationship. (Don't work with any attorney who won't provide one.)

- Live up to the terms of your written agreement or contract, or let you know ahead of time when something you agreed to needs to be changed. (You did make sure to get something in writing from your attorney, didn't you?)

- After becoming familiar with the facts of your case, lay out a game plan for your divorce and explain that plan to you. The plan does not need to be elaborate, but at a minimum it should give you a general sense of how your attorney intends to proceed with your divorce to achieve an agreement that works for you. Your attorney should also give you a rough timetable for the completion of your divorce.

- Provide clear explanations of all your options as your divorce progresses, answer your questions honestly, and show respect for your preferences and decisions.

- Pull out the stops to reach a negotiated settlement.

- Give you straightforward answers to your questions. Be prepared, however, to hear things you may not like — that your divorce expectations are unreasonable, that you should give up certain assets or pay money to your spouse, or that your spouse is unwilling to concede on an issue that is really important to you.

- Tell you when your divorce priorities and goals are not legally or financially feasible.

- Return your phone calls within a reasonable period of time (24 hours is acceptable) unless you are very clear that you need a quicker response.

- Consult with you before putting an offer on the bargaining table or taking other important actions related to your divorce.

- Copy you on all correspondence and documents sent out of his or her office that are related to your case.

- Keep your personal and financial information confidential.

- Store any important documents you turn over to him or her in a safe place. (Ask your attorney for copies of those documents.) Your attorney should return them to you promptly after your divorce is over or if you ask for them sooner.

- Act as your interim "counselor," as well as your attorney, by recommending certain services, other professionals, courses, seminars, and support groups that you may want to consider using to help you deal with the nonlegal aspects of your divorce. Believe it or not, good family law attorneys feel that they need to help with their clients' emotional or mental healing while they are handling the legal aspects of their divorces.

After your negotiations are underway, your spouse's attorney may do things that change the tenor or direction of your divorce. When that happens, your attorney's game plan will probably change and the cost of your divorce may increase as a consequence. These changes may also mean that your divorce takes longer.

Expect some disappointment and frustration along the way as the terms of your divorce are being negotiated. But don't take your feelings out on your attorney, assuming that he or she has been working hard on your case. Your attorney can't always produce instant solutions.

What Your Attorney Expects from You

To help get you the best divorce possible, your attorney will expect you to provide information, direction, and feedback when it's needed. Respond to your attorney's requests as quickly and completely as you can. Staying actively involved in your divorce and being responsive to your attorney's needs is the best way to help ensure that his or her legal help does not cost you a bundle and that your final divorce agreement reflects at least some of your goals and priorities.

Your attorney may tell you things that you should and should not do while you are getting divorced. These instructions are intended to help protect your legal interests or your safety. Don't disregard them! If you do, you may undermine your lawyer's efforts and put your interests or your children's interests in jeopardy. The following sections of this chapter describe what your attorney expects of you as a client.

How's that for a quickie?

One Web site we found touts the "Dominican (Republic) Celebrity Divorce" (it's located at www.global-money.com/products/divorce.html) as being quicker and easier than a U.S. divorce and "certified legal" to boot (whatever that means). Supposedly, after completing and returning the appropriate paperwork, you're single again in just three days, even if you and your spouse have not yet worked out the details of your divorce. You can even purchase a layaway divorce with a minimum initial payment of just $50. If you are tempted by this offer, consult with a family law attorney first before you sign any paperwork or pay any money for any kind of super-speedy divorce service.

Don't be afraid to ask questions and speak your mind

Trusting your lawyer's judgment doesn't mean that you can't ask your lawyer questions, or request an explanation when your lawyer says something that you don't understand, or speak up when you aren't sure that you agree with your attorney's recommendations.

When your attorney provides you with advice and options, carefully weigh what he or she says. In the end, follow your intuition — only you know what will really satisfy you and how far you're willing to go to get there. Remember, you call the shots; your attorney only recommends which shots to take.

Pay your bills on time

If you have trouble paying your legal bills, don't let them pile up. Instead, as soon as you feel financially pinched, find out if your attorney is willing to work out a payment plan or some other financial arrangement with you. Don't just disappear or become unavailable to talk with your attorney because of your money problem. You may hurt your case if you do.

If you don't pay your legal bills, your lawyer will likely file a motion with the court to withdraw from your case so that he or she can legally stop representing you. If the court approves the motion, you have to hire a new attorney and your divorce will take longer.

Keep your attorney up to date on any changes in your life

Your attorney wants to know about any changes in your personal situation or in your spouse's life that could affect your divorce or your safety. For example, inform your lawyer if your spouse begins threatening you with a custody battle, if your spouse's business is experiencing financial problems, or if your spouse becomes abusive.

Avoid using your lawyer as a therapist

Your attorney is your legal adviser, not your therapist. Taking up his or her time with tirades about your spouse, worries about your future, or laments about what could have been is a quick way to run up your legal bills. When you are having difficulty dealing with your divorce or just need a shoulder to cry on, talk to a trusted friend or relative, your religious adviser, or a mental health professional.

First Things First: Requesting Temporary Orders

If your divorce is contentious, one of the very first things your attorney may do is file motions asking the court to grant *temporary orders*. Temporary orders can help you make sure that certain things happen or don't happen while you are working out the terms of your divorce. For instance, your attorney may request temporary orders for

- Spousal support
- Child support, custody, and visitation
- Control of assets if you are worried that your spouse may waste or hide marital assets
- Inventories of all property in the marriage along with an appraisal of that property
- Appointment of a guardian or attorney *ad litem* to represent the interests of your minor children
- Court-ordered marriage counseling, alcohol or drug evaluations, or psychological counseling
- The right for you to remain in your home
- A temporary injunction against improper behaviors of many types on the part of your spouse
- The right to use certain property, such as a car or a bank account
- Payment of your attorney's fees
- The appointment of an independent receiver to save or sell certain assets

Your attorney may also request a temporary restraining order if your spouse is threatening your safety or your children's safety, or has already been physically violent.

If you are concerned that your spouse may disappear with your children, your attorney can also ask the court to prohibit your spouse from doing so or ask the court to mandate supervised visitation if your spouse has provided evidence that he or she may attempt to flee with the kids.

After your attorney has filed the appropriate paperwork with the court, the attorney or the court may arrange for a court hearing to discuss the attorney's motion for a temporary order. At this hearing, your spouse (actually your spouse's attorney, assuming that one has been hired) must argue why your motion should *not* be granted.

When you need action now: *Ex parte* orders

When the need for action is immediate, your attorney may be able to get a court order issued on an *ex parte* basis. *Ex parte* refers to a legal action ordered on behalf of one party without the other party being notified about it or having an opportunity to participate in the action.

With an *ex parte* order, your spouse will not learn about the court's decision and a hearing will not be held until after the court has approved your attorney's motion and issued

its order. Therefore, an *ex parte* order is normally of very short duration. Both parties in the action are usually ordered to attend a hearing to determine whether the terms of the *ex parte* order should be extended.

If you request an *ex parte* order, you may be required to post bond to protect your spouse against any damages he or she may suffer because no court hearing was held. However, in many family law situations, the bond requirement is waived.

Providing Your Attorney with Essential Information

You should provide your attorney with basic information about your family, marriage, finances, reasons for divorcing, and so on during your initial get-acquainted meeting. But after your client-attorney relationship is made official, your attorney needs to know a lot more about you.

Your attorney collects much of the information we mention here through one-on-one interviews with you, and by asking you to fill out forms and provide as much backup documentation as you can — tax returns, credit card statements, titles to property, insurance policies, lease agreements, phone bills, loan applications, business profit-and-loss statements and balance sheets, records of investments, household budgets, and other documents.

Don't decide for yourself whether your attorney really needs the information he or she requests. Do your best to provide everything your attorney asks for; don't hold anything back just because you think the information is unimportant or irrelevant. Failing to share that information may derail your attorney's negotiating strategy or complicate your divorce in other ways. For example, if you withhold information from your attorney that your spouse's attorney knows exists, your spouse's attorney may damage your case by introducing that information into evidence during a hearing.

If you read Chapter 6 of this book and followed its advice, you're a couple steps ahead of the game. But, if you delayed pulling together essential information because the whole process sounded oh-so-tedious and time-consuming — which it is — you can't avoid assembling the necessary paperwork after you hire a divorce attorney. Remember, the more information your attorney can get from you or through the cooperation of your spouse, the less you need any formal discovery and the less your divorce will cost. (Chapter 4 covers the discovery process in detail.)

The following sections of this chapter provide a rundown of some of the things your attorney needs to know.

Personal stuff

To help develop a strategy for ending your marriage and to determine what you may be entitled to in your divorce, your attorney needs information on your personal history, your marriage, and your minor children. Therefore, among other things, your attorney will question you about:

- ✔ Why you are getting a divorce
- ✔ The history of your marriage
- ✔ Biographical information about you and your spouse
- ✔ Your individual health histories, including whether either of you has a history of serious medical or emotional problems
- ✔ Your minor children — their ages; where they are living, if you and your spouse are separated; whether your children have special needs (educational, physical, emotional); whether they are attending public or private school, and so on

---

Writing it all down: The story of your marriage

Your attorney may ask you to prepare a written narrative describing your marriage: how you and your spouse shared child-care responsibilities, the personal habits of you and your spouse, what you think lead to your divorce, what you would like from your divorce and for your life after divorce, and what you believe your spouse wants.

The narrative can be a good way for your attorney to get at the facts and issues related to your divorce that may not be apparent from a review of the financial, legal, and personal data forms you fill out or from your client-attorney interviews. Furthermore, putting everything down on paper can be both cathartic and healing, and help you put your marriage and divorce in proper perspective.

Legal and financial stuff

Your attorney will also spend time reviewing the ins and outs of your finances and any legal agreements you and your spouse may have entered into. Among the things your attorney will want to know are:

- Whether you have a separation agreement. Your attorney will want to read the agreement if you have one. (See Chapter 5 for more on separation agreements.)

- Whether you and your spouse own any real estate, including homes, buildings, or land. Be prepared to provide your attorney with the *deeds of record* to this property and with any loan documents related to the property if you owe money on it.

- Whether you signed any prenuptial or post-nuptial agreements. (For the full scoop on prenuptial and post-nuptial agreements, turn to Chapter 20.)

- Whether you or your spouse have done any estate planning, such as writing a will, buying life insurance, or setting up a trust.

- Whether you or your spouse own a closely held business together or separately, or if you have other shared business interests.

- An accounting of your marital assets and debts and where you got the money to pay for any of the real property you may own. *Real property* includes your home and any other homes, buildings, or land you may own.

- How much each of you earns annually from all income sources — including salaries, bonuses, and other employment-related income, trust income, annuities, and royalties.

- Whether either of you made any special contributions to the other spouse's career or business. (You helped finance the business or worked in the business; your spouse supported you through college or graduate school; or you used your separate funds to purchase marital assets or to pay for your family's living expenses.)

- Whether either of you has wasted marital assets by gambling; engaging in phone sex or extramarital affairs; or through addiction to drugs, alcohol, or even the Internet.

- Your current household budget and your projected post-divorce budget.

- Proof of your spouse's fault, if you filed a fault divorce against your spouse, or proof of your innocence if your spouse filed against you.

Other important stuff

Finally, your attorney will ask you questions to understand what you expect from your divorce and what you are willing to do or not do to get what you want. Your attorney needs this information in order to meet your needs but also because your attorney has to be certain that you have realistic expectations about the possible or likely outcome of your divorce. Given this, you can expect your lawyer to ask you about:

- Your divorce goals and priorities
- Why you feel the custody arrangement you want is reasonable and why your spouse's desired custody arrangement isn't reasonable, assuming that you and your spouse don't agree on child custody
- Your expectations for your divorce
- Under what, if any, circumstances you are willing to go to trial to get what you want

Hammering Out the Details: Draft Agreements and Settlement Conferences

Your attorney will probably work out the details of your proposed divorce agreement and present them to you for your approval and then to your spouse's attorney in detailed written or oral form. Your spouse's attorney will do the same thing. These oral or written presentations can be little more than trial balloons to get your or your spouse's reaction to certain provisions or they can represent something closer to a final and complete divorce agreement.

After everyone feels that they are very close to a final agreement, both attorneys will prepare written draft *divorce agreements*. Depending on the complexity of your divorce and how willing you and your spouse are to do some compromising, a single draft agreement may be all that is necessary before you and your spouse have something you can both approve.

Expect to review all drafts, whether they are prepared by your attorney or your spouse's attorney, and then be ready to provide your attorney with feedback. Do not agree to any proposal if it makes you feel uncomfortable. You and your spouse are not obligated to accept any draft agreement you do not like. You can accept or reject the draft agreements, or you can use them as the basis for additional negotiations.

Settling disputes at a settlement conference

If your divorce is very complicated and involves a significant amount of property, after you and your spouse both feel as if you have at least the beginnings of an agreement, attorneys for both spouses may schedule a *settlement conference*. Usually this conference takes place after discovery has been completed but it can take place whenever you and your spouse are ready to make a deal.

The settlement conference offers your attorneys, and possibly you and your spouse as well, an opportunity to sit down face-to-face and try to hammer out the specific details of your divorce agreement. Whether you attend the meeting is something that you and your attorney should talk over before hand. It may or may not be in your best interest to attend. For example, if you have trouble controlling your emotions, you may want to stay away from the meeting. But, on the other hand, you may want to hear everything that is said at the settlement conference so you can provide your attorney with immediate feedback.

A successful settlement conference involves some old-fashioned horse-trading. So, if you have not been clear with your attorney about what you are willing to give up to get what you really want, your attorney will not be able to bargain effectively for you.

If an issue arises that you and your spouse simply cannot agree on, no matter how hard your attorneys try to craft a mutually acceptable compromise, they may recommend mediation, or even arbitration, both of which are described in Chapter 16. If you don't want to give these options a try and don't want to keep negotiating, your only other option, assuming that you and your spouse still want to get divorced, is to have your case tried in court (for more on what happens if you go to trial, see Chapter 17).

 After your attorney fully briefs you about key points and legal issues, he or she may suggest that you and your spouse work out the terms of your final agreement on our own instead of working through your attorneys (assuming that you and your spouse are communicating with each other). After that, your attorneys can draft a written divorce agreement.

Evaluating the Proposal

You have to evaluate whatever agreement your spouse may propose, or that either attorney may draft, and decide if you like the agreement, don't like it, or like it well enough to use it as the basis for your final negotiations in your divorce settlement. When you do your evaluating, ask yourself the following questions:

- ✔ Is the agreement fair to me?
- ✔ Can I afford the agreement?
- ✔ Is the agreement in my children's best interest?

✔ What was I looking for in a divorce agreement that this one does not have? Are items missing that are worth the cost and the time involved in continued negotiations?

✔ Is the reason that I don't yet want to settle because important items are missing from this agreement or because my emotions are getting in the way?

✔ If I really push for any of the missing items, what may I have to give up? Is it worth it to me? What are the risks of not settling now?

✔ Is my spouse likely to make any additional concessions?

✔ Will I be any better off if I refuse to settle and take this case to trial? What is the worst that could happen? (Your attorney should be able to give you a strong sense of how a judge would be likely to rule given your state's laws and guidelines and the past decisions of the judge who may hear your case.)

✔ What kind of financial and emotional toll is not settling likely to take on me and my children? Is not settling in order to gain what I want really worth it?

You and your attorney should discuss the pros and cons of the proposed agreement. Share your thoughts and concerns with your attorney and ask for an opinion about the agreement. Your attorney may tell you that the agreement is about as good as you're going to get, that you can probably get a few more concessions if you keep negotiating, or that the agreement is not in your best interest. In the end, however, how you respond to whatever offer is on the table is your decision.

Making a Deal: The Final Settlement

After you and your spouse come to a final agreement about the terms of your divorce, your lawyer or your spouse's lawyer drafts a formal version detailing everything you agreed to, including many standard provisions and boilerplate language — stuff you can find in every settlement agreement. If your attorney does the drafting, he or she submits it to your spouse's attorney for review and changes, or vice versa.

Don't get impatient with all the back-and-forth negotiations. Getting everything just right is important because after you and your spouse sign the agreement, it becomes a legally binding contract, which means that both of you are legally obligated to live up to what it says, like it or not.

Attending a hearing

What happens after you sign the settlement agreement depends on your state. In some states, in order to have your marriage officially dissolved or ended by the court, you and your spouse (or just one of you) may have to appear at a hearing. In other states, no hearing is required as long as your divorce is no-fault. (Chapter 4 explains the difference between fault and no-fault divorces.)

If you do attend a hearing, your attorney is with you. The hearing is more of a formality than anything else, and it's over quickly. You are legally divorced after the judge signs your divorce decree or judgment of divorce and makes that decree, together with your final settlement agreement, part of the court records.

Changing the agreement later

To change the agreement after it's signed, unless both you and your spouse agree to the changes, you have to hire attorneys again, and you may even end up back in court.

Some states allow judges to modify negotiated settlement agreements. Others allow judges to only accept or reject an agreement. If the judge rejects your agreement, you can go back to the drawing board to work out a new, more acceptable one. A judge may reject your agreement because he or she doesn't think it is fair to one or both of you, because it's unenforceable or violates your state's laws, or because it isn't in the best interests of your minor children, among other reasons.

When the Decree Comes In

After your attorney (or your spouse's attorney) submits the legal paperwork to the judge, the court then returns your divorce decree to your attorney. He or she then forwards the decree to your spouse's attorney. At that point, you and your spouse have a certain amount of time to appeal the court's judgment.

Realistically, unless you have a last minute change of heart or unless the judge makes changes to your divorce agreement that you do not like, an immediate appeal is unlikely. However, you or your spouse may try to get something changed later, after you have had a chance to live with the agreement and identify any problems with it or if changes occur that merit a modification. (Chapter 19 covers the topic of modifying divorce agreements.)

Keep a copy of your final settlement agreement and your divorce decree in a safe place.

Chapter 16

Using Mediation to Avoid a Divorce Trial

● ●

In This Chapter

▶ Defining mediation

▶ Understanding how the mediation process works

▶ Appreciating the benefits of mediation

▶ Asking about the mediators your attorney recommends

▶ Understanding the role of your attorney in mediation

▶ Wrapping up the mediation process

● ●

*W*hen you and your spouse are working out the terms of your divorce, no matter how hard you both may try, you're likely to encounter issues that you just can't resolve on your own. If that happens, you don't have to tear your hair out in frustration or toss in the towel and start hunkering down for a trial. Rather than let sticky issues derail your amicable divorce, you and your spouse may still be able to work out a negotiated settlement by using mediation.

This chapter explains what mediation is and how it works and describes the characteristics of a good divorce mediator. It also describes the role of your attorney when you use mediation (opting for mediation still doesn't eliminate the need for a divorce attorney).

Mediate, Don't Litigate

Mediation is a dispute-resolution method that relies on the open exchange of information, ideas, and alternatives to help individuals resolve their differences outside of court. Although mediation can help resolve a wide variety of civil law matters, it has proven to be an especially cost-effective tool for divorcing couples. When it works, mediation helps both spouses turn out winners and avoids a trial in which win-win resolutions are rare.

At the time of this writing, more than half of the U.S. states laws require divorcing couples under certain circumstances to participate in mediation before heading for a divorce trial. Those circumstances usually relate to unresolved custody issues. For the sake of the children, courts prefer for parents to make their own decisions regarding custody and visitation (rather than letting a judge decide).

States with laws requiring mediation include Alaska, Arizona, California, Delaware, Florida, Idaho, Illinois, Indiana, Iowa, Maryland, Michigan, Minnesota, Missouri, Montana, Nebraska, Nevada, New Hampshire, New Jersey, North Carolina, North Dakota, Ohio, Oklahoma, Oregon, Pennsylvania, Texas, Utah, Washington, West Virginia, and Wisconsin.

Do not begin mediation until you and your spouse have each spoken with a divorce attorney about your legal rights. Otherwise you risk agreeing to arrangements that are not in your best interest. In fact, a reputable mediator will tell you right up front that you need to hire an attorney.

If you are feeling a lot of anger or other strong emotions about your divorce, you may need to work with a mental health professional before you can use mediation successfully.

What Happens during Mediation

Mediation is about mutual understanding, cooperation, and problem solving; it's *not* about winning. During a mediation session, the *mediator* (a neutral third party), acts as coach, consensus builder, facilitator, and, if necessary, referee, and helps you to accomplish the following:

✓ Clarify exactly what you need to work out

✓ Organize your discussions by determining what you'll discuss first and how you'll approach each issue

✓ Keep your discussions moving forward

✓ Provide legal information as necessary (but not legal advice)

Who are mediators?

Some mediators may be mental health professionals, social workers, members of the clergy, financial professionals, or even volunteers. However, if you use a mediator to help you with your divorce, that person should either be a family law attorney or a non-lawyer mediator who has experience helping couples resolve issues related to divorce.

Working with a qualified mediator helps you ensure that whatever you and your spouse agree to complies with the laws of your state and will be legally enforceable.

A mediator who understands your state's laws and legal processes is better able to diffuse potentially explosive situations during mediation. For example, if your spouse threatens to storm out because you asked her exactly how much she makes, a mediator can remind your spouse that your attorney can get that information anyway through formal discovery if it isn't provided voluntarily.

Your attorney may accompany you to the mediation sessions or may just be available to consult with you by phone as needed. (See the section "How Your Attorney Can Help with Your Mediation" later in this chapter.)

What do mediators do?

A mediator does not take sides, interject opinions, or provide legal advice. (It is unethical for an attorney mediator, just as it would be for an attorney, to give legal advice to both you and your spouse.) Nor can a mediator make decisions for you or order you or your spouse to do anything you don't want to do. Nevertheless, the mediator does try to create an environment in which you and your spouse feel comfortable calmly expressing your opinions, talking over your differences, and working out your problems together.

At your first session, the mediator helps you establish the ground rules for your negotiations, clarifies the issue(s) that you want to resolve, and sets an agenda for your discussions. Depending on the complexity of the issues you need to resolve, and how well you and your spouse are able to work together, you may be able to resolve the issues in a single mediation session, or it may take a couple of sessions before you reach an agreement.

Sometimes, mediation isn't such a hot idea

Mediation is not for everyone. This method for avoiding a divorce trial is not the right for you if

✔ You are intimidated by your spouse.

✔ You have not clarified your own divorce priorities and goals so you don't know what to negotiate for.

✔ You do not have the information you need to negotiate on an equal footing with your spouse — you suspect that your spouse is hiding assets, for example. (A good attorney will not let you go into mediation unprepared.)

✔ You and your spouse can no longer communicate effectively.

The Benefits of Mediation

It takes two to tango, to sing a duet, and to make mediation work. So, if your spouse is not serious about making mediation work, you are probably wasting your time as well as the mediator's. However, if your spouse is uncertain about whether or not to mediate, ask him or her to consider these important mediation benefits:

- ✔ Working out the sticky issues in your divorce using mediation can be a lot cheaper than going to trial to resolve those issues. For example, according to the Academy of Family Mediators, a national membership organization of mediators, you may spend anywhere from a few hundred dollars to several thousand dollars, depending on the number of sessions required, to resolve the issues standing between you and a final divorce agreement. The cost of a trial on the other hand could run into five or six figures (that's right, more than a hundred thousand dollars).

  Depending on where you live and the experience and reputation of the mediator you work with, a mediator will charge anywhere from $60 an hour to $300 an hour for his or her services.

- ✔ A mediation session is considerably less formal, less intimidating, and less stressful than a trial.

- ✔ You get divorced faster. Depending on the caseload in your area's family court, it can be months — even a year or more — before your trial date arrives. On the other hand, after you decide to mediate, your first session can probably be scheduled within the month — although just how long it takes you and your spouse to work things out is in your hands.

- ✔ Mediation can help you and your spouse brainstorm about divorce agreement options. As a result, you may come up with options for child custody, for the division of your marital property, and for structuring your child support or alimony agreement that you may never have thought of otherwise.

- ✔ You are in control. You make the tough decisions in mediation, not a judge, and no one forces you to do anything.

- ✔ You preserve all your options. If mediation doesn't work, you can still go to trial.

- ✔ You preserve your privacy. If you end up in court, your "dirty laundry" becomes public knowledge. But, when you use mediation, only you, your spouse, and the mediator hear what you say.

- ✔ You and your spouse are more apt to be happy with your agreement and to honor it in the future because you are working it out together instead of having a judge decide.

Arbitration: Another out-of-court option

When you hear the word *arbitration,* you may think of labor union disputes. But did you know, arbitration can also be used to resolve marital disputes?

Arbitration is an out-of-court dispute resolution method that is more formal than mediation but less formal and less costly than a trial. During arbitration, you are represented by your attorney, witnesses can testify, written evidence can be presented, and so forth, just like in a trial. But during arbitration, you are not constrained by the formal rules of evidence or the usual courtroom procedures. You and your spouse, working with your attorneys and the arbitrator, set your own rules.

A fundamental difference between arbitration and mediation is that you and your spouse won't make the final decisions. The arbitrator will. Although this person is not a judge, an arbitrator's decisions may or may not be legally binding, *can* be legally enforced, and *cannot* be appealed.

Some states allow couples to have any of their divorce-related disputes arbitrated, although special arbitration rules may apply when a dispute relates to custody or child support. Other states prohibit any and all child-related issues from being arbitrated.

Arbitration can be a good alternative if you

✔ Don't want to try mediation or have already tried it and failed.

✔ Don't want to run up big legal bills or want to be divorced sooner than if you have to wait for your day in court.

✔ Are willing to let an arbitrator — often a retired judge or lawyer — make the decisions. Some arbitrators also work as mediators.

✔ Are willing to live with the arbitrator's decision even if you are not happy with it. Remember, unlike a judge's decision, an arbitrator's cannot be appealed.

Inquiring about the Mediators Your Attorney Recommends

If you tell your attorney that you want to mediate the sticky issues in your divorce so that you can avoid a trial, your attorney will probably recommend one or more mediators for you to consider, possibly after consulting with your spouse's attorney. It is a good idea to meet with the recommended mediators to learn about their backgrounds and training and to ensure that you hit it off and your personalities mesh.

Your and your spouse should agree on which mediator to use. Before choosing your mediator, ask your attorney questions about the ones he or she recommends, including

✔ How much do the mediators charge for their services? Do they charge by the hour or do they charge a flat fee?

✔ What are their professional backgrounds?

✔ Do they have any special mediation training or are they certified by any organizations?

✔ Do they belong to the Academy of Family Mediators or to another professional mediator organization?

The Academy of Family Mediators (800-292-4236) is a membership organization that sets standards of practice for its members and investigates complaints against them.

✔ Can they mediate all of the issues you need to resolve or just some of them? Some mediators handle the full gamut of divorce-related issues; not all mediate financial matters or custody battles.

✔ How many times have they mediated divorces that involved the same types of issues as yours? What is their success rate and how do they help other divorcing couples dealing with the same issues to come to closure?

Also, be sure to ask for client references — and check them, too!

In most states, mediators do not have to be certified or licensed. Also, no national certification standards exist for mediators. Therefore, even if a mediator your attorney recommends is not certified or licensed, that person may still be highly qualified to help you and your spouse resolve your differences. Nevertheless, do some investigating before you hire a mediator.

How Your Attorney Can Help with Your Mediation

If you decide to use mediation, your lawyer will not simply hand you off to a mediator and wait for you and your spouse to resolve all of your outstanding divorce issues. At a minimum, your lawyer will prepare you for mediation by helping you to:

✔ Develop a list of the specific issues you will try to resolve.

✔ Assess your options.

✔ Review any information your spouse may share with you prior to mediation so that you understand all of it and know the right questions to ask about it.

✔ Develop a mediation game plan or strategy.

Depending on your ability to negotiate with your spouse during a mediation session, the complexity of the issues you want to resolve, or your attorney's own preferences, your attorney may help you in other important ways:

- ✔ By serving as a sounding board before and after your mediation sessions.
- ✔ By being at your side during mediation.
- ✔ By serving as your on-site mediation consultant, brainstorming with you, and providing you with feedback.
- ✔ By confirming or denying any information the mediator or your spouse may give you.
- ✔ By reviewing any written agreement that the mediator may have drafted before you sign it.
- ✔ By doing your negotiating for you.

What Happens If Mediation Works?

If mediation works for you, the mediator puts your agreement in writing, provides a copy for your attorney so that he or she can review the agreement before you sign it, and then delivers the signed agreement to your attorney. The mediator also does the same for your spouse's attorney.

The agreement is incorporated into your final divorce agreement. After your divorce agreement has been filed with the court, everything in it, including what you and your spouse agreed to during mediation is legally binding on both you and your spouse.

Chapter 17

The Divorce Trial: Putting the Decisions in the Hands of a Judge

- -

In This Chapter

▶ Thinking long and hard before proceeding with a trial

▶ Analyzing your options if your spouse makes you a settlement offer

▶ Reviewing what happens at a pretrial conference

▶ Preparing for trial

▶ Understanding the role of the judge and the trial process

▶ Weighing the pros and cons of an appeal

- -

*W*e're going to give it to you straight: If you're headed for a divorce trial, the experience is not going to be pleasant. The cost of your divorce skyrockets; you'll probably have to pay for the litigation out of your marital property (which means you and your ex will each take less property from your marriage); your stress level soars; and after all is said and done, you still have no guarantee you'll like the judge's decision.

A trial is about winning and losing, not about compromise and cooperation. It's heavy, tough stuff, and both attorneys will do whatever they can to be on the winning side. Be prepared to be negatively portrayed by your spouse's lawyer and to have highly personal information used against you. People you consider to be friends may testify on your spouse's behalf, and your past mistakes may be blown out of proportion. Your attorney will use the same tactics against your spouse, which may please you to no end or make you feel dreadful over how badly your marriage ended.

If a divorce trial sounds like a kind of hell on earth, then you're getting the picture. Divorce trials are serious business. If you're headed for a trial, fasten your seat belts, because you're in for a bumpy ride.

To help prepare you for some major turbulence in your life, this chapter discusses out-of-court settlement opportunities and how to evaluate any offers that your spouse may send your way. It then explains what happens prior to a trial, and offers you general advice about proper, in-court behavior, and how to dress for a court appearance. This chapter also provides an overview of the trial process and concludes with information on appeals, in case the outcome isn't what you'd hoped for.

Making Certain You Really Want to Go to Trial

Before you move full speed ahead with a divorce trial, think long and hard about its financial and emotional costs. (Remember, you still have time to change your mind and get serious about a negotiated settlement!) Putting your divorce in the hands of a judge is a gamble.

The judge may not view things quite the way you do, and you may not get the divorce agreement you hoped for. Never assume that you have such a strong case that the judge will automatically decide in your favor. Be prepared to be disappointed.

Before committing yourself to a divorce trial, ask yourself the following questions:

✔ Does the risk of losing or having a disappointing outcome outweigh any benefits you may receive from going to court?

✔ Would you be better off compromising with your spouse to ensure that you get at least some of the things that are really important to you in a divorce agreement, rather than rolling the dice and hoping that you come up with the lucky number?

Temporary orders: A pretrial taste of the courtroom experience

Going to trial may not be the first time that you and your spouse have stepped foot in a courtroom during the course of your divorce proceedings. If your attorney or your spouse's attorney filed any *motions for temporary court orders,* you've already attended a hearing in a courtroom before a judge. Those court orders may have addressed issues such as temporary child support, child custody, visitation, or alimony.

Although the decisions of the judge regarding these motions are issued on a temporary basis, they often become a permanent part of a couple's divorce judgment. So, in effect, some aspects of your divorce may actually be decided at the temporary-order level. For that reason, a hearing on a temporary court order can be just as stressful and nerve-wracking as a divorce trial. (Chapter 4 has more information on temporary orders.)

✔ Do you have the time necessary to devote to a lengthy trial? Getting divorced takes longer if you go to court. Not only does preparing for the trial take a great deal of time, but you may also have to wait months for a trial date — as long as *a year* depending on how many other cases are in the pipeline ahead of yours and whether you have to postpone your original trial date. So if you are looking for a speedy divorce, going to trial is probably not the way to get it.

✔ Do you want to put your children through the emotional stress of a divorce trial? Although they may not fully understand what is going on, they will at least sense that you are under an unusual amount of pressure, which can scare them.

Despite all of the negatives associated with a divorce trial, sometimes, it's your best or only option. For example:

✔ Your spouse refuses to negotiate with you.

✔ You have tried to negotiate an agreement and it's gotten you nowhere.

✔ Your spouse is hiding information essential to a fair settlement.

✔ Your spouse is insisting on a custody arrangement that you do not think is in your children's best interest.

✔ You need more alimony than your spouse will agree to.

✔ You think your spouse may be wasting or hiding marital property or other assets.

✔ Your spouse has an alcohol or drug problem or has abused you or your children.

Do not let your selfish wishes to have your children live with you all of the time, or your desire for revenge against your spouse for ending your marriage, or your discomfort at having your children live with your ex and the new person in his or her life cloud your thinking about the best custody arrangement for your kids. It may end up pushing you into an unnecessary custody battle.

What to Do If Your Spouse Makes You a Settlement Offer

Most contested divorces never get to trial, although they may get as far as the courthouse steps. Therefore, while your attorney and your spouse's attorney prepare for your trial, they may also try to negotiate an out-of-court settlement agreement.

Big business in Splittsville, Nevada

During the first half of this century, divorce was legal in all states but generally frowned upon as something "nice people" did not do. In fact, to discourage couples from divorcing, state laws made certain the divorce process would drag out as long as possible. The one exception was Nevada — a free-wheeling frontier state that took a more open-minded attitude toward divorce, in part because divorce represented a potential financial boon to what was then a cash-poor state.

At the turn of the century, Nevada allowed a man or a woman who lived within its boundaries for a minimum of six months to walk into a courthouse, tell a judge why he or she wanted a divorce and walk out a divorced person. As a result, countless unhappy couples, including the rich and famous, flocked to Nevada to obtain their divorces. But, it was not until 1920 when "America's Sweetheart" Mary Pickford obtained her Reno divorce and immediately returned to California to marry Douglas Fairbanks, Sr., that the city's reputation as America's divorce capital really took off.

Recognizing the income potential from the state's new divorce-capital reputation, in 1931 the Nevada legislature shortened the residence period from six months to a mere six weeks, putting a Reno divorce within the

financial reach of the average person. After that, the Reno divorce business grew steadily, reaching a peak of more than 19,000 divorces a year by 1946.

Visitors to Reno in search of a quickie divorce included debutantes, movie ingenues, preachers, truck drivers, waitresses, businesspeople, and Hollywood executives. Some spent their six-week waiting period living in hotels and boardinghouses, while others chose to spend the time at one of Reno's "divorce ranches."

During the day, guests at a divorce ranch rode horses, swam, or skied (depending on the time of year) and in the evening wagered money at Reno's gambling casinos or whiled away the hours at the divorce ranch bar. Local cowboys who worked at these ranches were on hand to help the female guests forget their troubles and maybe even indulge in a little romance while they waited to end their marriages.

The divorce ranch is a thing of the past now, made antiquated by America's eventual acceptance of divorce and the liberalization of state divorce laws throughout the country. Men and women who want to end their marriages no longer have to leave their state and go into hiding in order to avoid the scandal and disgrace of divorce, or to just get a divorce at all.

Receiving the offer

After getting the go-ahead from their respective clients, one attorney may send the other a written offer, the other may counter it, reject it, or (if you are lucky) accept it. (By the way, your attorney cannot accept or reject an offer without your consent.)

Eventually, all of the terms of your agreement may be worked out. This back-and-forth process is a more formal version of what you and your spouse may have done if you tried to negotiate your own divorce by yourselves or during a mediation session. (To learn more about how mediation works, head to Chapter 16.)

During this back-and-forth process, you may get an offer that you believe is relatively reasonable and fair. The offer may not be everything you hoped for, but it may be close. You have to decide how to respond. Although your attorney should provide you with his or her opinions about the offer, the final decision is yours.

If you get an offer from your spouse, read it carefully. It may be obvious that the agreement isn't close to what you are legally entitled to, what your spouse can really provide, or what you think you need.

Deciding on the offer

Following are some questions that you should ask yourself to help you decide what to do when you get an offer:

- How close is the offer to what I am asking for?

- Does the offer reflect most, if not all, of my divorce priorities?

- Is the offer fair?

- Given what I know now about my legal rights and responsibilities, the value of the marital property my spouse and I own, and how my children are being affected by my divorce, am I likely to get more if I reject this offer?

- How much have I already spent on my case and can I afford to spend any more?

- Am I willing to take the offer just to stop the agony of going through a protracted and expensive legal process?

- Given what I know about the judge and his past rulings, am I likely to do better if I go all the way to trial than if I accept what my spouse is offering?

  To help you decide what to do, your attorney may be able to offer information regarding how the judge who is hearing your case has ruled on cases similar to yours.

- What are the advantages and the disadvantages of settling now?

- If I don't settle now, how long will it take for this case to come to trial and how long is the trial apt to take?

You may figure that threatening to take your divorce to trial will pressure your spouse to give in on certain points that are important to you. Before you try this tactic, you should think about which scenario is more likely: You hold your ground and your spouse agrees to a compromise, or your spouse holds his or her ground and calls your bluff.

Comedian Tom Arnold made $33 million when he divorced actress-comedienne Roseanne Barr in 1994. Cindy Costner topped that a year later with an $80 million divorce settlement from Kevin Costner. Who says divorce doesn't pay?

Settling Issues through a Pretrial Conference

A *pretrial conference* or *pretrial settlement conference* offers you and your spouse a formal opportunity to resolve your differences and come to an agreement. The judge participating in the conference may actively push for a settlement after he or she knows the facts of your case. Judges have been known to instruct divorcing spouses and their attorneys to talk over their case first. If the parties to the divorce are not able to reach a settlement, the judge will note his displeasure and demand to know exactly why the divorcing spouses did not come to an agreement.

In some jurisdictions, attorneys use pretrial conferences to settle issues related to temporary custody of the kids, temporary child support, and alimony. Attorneys may also try to resolve other immediate issues, such as who pays what bills while a couple's divorce is proceeding, how the legal costs will be paid, and so forth. For each of these issues, one side or the other has to file a pretrial motion. Although these back-and-forth negotiations increase the expense of your divorce, you may have no choice if your divorce is extremely hostile (for more information on pretrial motions see Chapter 4).

The pretrial conference is an opportunity for both lawyers, the judge (who may or may not be the same one who hears your case), and maybe even you and your spouse, to discuss your case outside of court and accomplish the following:

- Clarify the specific issues to be resolved during your trial
- Address all uncertainties that must be resolved before the trial gets underway
- Develop a timetable for *pretrial motions* (motions that are filed with the court before a trial)

The monetary costs of a trial

Going to trial can mean some serious expenses. The exact cost of a divorce trial depends on a number of factors: what part of the country you live in (divorcing in a major metropolitan area on either coast costs more than divorcing in the Midwest, the South, or in a rural area); the specific issues the judge is deciding on; your attorney's legal strategy; and the legal strategy of your spouse's attorney.

You can expect your legal bills alone to run into the five-or six-figure range — as much as four times the cost of a negotiated divorce.

At a minimum, you should be prepared to incur the following expenses:

✔ Lawyer's fees

✔ Filing fees

✔ Court reporter fees

✔ Expert fees

✔ Discovery fees

✔ Subpoena fees

✔ The cost of preparing exhibits and witnesses for the trial

✔ Miscellaneous legal expenses — copying, long-distance charges, postage, delivery fees, and so on

This list covers just the monetary costs of a trial. It can't begin to calculate the cost to your family's health and happiness if you're embroiled in an ugly divorce trial.

✔ Determine who will be called as witnesses

✔ Create a schedule for *discovery* (see Chapter 5 for information on the discovery process)

In some jurisdictions, pretrial conferences are mandatory; in other jurisdictions, pretrial conferences are used rarely. Also, in some jurisdictions, you and your spouse are required to try to resolve the outstanding issues in your divorce through mediation. Only after that can you get a court date, assuming that you still need one. This requirement is common in custody battles.

If you attend a pretrial conference, be on your best behavior. The judge at the conference may be the same one who decides your divorce. If you are unreasonable, overly emotional, or just downright unpleasant to be around, you may prejudice the judge against you, despite the merits of your case.

Attorneys sometimes use the pretrial conference to get a sense of how a judge is likely to rule on the issues in a case. If your attorney gets the feeling that things may not go your way in a trial, he or she will probably strongly urge you to settle out of court.

If you don't agree to a negotiated settlement at a pretrial conference, you and your spouse can agree to one later, even after your trial has begun.

Preparing for the Trial

Getting ready for a divorce trial is time-consuming work, which is why trials are so expensive. Your attorney reviews and gathers information related to your case, develops and refines his or her legal strategy, coordinates the production of exhibits, prepares witnesses to take the stand, and makes other preparations.

Setting the stage

Preparing for a trial is somewhat like staging a play, with you and your spouse as the reluctant "stars." The witnesses who take the stand are your supporting, or not-so-supporting players, depending on whether they testify for or against you.

To help stage your trial, your attorney will outline a trial strategy. This serves as an overview of everything your attorney will do to either get you a favorable out-of-court settlement as quickly as possible, assuming that is a realistic goal, or to win your case if it goes all the way to trial.

Your lawyer's strategy will also help set the stage for your trial. That strategy will be an aggressive or nonaggressive one.

- An *aggressive strategy* involves bombarding the other side with claims of abuse, indifference, child neglect, wasting assets, infidelity, or marital instability. To a lesser extent, an aggressive strategy can involve pressuring the other side with pretrial motions, interrogatories, requests for depositions, and requests to produce documents, among other things.

  Both tactics are designed to encourage an early out-of-court settlement, especially if your spouse's financial resources are very limited. Or, these tactics can make your spouse all the more determined to go to trial. An aggressive divorce strategy is almost guaranteed to make you and your spouse enemies for ever. But sometimes, it is your only option.

- A *non-aggressive strategy* tends to be less hostile than an aggressive one. It relies more on informal discovery to get at the facts of the case and cooperation between attorneys to work out the terms of your divorce.

The strategy that your attorney chooses depends on several factors, including:

✔ Your own desires and resources

✔ What your attorney thinks is best for the case

✔ The strategy that your spouse's attorney is likely to use

✔ Your attorney's style and the style of your spouse's attorney (some are scrappy street fighters and others are wily tacticians)

If you are contesting the validity of a prenuptial or postnuptial agreement, a judge has to rule on that issue before he or she can decide how to divide up your marital property and debts or decide whether one of you has to pay the other spousal support. (See Chapter 20 for more on prenuptial and postnuptial agreements.) To save time and money, your attorney should try to get this issue resolved as quickly as possible because the judge's decision determines exactly what issues your trial will address and influences how much discovery you may need to do.

Understanding the discovery process

One of the ways that your attorney gathers information is by using the formal *discovery* process, which involves the use of legal tools such as depositions, requests to produce documents, and interrogatories. (Your spouse's attorney will do the same thing.) This discovery is in addition to any that both attorneys may have already done — formally or informally — if you have been trying to work out a negotiated divorce agreement with your spouse.

Many states are passing discovery reform legislation in order to make the discovery process less overwhelming and costly, including requiring the parties to any lawsuit to exchange at least basic information and documentation up front in the process.

Discovery costs can skyrocket in a litigated divorce. Ask your attorney what he or she can do to keep those costs down.

Among other things, your attorney uses the formal discovery process to find out about the witnesses your spouse's attorney will be calling. He or she may also be able to get a short summary of what each witness knows relative to your divorce. If you know anything about their backgrounds that you feel may undermine their credibility — alcohol or drug problems, spousal abuse, criminal records — be sure to share that information with your attorney.

Producing physical evidence

Your attorney may use physical evidence to bolster his or her arguments or to undermine your spouse's position. Your attorney will also figure out how to address physical evidence your spouse's attorney may introduce that is damaging to your case. Among other things, physical evidence can include

- ✔ Financial records
- ✔ Police reports
- ✔ Appraisals
- ✔ Doctors' records
- ✔ Depending on your case, photos, letters, diaries, and videotapes and audiotapes
- ✔ Psychological evaluations

Calling witnesses

Your attorney and your spouse's attorney are likely to call witnesses to testify during your trial. In fact, your spouse's attorney may even put *you* on the stand and your attorney may put your spouse on the stand.

Your friends, family members, coworkers, business associates, and even your children may be called as witnesses. *Expert witnesses* who have special training, education, or knowledge, such as, psychologists, business valuation specialists, doctors, real estate agents, social workers, and others with professional expertise may also be called.

Expert witnesses expect to be paid for their time. Depending on the kind of witness and his or her reputation, an expert witness may charge several hundred dollars an hour! If these witnesses are asked to do certain things in preparation for testifying — review documents or write a report, for example — they will bill you for the time it takes them to do that work as well as for their time on the stand.

Witnesses are formally ordered by the court to appear and testify in court via *subpoenas*. Subpoenaed witnesses who do not show up will be escorted to court by a law enforcement officer or charged with contempt of court. (For more on subpoenas see Chapter 4.)

Ordinarily, witnesses are used to help establish certain facts. For example, if you and your spouse are fighting over the custody of your kids, witnesses may be called to help establish which of you is their primary caregiver and *go-to-parent* — the parent who takes them to the doctor, attends parent-teacher conferences, takes them to and from day care, feeds them, clothes them, chauffeurs them to and from their extracurricular activities, helps them with their homework, and so on.

The following is a list of the sort of witnesses who are commonly called to attest to a parent's role in his or her children's lives or to discuss a spouse's parenting abilities:

- ✔ Doctors and their staffs, including psychologists and psychiatrists
- ✔ Teachers
- ✔ Child care workers
- ✔ Soccer coaches, music teachers, scout troop leaders, and similar others
- ✔ Relatives
- ✔ Baby-sitters
- ✔ Next-door neighbors

Before the start of your trial, your attorney interviews witnesses on your behalf to get a sense of what they will say on the stand. Your attorney may advise them about the points that they should try to make and the best way to get those points across. However, your attorney does *not* tell witnesses what to say.

Rehearsing for your big day (or days)

Prior to the start of your trial, your attorney should spend time with you, preparing you for what's to come. For example, your attorney may

- ✔ Walk you through the trial process.
- ✔ Review his or her strategy with you.
- ✔ Explain the points that you should make when you testify, even suggesting words or phrases to use to help clarify your thoughts or add weight to your statements.
- ✔ Anticipate the questions that your spouse's attorney is likely to ask you and help you come up with answers for the more sensitive or difficult ones.
- ✔ To build your confidence, do some role playing by grilling you as your spouse's attorney would if he or she were trying to unnerve you or make you angry.
- ✔ Advise you about how to look and act in the courtroom.

Tell your attorney about any concerns you may have about the trial. Your attorney can probably help alleviate your worries.

Dressing the part

Your appearance can detract from the real issues in your divorce and even undermine your attorney's legal strategy. Appearances do count! Therefore, be sure that you and your attorney talk about how you should dress for your trial.

Most likely, your attorney will suggest that you wear something simple and understated (no loud colors, plaids, or prints), that you steer clear of flashy jewelry, that your hair is clean and neat with no wild hairstyles, and that you avoid excessive makeup. Even if understatement is not your style, make it yours during the trial.

Acting the part

You may seethe with anger, quake with fear, or feel totally defeated when you are in the courtroom, especially when you are on the witness stand, but try to keep your cool. Also, be polite to everyone — including your spouse's attorney and, yes, even your spouse!

Your attorney may tell you not to hold back your tears when you are on the witness stand. Sincere tears can work to your advantage.

Listen attentively to the courtroom proceedings. Take notes and when you hear someone say something that you know is not the truth, let your attorney know. The best way to do that is by passing your attorney a note, rather than whispering in your attorney's ear. Whispering may make your attorney miss important testimony and someone on your spouse's side may overhear your comments.

When you are called to the witness stand, keep a few things in mind:

✔ Answer the questions you are asked in as few words as possible. If you give long, involved answers, you may say too much and hurt your case. If the attorney wants to know more, let him or her ask you another question.

✔ Pause before you answer a question so that you give yourself time to think about what to say and so that your attorney has time to object to the question you are asked. If your attorney does object and the judge sustains the objection, the judge will tell you not to answer the question. Otherwise, you will be expected to answer any question you are asked.

✔ If you are unnerved by a question or not sure how to respond to it, buy some time to compose yourself and to think about your answer by pouring yourself some water and having a sip. A pitcher of water and a glass should be sitting on the witness stand. If not, ask the judge for a glass of water.

✔ Sit up straight; don't slouch. Keep your hands folded in front of you on your lap. Avoid wild gesticulations.

✔ Do not be rude, sarcastic, or argumentative with your spouse's attorney, even if his or her questions are offensive or upsetting to you. Offending or upsetting you may be part of the attorney's strategy.

✔ When you get off the stand, do not send dirty looks or expressions of exasperation in the direction of your spouse or your spouse's attorney. Maintain your dignity no matter what.

Testifying on the stand is very much like giving a deposition. The same rules apply for what to do and not do when you are asked a question. For a list of deposition do's and don'ts, read Chapter 4.

Understanding the Judge's Role

The judge who hears your case is responsible for ensuring that you get a fair trial and that the attorneys follow the appropriate trial procedures. The judge also rules on any objections the attorneys may make to the introduction of evidence. If the attorneys get into a disagreement with one another or if someone in the courtroom gets unruly, the judge steps in.

During the trial the judge listens to the testimony and the attorneys' statements and reviews any exhibits that are entered into evidence. He or she may also ask questions of the witnesses and will almost certainly take notes, although a court reporter is there recording every word that is said.

Many family court judges used to be divorce attorneys. Most judges have reputations for the kind of courtroom they run and for the way they tend to rule on certain issues. For example, some run their courtrooms with an iron hand, and others give attorneys a great deal of leeway. Some favor mothers over fathers in custody battles, and some are less inclined than others to order permanent alimony.

If your attorney knows which judge will hear your case and if your attorney has been practicing in that judge's jurisdiction for some time, your attorney should take the judge's style and reputation into account when preparing for your trial. If your attorney isn't familiar with the judge, he or she should talk to an attorney who is.

In some jurisdictions, you may not know which judge will hear your case until the day of your trial. Therefore, your attorney may have to "fly blind" as far as preparing for trial with a particular judge in mind.

When Your Day in Court Arrives

Weeks, maybe months, after your divorce is filed, you and your spouse finally get your day in court (assuming that you still have not been able to settle the issues in your divorce out of court).

In the courtroom, you and your spouse will sit with your respective attorneys at tables directly in front of the judge. If you haven't seen or spoken with your spouse in a while, the sight of your spouse in the courtroom may be unnerving and upsetting; on the other hand, you may feel just plain glad that you are finally getting divorced.

You will probably be nervous about what to expect as your trial date approaches. A great way to alleviate some of those pretrial jitters is to visit the court ahead of time so that you can see the courtroom setup and watch and listen to some other couples' divorce trials. If you know which judge is going to hear your case, try to sit in on a divorce he or she is presiding over.

Trials often move along slowly with many starts and stops. The courtroom dramas that you've read about in books or seen on reruns of *Perry Mason* (or even on real-life dramas like the O. J. Simpson trial) rarely occur! So be prepared to be bored or confused at times, unless you are a regular viewer of Court TV.

Judge or jury?

In some states, your divorce case (or some parts of it) may be decided by a jury. If your state is one of them, you can opt for either a jury trial or a *bench trial.* (A bench trial is a trial decided by a judge.) This is an important strategic decision that you have to make with your attorney. Whether you opt for a judge or a jury trial, the basic trial process is the same.

Before your attorney and your spouse's attorney can begin presenting their cases in a jury trial, they must select the members of the jury through *voire dire.* The *voire dire* process involves asking potential jurors questions in order to assess their biases and prejudices so that the attorneys can decide who they want and who they don't want on the jury. (Each attorney gets to eliminate a certain number of potential jurors.)

Once a jury is selected, the jury members will be sworn in by the court.

Trials follow a very predictable sequence of events. So, to help you make sense of what is happening in yours, here is a brief rundown on what to expect:

1. **Opening statements.**

   Each attorney makes an initial statement to the judge about what he or she will prove during the trial. These statements set the stage for the evidence and arguments to come. Opening statements may be waived if the trial is resolving just a few issues.

2. **The plaintiff's or petitioner's case.**

   The attorney for the spouse who sued for divorce (the *plaintiff*) gets to go first. The plaintiff's attorney presents evidence as to why that spouse should get what was asked for in the complaint that initiated the couple's divorce. To help prove the attorney's arguments, witnesses are called to the stand and questioned, first by the plaintiff's attorney and then by the defendant's attorney. When the defendant's attorney asks questions, it's called a *cross-examination.*

3. **Redirect and re-cross examinations.**

   During the redirect examinations, the plaintiff's attorney asks more questions of some of the witnesses who testified earlier. (This may or may not happen during the trial.) Redirect and re-cross examinations are more apt to be used if a witness damages the plaintiff's case during cross-examination and needs to be *rehabilitated,* that is, something he or she said needs to be clarified or explained in a way that is more favorable to the plaintiff.

4. **The defendant's case.**

   The attorney for the defendant spouse presents his or her case following the same procedures used by the plaintiff's attorney.

5. **Rebuttal by plaintiff.**

   This may or may not happen. If it does, the plaintiff's attorney responds to the comments made by the defense. However, the attorney cannot introduce any new evidence; the attorney can only address what the defendant has already introduced.

6. **Surrebuttal by defendant.**

   This rarely happens in a divorce trial, but if it does, the defendant's attorney denies or counters what the plaintiff's attorney said in his or her rebuttal. The attorney cannot address anything else in the plaintiff's case.

7. **Closing arguments.**

   During closing arguments, both attorneys get one last chance to make their cases. The plaintiff's attorney goes first. If only a few issues need to be resolved, final arguments are waived.

8. Judge's ruling.

Depending on the complexity of the case, the judge may issue his or her decision right away or may take time to deliberate and return with a decision later. If more than one issue is to be decided, the judge makes multiple rulings.

No matter how long you think you'll be sitting in front of the judge, never bring food, beverages, or reading materials into a courtroom.

Finally, the Judgment

After the judge issues his or her decision, your attorney or your spouse's attorney, but usually the attorney for whichever spouse *prevailed* or won, drafts your divorce judgment or divorce decree — a formal term for the summary of what the judge ruled and of anything you and your spouse may have agreed to on your own.

The attorney who drafts the decree sends it to the other attorney for review and approval. The non-prevailing attorney usually has a certain amount of time to object to the draft if he or she feels that, as worded, it does not accurately reflect what the judge ordered. Once both attorneys agree, or if the time limit expires without an objection, the decree is submitted to the court for approval.

Once the judge approves your divorce decree, you can expect the following to happen:

- ✔ The provisions of the decree usually replace any temporary pretrial court orders.

- ✔ Your attorney gives you a copy of your signed divorce agreement. You will receive a copy of the judgment at a later date after the court has processed all the paperwork. Make sure that your copy is certified.

- ✔ A record of your divorce is filed in the vital records section of your state's Public Health Department.

- ✔ You are officially divorced once your decree has been signed.

Yes, your divorce is officially over and for better or worse, you are single again. You and your now ex-spouse must comply with all of the decree's provisions, including transferring and returning property, paying money, adhering to a specific visitation schedule, and other terms of the decree.

In 1968, the late Tammy Wynette, one-time first lady of country music, divorced her second husband. In that same year, two of her songs — "Stand by Your Man" and "D-I-V-O-R-C-E" — became number-one hits on the music charts (creating a sort of C&W hit-song contradiction).

If You Want to Appeal

You can appeal the judge's decision if you are unhappy with it, but an appeal takes yet more time and money. In addition, you have to file your appeal within a certain period of time. How long you have to file depends on your state. If you are considering an appeal, ask your attorney about your state's deadlines for filing.

You can't appeal a judge's decision just because you want to. You must have a legal basis for the appeal.

Time and money are not the only factors you should consider when you are deciding whether to appeal. You should also consider these facts:

- Your appeal may not be heard for months, and once it is, assuming that the judge's decision is overturned, you face yet another divorce trial.

- While you are waiting to learn the outcome of your appeal, you, your spouse, and your kids are living in a sort of limbo. If the appellate court decides to overturn your divorce, its action will make you married again. The result: You're still not divorced.

- Everyone in your family already may be emotionally worn out by the first trial.

- You may have to find a new attorney, especially if your current attorney thinks that filing an appeal is risky or pointless given the facts of your case.

- The judge's decision may not be thrown out and, even if it is, you have no guarantee that the outcome of your next trial will be more to your liking. In fact, you could end up with a judgment you like even less!

- A faster and less expensive way to deal with some aspect of the judge's decision is to leave the court judgment in place and to ask the court to modify the specific provision or provisions you do not like. To do so, you have to file a petition for modification. Chapter 19 talks about modifications to a divorce decree.

Wrapping things up

You and your attorney should review the details of the judge's decision and any aspects of your divorce that you may have negotiated with your now ex-spouse so that you understand your legal responsibilities to one another and are clear about any other steps you may need to take as a result of your divorce. You may need to

✓ Transfer titles, deeds of trust, and other ownership documents.

✓ Exchange cash and other valuables. You may want to make this exchange in front of a neutral third party so that neither of you can accuse the other of dishonesty.

✓ Amend your insurance policies as necessary or purchase new ones.

✓ Make changes to your will and to other estate planning documents.

✓ Notify your creditors and the Big Three credit bureaus about your name change if you take back your maiden name. (You can find information about how to contact the Big Three in Chapter 2.)

Part V
After Your Divorce Is Finalized

The 5th Wave · By Rich Tennant

"I don't know if we had irreconcilable differences or not. We never talked."

In this part . . .

This part of the book helps prepare you for the post-divorce experience. We give you advice on handling your personal finances, seeking a well-paying new job, and getting the education you need to pursue that new career. We also alert you to some of the more common (and serious) problems newly divorced people face, give you advice on how to deal with those problems, and point you toward other resources that can help. Finally, for more peace of mind the next time you marry, we offer information on prenuptial and postnuptial agreements (they're not just for the rich anymore).

Chapter 18

Handling the Practical Matters of Life after Divorce

. . . .

▶ Attending to post-divorce legal and financial matters
▶ Rethinking your estate planning
▶ Managing your money after you're divorced
▶ Locating the job you need
▶ Addressing personal and family issues

. . . .

*N*ow that you're divorced, what do you do first? Depending on the details of your divorce judgment, you may have plenty to take care of in the way of paperwork and payments. You will have to begin managing your own money, perhaps find a job outside the home, and build a new social life for yourself or pick up your old one where you left off. You may also have to figure out how you're going to care for your kids now that you're on your own.

Although all of this may sound like a formidable challenge, with the right information and a positive attitude you *can* put the pieces of your life back together again. In fact, you can even create a life for yourself that's more satisfying than you ever imagined it could be.

This chapter provides you with the information and advice you need to tie up the loose ends of your divorce and face the challenges ahead. It highlights estate planning issues to consider, offers information that can help you reach your educational and career goals, and suggests things you should do to manage your money wisely, no matter how much (or how little) income you have. The chapter also offers some valuable advice about post-divorce parenting and developing new friendships.

Studies show that a whopping 85 percent of divorced women say they are happier after their divorce than they were when they were married. Only 58 percent of men say the same thing.

Tying Up the Loose Ends of Your Divorce Decree

Read the details of your divorce decree carefully, and do exactly what the decree says. If you thumb your nose at your legal obligations (and that is exactly what they are), the battles that may have plagued the end of your marriage are likely to continue. If your ex-spouse decides to take you to court, you may find yourself in legal trouble all over again.

Ask your attorney which of the loose ends related to your divorce you should handle yourself and which he or she must take care of. Your attorney should clearly state who should do what in writing. Use your lawyer's letter as a checklist to make sure that you don't overlook any of your legal responsibilities.

Your divorce decree may require you to accomplish specific tasks by a certain date, such as closing a joint checking account or returning your former spouse's record collection. You may also have to begin paying a fixed amount of child support or alimony by a certain date every month. Depending on the terms of your divorce, you may also have to take care of other details (some of which can be a little complicated).

Transferring real property

If your former spouse will become the sole owner of real property you own together, you must transfer your interest in the property by giving your ex a signed copy of the deed to that asset. The deed will later be recorded in the public records of the county courthouse where the property is located. Real property can include your home, rental property, other buildings, and land.

If the transferred property has an outstanding debt, you will still be liable for it, even if your divorce decree says that your former spouse must pay it off. (See Chapter 9 for a discussion of the legal actions you can take to protect yourself legally if your ex-spouse defaults on the loan associated with the transferred property.)

If your divorce decree obligates your former spouse to pay you money, you should secure that debt with an asset — just as a bank may do. That way, you increase the likelihood of seeing that money. For example, if your former spouse is getting the house and, in return, your ex is going to pay you $30,000 over the next five years, you can secure that debt by placing a $30,000 *lien* on the house. If your former spouse doesn't pay up, he or she won't be able to sell, borrow against, or transfer the collateralized asset without paying you first, assuming that you record the lien at the county courthouse where the property is located.

If you place a lien on the house, you can foreclose on your former spouse and sell the house. Foreclosure and sale can be a good option if you have enough equity in the house so that, by selling it, you get sufficient funds to

- ✔ Pay off the mortgage.
- ✔ Pay the costs of having a sheriff or a trustee sell it.
- ✔ Keep some money for yourself.

Transferring other property

If you transfer stocks, bonds, or mutual funds to your former spouse, you will *not* have to pay a capital gains tax if their value has appreciated since they were first purchased.

States differ in their legal requirements for transferring ownership of vehicles, boats, and motorcycles. Your attorney should be able to advise you about your state's requirements.

Paying off debts

At all costs try to avoid a divorce agreement that requires your former spouse to pay off your debt. If your ex fails to honor that agreement, your credit history will be damaged, despite what your agreement says. This is a real concern if your ex is angry about your divorce and you think he or she may try to get revenge by not paying your debts.

However, if your former spouse does take over some of your debts, notify your creditors in writing and ask them to transfer those debts into your ex-spouse's name in order to relieve you of responsibility for them. Although the creditors are not legally obligated to comply with your request and although they can still collect from you if your former spouse does not pay, your letters help underscore who is supposed to be satisfying those debts. And, as a friendly reminder of what you expect, send your ex a copy of those letters.

If you want to be sure that your ex-spouse is paying off the debts that used to be yours, see if you can get your ex to provide you with proof of each payment — a canceled check will do.

Arranging for your own health insurance

Under the provisions of COBRA (Consolidated Omnibus Budget Reconciliation Act), your divorce decree may allow you to remain on your former spouse's health insurance plan for up to three years, giving you time to get your own health coverage. (You may or may not have to pay the cost of your coverage depending on the terms of your divorce.) However, continuing your coverage does not happen automatically — you must notify your ex's employer within 60 days of your divorce judgment.

If your former spouse will be paying the cost of your COBRA health insurance benefits, ask for proof of payment so that you can be assured that your coverage is not about to lapse due to nonpayment. The same advice applies if your former spouse is maintaining life insurance on your behalf.

Protecting your pension rights

If your divorce judgment gives you the right to collect a portion of your former spouse's pension benefits, profit sharing money, 401(k) funds, or other deferred retirement income when your ex becomes eligible to retire, you need to have a special legal document called a QDRO (Qualified Domestic Relations Order) prepared during your divorce. Without it, you cannot be assured that you will get your share of those moneys when the time comes. The completed QDRO must be sent to the bank, brokerage firm, or employer administering the retirement benefits. (Chapter 9 provides a more complete explanation of QDROs.)

If you are unhappy with something in your divorce decree, comply with it anyway. However, if you believe that the terms of your divorce should be modified due to changes in the circumstances of your life or your former spouse's life, you can petition the court for a modification.

Rethinking Your Estate Planning

If you had a will when you were married, you need to revisit that legal document now that you're divorced. Most likely, you want to excise all mention of your spouse from your will. Furthermore, if you created a trust during your marriage for the benefit of your now-former spouse, you no doubt want to change that estate planning document, too. An estate planning attorney can advise you about your state's legal requirements for changing or voiding any or all of your estate planning documents.

In many states, your entire will or, in some cases, just the parts of your will that relate to your former spouse are revoked automatically when you get divorced.

If you don't have a will, now's the time to write one

Getting divorced is a good excuse for writing a will (if you don't have one already). A will isn't just for multimillionaires. Wills are for everyone who cares about who inherits their property after they die. Without a will, the laws of your state determine who inherits everything you own.

If you have minor children, you have other important reasons to draft a will. You can use a will to

- ✔ Provide for your children should you die while they are still financially dependent on you.

- ✔ Designate the adult who will manage the assets you leave to your minor children in your will. That person is called a *property guardian*.

  All states limit the value of the assets that minor children can own on their own. The maximum varies but ranges from about $2,500 to $5,000 in most states. Therefore, if you use a will to leave your children more than your state's maximum, their property guardian will manage your children's assets on their behalf until they become legal adults. If you do not name a property guardian in your will, the court will probably appoint your ex-spouse to play that role.

- ✔ Designate the adult who will raise your children if you and your former spouse both die while your children are still minors. This designee is called a personal guardian. Many parents name the same person to serve as property and personal guardian.

Depending on your state, if you write a will and your estate is relatively simple and small in value, when you die your estate can go through an informal probate process, which is less expensive and time-consuming than the traditional probate process. (Among other things, *probate* is used to formally affect the legal transfer of your property to others — to your beneficiaries if you write a will, or to your legal heirs if you do not.) However, if you die without a will, no matter how small and simple your estate may be, your estate must be probated.

Ordinarily, if you are the custodial parent and you die, your former spouse raises your children. But, if you don't want that to happen, you can state your preference in your will. Be sure to provide your executor with a written statement of your rationale. (An *executor* is the adult responsible for making sure that the provisions of your will are carried out after you die. You designate your executor in your will.) However, despite your stated preference, a judge would probably award custody of your children to your ex-spouse unless he or she does not want custody or is an unfit parent.

In some states, the only way a parent can legally designate a personal guardian for his or her children is by using a will.

Estate planning tools you should know about

In the event of your death, you can make sure that your minor children are financially provided for in other ways besides including them in your will. To find out which estate planning tools are most appropriate for you, talk with an estate planning attorney.

Custodial accounts

One easy and inexpensive option is to set up a *custodial account* for each child according to the terms of the federal Uniform Gifts to Minors Act or Uniform Transfers to Minors Act. The account can be set up at a bank or at a brokerage house. You can make *intervivos* gifts (gifts that you make while you are alive) of assets that you own to each child and transfer whatever you give them into their custodial accounts. You need to designate an adult *custodian* for each account. That person will manage the account assets and possibly disperse money generated by the assets to each child until they become legal adults.

The specific types of assets you can transfer into a custodial account — money, securities, real property, and so forth — depends on which version of the Uniform Gifts to Minors Act or the Uniform Transfers to Minors Act your state has adopted.

Trusts

A second option is to establish a *trust,* a legal entity that's established to hold and manage assets for one or more beneficiaries. A trust can be *revocable* (one you can change later on) or *irrevocable* (a trust you won't be able to change). You must designate a *trustee* to oversee and manage the assets held in trust for the benefit of a young child or children. To help you determine whether a trust is appropriate, consider the following facts about trusts:

✔ You may prefer to use a trust to transfer property to your minor children (rather than one of the estate planning tools described earlier in this chapter) because a trust gives you maximum control over when your children can receive the trust assets.

✔ Depending on the type of trust you set up, it can provide you with tax benefits and can help you reduce the number of assets in your estate that must go through probate.

✔ Because a trust is relatively expensive to set up and maintain, it is most appropriate when you are leaving your children a substantial amount of property.

✔ Trusts are complicated legal entities. To establish one, you need the help of an estate planning attorney.

Other estate planning options

Yet another option is to name your children as the *beneficiaries* of your life insurance policy, employee benefits plan, or IRA. Again, depending on the value of the benefits, you may have to name an adult to manage them for your children should you die. Depending on whether you arrange to have the benefits paid directly to your children, placed in a trust, or deposited in a custodial account, the adult you name will be the formally titled property guardian, trustee, or account custodian. Your estate planning attorney, financial adviser, or plan administrator can provide helpful advice.

The Will Kit by John Ventura (Dearborn Financial Publishing, Inc.) is an easy-to-understand primer about estate planning for everyday people. To help make a potentially intimidating subject interesting and even fun, the book features anecdotes about the estate planning successes and failures of such notables as Kurt Cobain, Clark Gable, Jerry Garcia, Henry Fonda, and Elvis Presley, among others.

Assessing Your Financial Situation

What you asked for during your divorce process and what you actually ended up with are probably somewhat different. For example, you may have received fewer assets, been saddled with more debt, and received less child support and alimony then you had hoped for. On the other hand, if you're the one making those child and spousal support payments, those payments may be higher than what you expected. Either way, money is likely to be tight right now. Developing a budget helps you determine just how much you can afford to spend and where you should be cutting back.

After comparing your current income with your current outgo, it may be obvious that to stay afloat financially you need to cut expenses, get a job (maybe even a second one), or find one that pays more. If your children are old enough, ask them for ideas on how everyone in your family can cut back a little or find extra sources of income. Consider suggesting that they help pay for some of the extras you may not be able to provide them — that new pair of athletic shoes, that prom dress, their portion of the gasoline and insurance expenses if they drive — by working at a part-time job after school or on weekends.

If you are obligated to pay spousal or child support, managing your money is particularly important because the law expects you to make those payments on time and in full. If you don't, and your former spouse takes you to court to collect back support, arguing that you "just ran out of money" won't cut it with any judge! You may find yourself spending time in jail.

Consider wiping out high-interest credit card debt by selling an asset you don't need or by applying for a debt consolidation loan. The more debt you have, the harder it is for you to finance major purchases (a home of your own, a reliable car, or educational opportunities for you or your children) at reasonable terms.

Using the services of a financial planner

Some of you may be lucky enough to exit your marriage with enough money and other assets to meet your day-to-day financial needs and to help finance your future. Although you may not have to worry much about how to pay your bills, you do have to decide how best to maximize the value of those assets so that you can achieve the short-term and long-term goals that you have for yourself and for your children.

Unless you are a savvy financial manager, planning and implementing an appropriate investment strategy takes the help of a qualified financial planner or adviser. When you are looking for one, as a general rule steer clear of professionals who sell specific financial products and who make their money from the commissions they get by selling those products. Because they have a monetary incentive to push you toward what they are selling, their advice and recommendations tend to be biased and may not be in your best interest.

Working with a financial planner who makes money by charging you a percentage of the total value of the assets he or she manages or invests for you or hiring a financial planner who charges you by the hour for advice and assistance are far better alternatives. Financial planners who charge you by the hour are most likely to consider *all* your investment alternatives — mutual funds, stocks, bonds, real estate, and so on.

Shop for a financial planner or adviser just as you would for any other professional you'd hire to help you make important decisions. Interview several possible candidates, come prepared with a set of questions to ask, learn about his or her credentials to do the job, and don't forget to get references.

As a general rule, your mortgage payment (principal and interest) should not consume any more than 25 percent of your pretax income, and your debt should not exceed 40 percent of that income.

For help in putting your budget on a diet or to increase your financial IQ, get in touch with the Consumer Credit Counseling Service office (CCCS) nearest you. The CCCS may offer beneficial money management and budgeting seminars. Also, if you owe more than you think you can pay given your monthly income, a CCCS counselor may be able to help you negotiate lower monthly payments to your creditors. If you can't find a CCCS office in your local phone book, call the organization's national office at 800-388-2227.

A year after her divorce is over, a woman's financial situation is likely to be 70 percent worse than it was when she was married. And a man's financial situation is likely to be 40 percent better than during his marriage. This is largely owing to the fact that most women end up with custody of the children, the amount of support they receive is often inadequate (or they don't receive it at all), and working women tend to earn less than men.

Finding a Job or Landing a Better One

After you take a hard look at your budget and assess all your options, you may determine that if you are going to be financially solvent, you will have to work outside the home (if you don't already) or land a better-paying job.

If you are unsure about what kind of new career you may be suited for, meet with a career counselor. He or she can help you assess your skills and interests and discuss the types of jobs for which you may be suited. Other possible sources for this service include your local community college and your state's employment commission. Some of these state agencies have a "rehabilitation" office specifically designed to help the newly divorced who are entering the work world with few if any job skills.

What Color Is Your Parachute? by Richard Bolles (Ten Speed Press) is a classic must-read for job-seekers who want to analyze their strengths and weaknesses prior to joining the work world or making a career change.

The federal government's Bureau of Labor Statistics publishes brochures on a variety of specific occupations. For each occupation, brochures on job growth and salary information tell you about the kind of education and training the jobs require, and offer job-finding advice. Go to `http://stats.bls.gov/emphome.htm` to learn more about these publications.

Acquiring the education you need

If you already have a job but need to make more money, finding more-lucrative work may simply be a matter of updating your résumé and beginning a job search (especially if you have good job skills and strong credentials). But, if you're reentering the work world and your skills are outdated or very limited, or if you want to change careers, you'll probably need job training or continuing education to achieve your employment goals.

Financing a college degree

Depending on your job skills and education level, achieving your career goals may require getting a degree from a four-year college or university, completing a community college program, or attending a trade or technical school (see the next section of this chapter for more on choosing a good technical school). But, financing the cost of higher education can be tough to do when money is tight, especially if you need to put money away for your children's own education. If you do need help in funding your schooling, the federal government's loan, grant, or work-study programs may be able to help you.

The Student Guide to Federal Financial Aid published by the U.S. Department of Education (DOE) offers a good overview of the full range of federal educational assistance programs for which you may qualify. Call 800-433-3234 to obtain a copy. You can also obtain information at the DOE's Web site, www.ed.gov.

Some states offer their own educational assistance programs. Call your state's department of education to find out if your state is one of them. In addition to government educational assistance programs, you may be eligible for a special scholarship or grant. (You can find a directory of scholarships and grants at your local library or by doing an Internet search.) A financial aid officer at the college or university you are interested in can tell you about the school's tuition assistance programs.

We also recommend a really helpful title that happens to be from the publishers of this book — *College Financial Aid For Dummies* by Dr. Herm Davis and Joyce Lain Kennedy (IDG Books Worldwide, Inc.).

If you are going to college with the goal of getting a well-paying job after you graduate, select your program of study carefully. Some college majors provide a bigger and more immediate financial payoff than others.

Choosing a trade or technical school

You can find both good and bad trade and technical schools. Attending one of the good ones can be a great way to gain very specific job skills. The bad ones will take your money and give you little in return.

Before you enroll in a trade school, find out if your community college offers you the same education at a cheaper cost.

The following tips can help you shop wisely for a trade or technical school program:

- ✔ Visit the school. Check out its classrooms, computers, and other classroom resources. Do the surroundings look well-cared-for and is the equipment state-of-the-art?

- ✔ Find out what, if any, organizations have licensed or accredited the school. For example, has it been accredited by your state's board of higher education or by another licensing or regulatory agency that accredits trade schools in your state?

- ✔ Find out if the school is facing any consumer complaints by calling the consumer affairs division of your state attorney general's office and by checking with the Better Business Bureau in the town where the school is located.

- ✔ Ask to sit in on some of the classes you will be attending if you enroll in the school.

- ✔ Get written information about the school's curricula, teaching staff, costs, and refund policy.

- ✔ Talk to students who have completed the program you hope to enroll in. Get their opinion of how well the program prepared them for a career. If they are willing to share the information with you, find out what kind of salaries they are earning.

- ✔ Talk with the human resources or personnel departments of the companies you would like to work for to get their opinions of the trade or technical school program you are considering. Would they be more or less likely to hire you knowing that you had completed that program (or do they recommend any others)?

- ✔ Find out about the kind of job-finding assistance the school offers its students and ask about the school's placement rate. According to the Accrediting Commission of Career School and Colleges of Technology, most trade and technical schools have a placement rate of at least 70 percent.

Students who attend disreputable or unaccredited trade schools are often unable to find the employment they need to repay their student loans. If you default on your student loan, to collect what you owe the lender may have a legal right to place a lien on property you own after getting a court judgment against you. To be on the safe side, call the Federal Information Center at 800-688-9889 to find out about the loan default rate of a particular school.

Searching for the right job

Many avenues are open to you when you begin looking for a job. The right method for finding that perfect job depends on your particular job skills, work experience, and the kind of job you want. You may want to consider the following job search methods:

- ✔ Read the classified ads in your local paper.

- ✔ Go to job fairs. They can be a great way to learn who is hiring in your market and what kinds of skills those companies are looking for.

- ✔ Talk with some of the larger job placement or personnel agencies in your area.

- ✔ Work with an executive recruiter, better known as a *head hunter*.

- ✔ Check out your local, county, or state human resources department to learn about job vacancies.

- ✔ Visit your state or local job service or public employment service agency to find out about job vacancies in the public sector.

- ✔ Let your friends and professional associates know that you are looking for a new job. Many better-paying jobs are filled via word of mouth, not through the classifieds.

- ✔ Attend professional networking meetings. Their luncheons, breakfasts, and happy hours may be listed in the business section of your local newspaper.

- ✔ Use your Internet browser. Entering key words such as "job openings," "employment opportunities," or "careers" yields a wide variety of job openings all over the country. You can narrow your search by specifying the state or community you want to work in or by indicating the type of job you want, or you can go directly to the company you want to work for and click onto its "employment" link. Other sources of job information on the Internet can include your local chamber of commerce, your state employment commission, and your local branch of government.

Some career-oriented Web sites offer more than just job listings. They also allow you to post your résumé at the site, conduct your own job search, arrange for a personal search agent to e-mail you information about listings that match your job criteria, and get advice from career counselors. If you're interested in these online services, check out the following pages:

- Infoseek's The Career Channel: `www.infoseek.com/Topic?tid=421&sv=N5&svx=nscrerR1`
- Career Builder: `careerbuilder.com/index.asp`
- Career Mosaic: `www.careermosaic.com`
- The MonsterBoard: `www.monsterboard.com`

Dealing with Personal and Family Issues

After your divorce is over, you enter a new phase in your life. You may feel happier than you have felt in a long time, free of the tension and strife that plagued your marriage. Life after divorce can represent a time of personal growth, rediscovery, and new opportunities.

On the other hand, being single again can be an intimidating and lonely experience — particularly if divorce was not your idea and you are unprepared for life on your own or if you have sole custody of your children. Even if you sought that custody arrangement, having full-time responsibility for your children seven days a week, night and day, can be overwhelming, not to mention exhausting.

Being easy on yourself

To help you adjust to all the changes in your life, avoid piling unreasonable expectations on yourself. Just do what you must to tie up the loose ends of your divorce; otherwise, take a breather and regroup mentally and physically. Although you may have big plans for what you want to do with the rest of your life, give yourself the opportunity to recover from what you've just gone through.

In other words, being a little lazy — letting your house get messier than it usually is, eating fast-food dinners once in while, skipping a few workouts at the gym — is okay. Pressuring yourself to make important decisions right away, before you can think them through with a clear head, may cause you to make some mistakes you'll regret later on.

On the other hand, you need to maintain those habits that make you feel good about yourself and about life in general. If you get too lazy, you may slip into a funk you can't crawl out of, which will definitely interfere with your ability to get on with your life as a single person.

Taking time to reflect on what happened

Try to put your recent experiences into perspective. Take time to understand why your marriage didn't work out and how you may have contributed to your marital problems. Otherwise, you may end up making the same mistakes twice. Keeping a journal is a good way to do this and therapy can be a big help, too.

Rebuilding When a Relationship Ends, Second Edition (Impact Publishers, 1995) by Dr. Bruce Fisher can help validate the feelings you may be experiencing about the end of your marriage and provide you with useful advice about how to have a more successful marriage next time around.

Accept the fact that your life is no longer the way it used to be and it never will be again. This doesn't mean that your new life has to be a disappointment — it's just different. Try to identify some benefits to your being single again (they may be hard to find at first but they do exist). For example, you have more privacy and time to yourself, your relationship with your children is stronger, and you can sleep better because you're no longer stressed out by your divorce.

Finding a support group

Consider joining a divorce support group. Its members can help bolster your confidence through the inevitable down times as you rebuild your life and can provide you with advice and feedback when you encounter problems you're not sure how to best handle.

Becoming handy around the house

Being divorced usually means having to take on new household chores — cooking, grocery shopping, balancing the checkbook, home repairs, mowing the lawn — chores your ex-spouse used to do. If you need to get up-to-speed quickly on unfamiliar household tasks, relatives and friends may be willing to give you a quick lesson (don't be ashamed to ask them for the help you need). Reading how-to books or taking classes are also good ways to acquire new skills. Soon you'll feel proud of what you can accomplish on your own and gain confidence in your ability to learn even more.

Focusing more attention on your kids

If you have children, much of your energy should focus on helping them adjust to life after divorce. If you and your spouse were separated while you were getting divorced, your kids probably began making the adjustment back then. Now that your divorce is final, they may have to deal with a new set of changes and will need more of your love and affection as a result (provided you don't smother them or become overprotective).

Your divorce may actually provide an opportunity for you to improve your relationship with your children. Now that you are no longer distracted by the troubles of your marriage or by the process of your divorce, you can refocus some of your energy on your children.

Research shows that even in amicable splits, the effect of divorce on both boys and girls tends to be greatest during the year immediately following a divorce, and boys tend to have a harder time adjusting overall than girls do.

The experts at the Parenting Q&A Web site (www.parenting-qa.com) can answer questions you may have about your children's behavior, as well as their development and growth. The online experts include social workers, educators, psychologists, and pediatricians.

Finding activities you and your children enjoy

If you are a noncustodial parent, being with your kids may be awkward for all of you at first. Seeing you living in a new place and not having you in their everyday lives may feel weird to your children.

To help everyone feel more comfortable and adjust to the new situation, try to avoid making every get-together a special event. Simple activities such as a trip to the grocery store, a bike ride, doing homework together, or watching a video — the kinds of things you used to do with one another — take some of the pressure off and helps reassure your kids that not everything in their lives has changed.

You can reassure your kids that you're still an active parent by attending their school's open house, attending their recitals or sporting events, or joining in their scouting activities. Even if you live out of town, making it a point to show up at least a couple of times a year to lend moral support means a lot to your children and assures them that they're very important to you.

If you are a noncustodial parent, don't be upset if your kids don't act overjoyed to see you when you pick them up, but then seem sad to leave you. Their initial nonchalance may be their way of protecting themselves emotionally, or it may reflect their confidence that you will always be in their lives and divorce hasn't changed your love and concern for them. Don't make assumptions about the ways your children are responding to the changes occurring in their lives. Instead, observe your children and try to understand the true reasons for their behavior.

If your children are living with you but spending some nights with your former spouse, give your kids time to get used to their other parent's home and the different rules your ex may expect your children to follow. Your children may have a hard time falling asleep when they spend the night at your ex's or may act reluctant to spend time there at first, but most likely they'll adjust fairly quickly to their new living arrangement.

Working at rebuilding a sense of family

As you recover from your divorce, rebuilding a sense of family with your children is important. This is particularly critical if your marital problems have affected how your entire family functions.

Whether you are a custodial parent, a noncustodial parent, or share custody with your spouse, your children need to feel that they're still part of a real family, which is essential to your child's sense of self-worth. To help maintain a sense of family, hold on to as many family rituals as possible, such as attending religious ceremonies with your children or arranging for all of you to spend holidays with your extended family.

Think about establishing new family customs (going on an annual family vacation or taking up a new hobby with your children, for example) to make them feel as if some benefits to their new life do exist and to help your children enjoy spending time with you as a family.

Special family time doesn't have to cost a lot of money. It can be as simple as a walk after dinner, weekend bike rides, playing Monopoly, or decorating the holiday tree. Whether you have a one-parent, two-parent, or blended family, your children will benefit from spending time together as a group and growing up in a household where open communication, humor, clear values and rules, nurturing, and respect for one another exist.

If your children are preteens or teenagers, be sensitive to their need for peer support, but insist that they do something with your family at least once a week. They, too, will benefit from that special family time. Getting your older children to participate in family activities is easier if you choose activities that the whole family enjoys or if you let each of your children take turns picking a family activity.

Making New Friends

When you get divorced, you will almost inevitably lose touch with some of your friends. Most likely, they will be people you knew through your spouse, or people who may have related to you solely as one-half of a couple. Some of your friends may feel the need to choose sides in your divorce, some will side with you, and some with your ex-spouse. Other friends may drop out of both of your lives, perhaps because their own marriages are shaky and they feel uncomfortable around people who are recently divorced.

Divorce changes friendships in different ways. Now that you are single, you may find that you have less in common with certain friends or that you feel awkward going to their dinner parties and other social gatherings by yourself. As a result, you may drift apart from some people.

Hopefully, your most important and significant friendships will remain intact. Even so, try to make new friends, too. Meeting new people can be fun and can bring new energy and hope to your life. To make new friends, volunteer for a cause you care about; take a class; join a singles group (a group for divorced people is a particularly good idea), a book discussion group, or a health club; or try some other new activity.

Make a point of rediscovering your community and all that it offers you and your kids. Learn to do something you have always wanted to do but never got around to doing, or take up a hobby you put aside after your marriage. The point is this: Get out of the house and add some variety to your life!

Avoid alienating your friends and family members by constantly griping about what a raw deal you think you got in your divorce or about the people your spouse is dating. Although your friends may have been ready to offer you a shoulder to lean on while you were *getting* divorced, they may be less willing to listen now that you've finally split from your ex. If you need to vent, talk to someone who is a patient and impartial listener or seek professional counseling.

Chapter 19

The Toughest Post-Divorce Problems (And How to Solve Them)

- -

In This Chapter

▶ Your ex won't let you spend time with your kids

▶ You don't get your child support payments

▶ Your former spouse skips out

▶ Your ex disappears with your children

▶ Your former spouse fails to pay court-ordered child support

▶ You want to change your divorce agreement

▶ Your ex-spouse declares bankruptcy

- -

ivorce doesn't always bring to an end the problems that destroyed a marriage. Some divorced couples persist in arguing and going out of their way to make each other miserable instead of getting on with their lives. Consumed by anger and a desire for revenge, they fight over the outcome of the divorce, withhold court-ordered child support or alimony, purposely delay making support payments, or interfere in each other's custodial or visitation rights.

Some former spouses develop serious financial trouble after they get divorced, so serious that they end up filing for bankruptcy. When that happens, the financial troubles of one spouse can jeopardize the finances of the other. Some former spouses go so far as to file bankruptcy in a deliberate effort to renege on their divorce-related financial obligations. None of this paints a pretty picture, but it's reality in many divorce cases.

This chapter can't solve everyone's post-divorce problems, but it can provide specific information about some of the most common (and serious) problems divorced couples face and what can be done about them.

Your Ex-Spouse Interferes with Your Visitation Rights

If you are a noncustodial parent and your ex-spouse makes exercising your visitation rights difficult, or even impossible, your ex is violating the terms of your divorce, plain and simple.

If you are the custodial parent, you cannot force your former spouse to exercise his or her visitation rights. No law requires a noncustodial parent to use those rights. On the other hand, you can use your former spouse's repeated failure to exercise his or her visitation rights as justification for why the court should modify your current custody agreement. You may even be able to ask the judge to restrict your former spouse's visitation rights.

Don't retaliate by withholding payments

If your spouse is interfering with your visitation rights, you may be tempted to withhold payment for child support or alimony. Don't do it! Not only will you be breaking the law — just like your former spouse is doing — but you may also jeopardize your children's well-being. Two wrongs in this case definitely *do not* make a right.

A far better course of action is to continue paying your child support (and alimony, too) and try to work things out with your former spouse. Mediation is probably your best bet if you want to resolve your disputes outside of court. (See Chapter 16 for more on the subject of mediation.) But mediation will not work unless you both are willing to give it a try. If your ex-spouse is unwilling, going back to court may be your only option.

Do file a contempt of court complaint

If you and your ex-spouse are so estranged that you can't attempt a non-court resolution of your problems, file a complaint for contempt of court against your ex. Although you have to pay certain fees to file, if the court finds your ex to be in contempt, you can probably recover your filing costs from him or her. From start to finish the complaint process takes relatively little time — certainly less time than your divorce took.

Unless your former spouse can prove that he or she has good reason to keep you from seeing your kids — you've abused them, sexually molested them, you have a drug problem, and so on — your ex will be ordered to allow you to exercise your visitation rights.

Where did our love go?

The following couple of stories demonstrate what can happen when a divorce turns particularly bitter.

A Rhode Island couple divorced after 20 years of marriage. She got custody of their kids, their house, their car, and the camera shop business the couple had built together. He got the shop's phone number, thousands of dollars in camera equipment and repair tools, and cash. Although her divorce attorney said that she didn't need a noncompete clause in her divorce agreement based on a conversation the attorney had with her spouse's lawyer just before their divorce was final, her husband opened his own camera shop, just a few doors away from hers! Now, their long-time customers are caught in the middle, and both business owners are competing with one another to survive.

In a lawsuit that received national media attention, a North Carolina woman used her state's little known alienation of affection law to sue the woman she claims lured her husband into an extramarital affair, destroyed their happy marriage, and convinced her husband to divorce her. Two months after the divorce was final, the husband married his former mistress. A jury of nine women and three men ordered that Wife Number Two had to pay Wife Number One a million dollars for breaking up her marriage.

The Child Support Payments Don't Arrive

The sad reality is that literally millions of divorced parents (mostly mothers) with court orders for child support never receive their court-ordered child support, or receive it only on a sporadic basis. As a result, many of these parents struggle to provide for their children, some are pushed into bankruptcy, and still others fall into poverty.

The formal term for past due child support is an *arrearage.* According to the 1992 U.S. census, only about half of the 5.3 million parents with court orders for child support were receiving full support payments. The average *annual* amount of child support they received was a meager $2,961.

If your ex is a *deadbeat,* a person who can pay but won't, you can scream, cry, tear your hair out, or you can use legal means to force your ex-spouse to pay up. If you choose the latter option, you can

✔ Get help from your state's Child Support Enforcement (CSE) Program. Although the CSE office charges you little or nothing for its assistance, don't expect overnight results.

✔ Hire an attorney to do much of what the CSE will do. An attorney's help can be expensive, but unlike the CSE office in your state, your attorney may be able to get you some quick results. Also, you can try to recover your attorney's fees and legal costs from your former spouse.

✔ Work with a private child support collection agency. If you go with this option, select the agency carefully because some of these agencies take a large percentage of any child support they collect. For solid advice for choosing a private agency, see the section titled "Using a private child support collection agency," later in this chapter.

Some counties have domestic relations departments that are independent from the state agencies and handle child support enforcement.

One of this country's most famous deadbeat parents sat in jail for contempt of court while Vermont auctioneers sold off most of his furniture, jewelry, artwork, and other household possessions to raise some of the $640,000 he owed in back child support. Since his divorce 17 years earlier, the commodities consultant, who earned a six-figure income, had moved from New York to Florida to Canada and then to Vermont all in an attempt to avoid paying up. Guess he figured all those moving costs and real estate fees were worth not meeting his $10,000 monthly child support obligation.

Calling on your state's Child Support Enforcement (CSE) Program for help

The Child Support Enforcement (CSE) Program is a joint effort of the federal and state government. The program's goal is to increase the number of custodial parents receiving court-ordered child support. (The CSE program also helps parents obtain court orders for child support.)

The federal government helps fund and develop state CSE programs in accordance with federal law. Generally, state-level efforts are planned and coordinated by state Social Service Departments, Revenue Departments, or through the offices of state Attorneys General. To implement their programs, most states work with local prosecuting attorneys, other local law enforcement agencies, and with family law courts.

CSE services are available for free or at very little cost to any parent who needs them. However, if you seek help from your state's CSE office, be prepared for delays and frustrations. Working with any government bureaucracy can be frustrating, and given the extent of the child support collection problem in this country most CSE offices are chronically understaffed, so getting results can take time.

To more fully understand how the CSE office in your state can help you with your child support problems, request a free copy of the U.S. Department of Health and Human Services *Handbook on Child Support Enforcement.* You should be able to obtain a copy of this handbook from your state CSE office. Table 19-1 provides CSE office phone numbers for every state.

How the CSE office gets your payments for you

 CSE programs vary from state to state. To find out the particulars of your state or local CSE program and how it can help you, call the number for your state listed in Table 19-1. Your local CSE office can help you collect your court-ordered child support in a number of ways:

- ✔ Order your former spouse to meet with the district attorney's office to discuss how your ex can get current on his or her child support payments.

- ✔ Seize your ex's federal tax refund. If your state has its own income tax agency, federal law requires that the state's tax collection agency intercept any state tax refunds your spouse may receive.

- ✔ Ask the IRS to start collection proceedings against your former spouse. (This collection process is the same one that the IRS uses to collect back taxes.) If the IRS responds to the request, it will offer your former spouse an opportunity to negotiate a payment plan to wipe out the child support debt. If that doesn't work out, the IRS may seize assets your ex-spouse owns including bank accounts, real estate, equipment, and other property.

- ✔ Place a lien on your former spouse's real and personal assets, including real estate, vehicles, computer equipment, and so on. (However, most states will not put a lien on a parent's primary residence or on any property he or she needs to make a living.)

- ✔ Placing a lien on property is no guarantee of payment. However, it will prevent your former spouse from selling, transferring, or borrowing against the property until he or she pays the child support debt.

 If you did not get a lien on assets through your divorce and your former spouse fails to pay you your court-ordered child support, you can sue your ex and get a judgment to place a lien on his or her assets after the fact.

- ✔ Require that your ex-spouse pledge real or other property to you, or give you a lien on any real estate (home, land, or buildings) that he or she may own as a guarantee of payment. In the case of nonpayment, your ex will lose the property to you as payment for the back support.

- ✔ Seize the assets of your former spouse, sell them, and use the proceeds to pay off his or her child support debt. Because this option also has issues related to the value of the seized property and transfer of ownership, this is a matter to discuss with an attorney, the CSE office, or a private collection agency if you hire one to help collect on past-due child support.

✔ Use state nonsupport statutes to prosecute your ex-spouse. This option is usually a last resort. However, if it is used and your former spouse does not pay up, the judge can order your ex to be jailed.

The federal Health and Human Resources office (the department in charge of the CSE) has a Web site that provides up-to-date information on the CSE program as well as links to state programs that have their own Web pages. Point your browser to

`www.acf.dhhs.gov:80/ACFPrograms/CSE/`

Table 19-1	Your State's CSE Office Phone Number		
Alabama	334-242-9300	Montana	406-444-4614
Alaska	907-276-3441	Nebraska	402-471-9125
Arizona	602-252-0236	Nevada	702-687-4744
Arkansas	501-682-8398	New Hampshire	603-271-4426
California	916-654-1556	New Jersey	609-588-2361
Colorado	303-866-5994	New Mexico	505-827-7200
Connecticut	203-566-3053	New York	518-474-9081
Delaware	302-577-4863	North Carolina	919-571-4120
DC	202-724-8800	North Dakota	701-224-3582
Florida	904-488-9900	Ohio	614-752-6561
Georgia	404-657-3851	Oklahoma	405-424-5871
Guam	671-475-3360	Oregon	503-986-2417
Hawaii	808-587-3700	Pennsylvania	717-787-3672
Idaho	208-334-5710	Puerto Rico	809-722-4731
Illinois	217-782-8768	Rhode Island	401-277-2409
Indiana	317-232-4894	South Carolina	803-737-5870
Iowa	515-281-5580	South Dakota	605-773-3641
Kansas	913-296-3237	Tennessee	615-741-1820
Kentucky	502-564-2285	Texas	512-463-2181
Louisiana	504-342-4780	Utah	801-538-4400
Maine	207-287-2886	Vermont	802-241-2319
Maryland	410-767-7619	Virgin Islands	809-775-4331

Massachusetts	617-577-7200	Virginia	804-692-1428
Michigan	517-373-7570	Washington	360-586-3162
Minnesota	612-296-2542	West Virginia	304-558-3780
Mississippi	601-359-4415	Wisconsin	608-266-9909
Missouri	573-751-4301	Wyoming	307-777-7747

Other ways a CSE office can put pressure on your ex

Your state Child Support Enforcement (CSE) office may use other tools as well to pressure or embarrass your former spouse into paying up or to make meeting his or her child support obligation as easy as possible. Depending on where you live, some of those other tools the CSE may use include

- Automatic billing, telephone reminders, and delinquency notices.
- Electronic fund transfers from the bank account of your former spouse to your account (a good tool when the support-paying parent is self-employed, because automatic wage deductions are not possible).
- Reporting a child support delinquency to major national credit bureaus.

    Federal law requires that states report all child support arrearages of more than $1,000 to the major credit bureaus; they can report smaller arrearages if they want. When a consumer has this kind of negative information on his or her credit record, the consumer may have a more difficult time getting new or additional credit at reasonable terms.

- Revoking a parent's license to practice law, medicine, or another profession, and revoking the parent's driver's license, hunting or fishing license, or other government-issued license.
- Using local or state "most wanted" campaigns to embarrass parents to pay up and to flush out deadbeat parents.
- Using the media to promote "amnesty" campaigns. Parents who come forward to pay their child support debt during the amnesty period will not be prosecuted or will be punished less severely than they would be otherwise.
- Posting information about delinquent parents on the Internet.

Collect Your Child Support: A Step-by-Step Guide to Successfully Collect Child Support for You and Your Children by Richard Todd (National Legal Services, Inc.) provides a good overview of the basic child support collection techniques and how to use them. Although trying to collect on your own is usually a thankless task, the more you know about what to do, the better able you are to make CSE services work for you.

Working with an attorney to collect support payments

Some family law attorneys specialize in helping parents collect past due child support (and alimony as well), but paying for more legal help may be unrealistic given the state of your post-divorce finances. Furthermore, these attorneys cannot do anything that Child Support Enforcement (CSE) program staff can't do, but they can probably do it faster.

If you have hired an attorney to help you collect your child support, he or she can work with your area's CSE office, coordinating his or her collection efforts with CSE staff to prevent duplication of services and conflicting enforcement decisions.

Using a private child support collection agency

A growing number of parents with child support collection problems are hiring private *child support collection agencies* to help them. These agencies tend to get quicker results than CSE offices and cost less than attorneys.

A cross between a detective agency and a traditional debt collection agency, private child support collection agencies can help you collect your back support and track down your ex-spouse if he or she has disappeared in order to avoid paying child support. For these services, you pay the agency a percentage of the child support it collects for you. You may also have to pay an up-front fee.

Although most private child support collection agencies truly want to help, some victimize desperate parents who are already being victimized by their former spouses. These agencies may take a bigger percentage of the child support they collect than they said they would, demand exorbitant up-front fees (and do little or nothing to earn that money), or fail to turn over the money they collect to the parent who hires them.

To protect yourself from getting ripped off, be sure that you get

- ✔ **Written information about the agency's services.** The information should include background on the company's management and its legal expertise.

- ✔ **References.** Check them out. Also, call your local Better Business Bureau and the consumer protection office of your state Attorney General's office to find out if they have received any complaints against the private child support collection agency.

> ✔ **A written contract from the agency**. The contract should spell out exactly what the agency will do for you, the terms of payment, and how quickly any money the agency collects on your behalf will be turned over to you. Read the contract carefully before you sign, and get all of your questions answered.

Do not sign a contract that requires you to pay a percentage of your child support until your child reaches the age of 18 or 21 or that prohibits you from seeking help from other resources.

Your Ex-Spouse Skips Town

Unfortunately, some parents are so intent on not paying their child support that they move out of state (or even out of the country), often without leaving a forwarding address. When that happens, enforcing a child support court order and collecting that support can be particularly difficult.

The federal government requires state Child Support Enforcement (CSE) offices to pursue interstate cases as vigorously as in-state cases, but in reality, they often get short shrift given the amount of staff time interstate cases take and the many obstacles to success. Nevertheless, in recent years, Congress has passed new laws intended to improve the effectiveness of interstate child support and collections.

A law to track down deadbeats

Signed by President Clinton in 1996, the federal Personal Responsibility and Work Opportunity Act aims to increase child support collections by $24 billion over the next ten years. To do so, the law established a federal/state National Directory of New Hires to help governments keep track of divorced parents who frequently change jobs in order to avoid paying their child support. The law also mandated that all states computerize their collections efforts and implement tough new penalties for child support deadbeats.

The law also expands and simplifies the automatic wage deduction process and requires all states to adopt the Uniform Interstate Family Support Act (UIFSA), which, among other things, facilitates cooperation between states in expediting interstate enforcement of child support orders.

Under earlier legislation, a parent who was obligated to pay child support could avoid paying or could pay less by moving to a new state and getting the new state to modify his or her child support court order. Now, as long as either parent remains in the state where the court order was originally filed, that state has continuing and exclusive jurisdiction over the court order.

A law to prevent fleeing to avoid child support obligations

The Child Support Recovery Act of 1992 makes it a federal crime for a parent to move to another state to avoid meeting his or her child support obligation. However, to be prosecuted under this law, the fleeing parent must owe more than $5,000 in back child support or must have owed back support for more than one year. Also, the parent must have been aware that he or she had an obligation to pay child support and been able to meet that obligation when it was due.

Your Ex-Spouse Disappears with the Kids

If you have custody of your kids and your ex-spouse kidnaps them or refuses to return your children to you, your former spouse is breaking the law. Under most circumstances, the federal government and a majority of states will treat the kidnapping as a felony.

Leave no stone unturned if your ex takes off with the kids. The longer you wait to act, the harder finding them will be. You should

- **Call your local police department immediately.**

- **Contact the FBI yourself.** Don't wait for your local police department to contact the FBI, but let them know that you have. If kidnapping is a felony in your state, the FBI will help you.

- **Contact your Congressperson.** Sometimes a call from your representative can make government offices move more quickly than they would otherwise.

- **Make sure that your state CSE office contacts the Federal Parent Locator Service about your missing spouse.** (This service in Washington, D.C., can also be used in child support enforcement and collection matters.) Your state or county government may also have a parent locator service.

- **Get in contact with organizations that can help you.** Those organizations include the National Center for Missing and Exploited Children (800-843-5678), Child Find of America (1-800-I-Am-Lost), and Missing Children Help Center (800-USA-KIDS).

- **Hire your own private investigator.** *Skip tracers,* individuals who track down missing persons using national computerized databases, are very effective at turning up missing people through Social Security numbers, driver's license numbers, and plenty of asking around. Plus, they're relatively inexpensive.

If you suspect that your spouse may be thinking about taking off with your children, contact your family law attorney, or the CSE office in your area, or contact both to find out what to do. You should also alert your child's school or day care center about your concerns. Instruct them to release your child only to you or to someone you have specifically designated.

If you think that your ex-spouse may be planning to leave the country with your kids, contact the U.S. Passport office and ask that your child not be granted a passport if your ex applies for one. Should your former spouse manage to get out of the country with your children, contact the Department of State's Office of Citizen and Counselor Services. It will provide you with helpful information and forms to fill out.

Your Ex-Spouse Owes You Alimony

Many former spouses who are legally obligated to pay alimony fail to make the payments or don't make them consistently, often because they resent having to pay the money or because a new spouse pressures them not to pay. Other former spouses don't pay because they develop serious money troubles after their divorce and instead of asking the court to let them pay less they simply stop paying or pay only when they can afford to.

If your former spouse falls behind on his or her alimony payments to you, the Uniform Interstate Family Support Act (UIFSA) may be able to help you. The federal government has ordered all states to adopt the law. Also, some courts are becoming more aggressive about enforcing court-ordered alimony agreements.

In some states, the wages of an ex-spouse who's fallen behind on alimony payments can be attached. In addition, the former spouse can be held in contempt for violating a court order to pay alimony and jailed as a result.

If contempt of court is not an option in your state, you may be in the same boat as anyone else your ex owes money to when your alimony isn't paid. Making matters worse, your state's debtor protection laws may make all or most of the property owned by your ex-spouse exempt (that is, protected) from your efforts to collect what you are owed, effectively making the past-due alimony not collectable.

Your best option when your spouse owes you alimony is to contact your divorce attorney who can both lay out your options and help you carry out a plan of action.

The time to ask your attorney about potential problems with collecting alimony is when the terms of your divorce agreement are being written. One option your attorney may recommend is requiring your spouse to pledge property to you as a guarantee.

You Want to Change Some Terms of Your Divorce Agreement

Sometimes things change, and the divorce agreement or judgment that seemed fine at the time it was written may no longer be what you need or want now. Or maybe you've never been happy with the outcome of your divorce — you've done your best to abide by your divorce agreement but have decided it's time to do something about it.

If you and your former spouse see eye-to-eye on the changes, then modifying your agreement or the judge's order may be relatively hassle-free, assuming that the judge shares your perspective and assuming that the changes will not harm your minor children in any way. However, if one of you wants things changed and the other doesn't (which is more likely), then you may be in for a replay of your divorce battles.

Demonstrating a change in your circumstances

Ordinarily, if you ask the court to modify the terms of your divorce, you must justify your request by demonstrating that a definite change in your circumstances exists. It's unlikely that a judge will regard your simply "not liking" the terms of your divorce as a sufficient justification for a change.

To modify the terms of your custody and visitation agreement, you must be able to demonstrate a legitimate need for the change due to significant changes in your life, in your former spouse's life, or in the lives of your children. Those changes may include the following:

- You are moving a long distance away.

- The income of the spouse who is paying child support has increased or decreased.

- Your children are not being properly supervised when they are with their other parent. This may be due to a substance abuse problem, because his or her work hours have changed and the children are left alone for long stretches of time, because your former spouse is busy partying into the wee hours of the morning, or other similar situations.

- Your child has become seriously ill and you need more financial assistance to treat that illness.

- One parent has become seriously ill, been arrested for a violent crime, or has been accused of child molestation or child abuse.

✔ You and your teenage children are in constant conflict, and you can no longer control them.

✔ Your ex's new spouse is trying to take over your position as parent to your children or is otherwise improperly influencing your children.

✔ You believe that your former spouse is abusing or sexually molesting your children.

✔ The arrangements in your divorce agreement or judgment are simply not working out.

Whatever the reason(s) you give to justify your request for a modification, the judge makes his or her decision according to what is in the best interests of your children.

After you are divorced, you or your former spouse may also want to make changes in your child support court order. Usually, the parent who is receiving the support wants more money, and the parent who is paying the support wants to pay less. What a surprise! The parent who is requesting the modification must provide the court with proof that changes in his or her life, changes in the life of the other parent, or changes in the lives of the children merit the modification. If the court denies the parent's request, in most states that parent is limited in his or her ability to file a new request.

If you have more children with another partner after you get divorced, a judge will view that as a valid reason for lowering the amount of child support you are obligated to pay to your former spouse.

Courts are unlikely to agree to a modification of a couple's property settlement agreement, and in fact, many states prohibit such a change. Those states that do allow modifications in the property settlement agreement usually provide only a very short window of opportunity — typically 30 days — for requesting it. Courts are much more willing to consider changes related to the terms of custody, child support, or alimony, assuming circumstances merit the change.

Securing a court order if you change the agreement yourselves

If you and your ex-spouse informally decide to change your child custody and visitation agreement, be sure to get a new court order that reflects all of your changes. Otherwise, despite what you and your spouse agree to, it won't be enforceable by contempt because the court continues to recognize the original court-ordered agreement.

Put your new agreement in writing, and, to be certain that it is enforceable, get an attorney's help in wording it. Make sure that you both get copies of the new agreement.

If you are paying court-ordered child support and you and your ex informally agree that you can begin paying less child support than what was ordered, or that you can suspend your payments for a while, or that you don't have to pay any child support at all, your state may view your new informal agreement as nonbinding and void, even if you put it in writing. In that case, the court order for child support remains in effect.

Even if your requested changes are mutual, a judge may not consider them to be in the best interests of your children. Therefore, if you and your ex-spouse reduce, cease, or suspend your child support payments, the court may consider the non-paying party to be in contempt and that parent could end up in legal hot water. If you want to modify your current court order, do so by entering a new one.

Your Ex-Spouse Files for Bankruptcy

Considering that consumer bankruptcies are at an all-time high and the finances of many people take a turn for the worse after divorce, the possibility exists that your former spouse may file for bankruptcy.

If you believe that your ex-spouse may be thinking about filing for bankruptcy, and if he or she is currently paying you alimony, child support, or both, get in touch with a bankruptcy attorney immediately!

The two types of bankruptcy

The two types of consumer bankruptcy are *Chapter 13 reorganization of debt bankruptcy* and *Chapter 7 liquidation bankruptcy.*

If your former spouse files Chapter 13, your ex has between three and five years to catch up on all of the past due alimony or child support payments that you are owed. During this same time, your former spouse is required to make all of his or her support payments in full and on time.

If your former spouse files Chapter 7, you can try to collect your back child support and your back alimony from your ex by using any or all of the collection options previously described in this chapter. Also, just as with a Chapter 13 bankruptcy, your former spouse must stay up to date on all of his or her support obligations to you while in bankruptcy.

Bankruptcy just isn't the excuse it used to be

If your divorce occurred prior to 1994, your former spouse would have been able to use bankruptcy to void certain divorce-related obligations, including a promise to pay off some of your debts or to give you a set amount of money over time in exchange for being able to keep certain assets.

If this situation happened to you prior to 1994, you may have ended up with considerably more debt to pay than you had anticipated at the time of your divorce and possibly not enough money to pay it. In fact, your ex-spouse's bankruptcy may have forced you to file for bankruptcy as well!

Since 1994 when the law changed, a former spouse has a much harder time using bankruptcy to wipe out certain kinds of financial obligations. Now if the court believes that your former spouse has sufficient resources to cover basic living expenses and meet his or her financial obligations to you, then those obligations may remain unaffected by bankruptcy. This is especially true if the court believes that by releasing your former spouse from the obligations, you would suffer more than your former spouse would benefit.

To take advantage of the 1994 change in the law, you must file an *adversary proceeding* — the equivalent of a minilawsuit — in your ex-spouse's bankruptcy within 60 days of the date of your ex's first creditor's meeting. This assumes that you know that your former spouse has filed for bankruptcy and that you have the financial wherewithal to hire an attorney to help you initiate an adversary proceeding.

Support obligations remain unaffected

Although going bankrupt wipes out many of your ex-spouse's debts, including some of the debts your ex-spouse may have agreed to pay you according to your divorce agreement or court order, the bankruptcy will *not* affect his or her obligation to pay you alimony or child support. (Nor will your ex-spouse's child support debt be wiped out through bankruptcy if you are working with the CSE to collect on it.)

Two exceptions to the law

Child support and alimony obligations are considered *priority debts* in a bankruptcy. That means that your former spouse must pay them in full. They cannot be wiped out or discharged through bankruptcy, *except in two situations:*

✔ Your former spouse fell behind on his or her child support or alimony payments, and you turned those debts over to a private collection agency. However, your former spouse is still legally obligated to make all *future* support payments to you in full and on time.

✔ The bankruptcy court rules that your ex's alimony debt is really another type of divorce-related financial obligation — a debt related to your property settlement, for example.

The obligations may also be wiped out if your ex-spouse owns a business and the court believes that there will not be enough money to continue running the business if your ex must continue to meet his or her financial obligations to you.

Chapter 20

Thinking Ahead: Prenuptial and Postnuptial Agreements

In This Chapter

▶ Bringing up the subject of prenuptial agreements with your spouse-to-be

▶ Figuring out what to put in your prenuptial agreement

▶ Making your agreement meet the letter of the law in your state

▶ Calling on an attorney to help you with your agreement

▶ Negotiating a postnuptial agreement

. . . .

*S*ooner or later, you'll probably meet someone new, fall in love, and maybe even think about tying the knot again. If you've been divorced before, you may know that marriage can be something of a gamble, and when it ends it can drain your emotions and your pocketbook. So you may be wondering if you can do anything to make splitting up a little bit easier, just in case things don't work out the way you'd hoped the next time around.

A prenuptial agreement may be what you need for some peace of mind because it lets you and your future spouse work out some of the details of your divorce *before* you get married. Although it may seem somewhat cynical (let alone unromantic) to discuss such an arrangement with your spouse-to-be, drafting a prenuptial agreement may make good sense given today's divorce rate. (However, we hope you won't need to use it.)

This chapter tells you all about what a prenuptial agreement can do (and can't do), what makes such as agreement legally binding, and the role that attorneys play in the prenuptial agreement drafting process. (We also offer you some advice for raising the subject with your intended.)

This chapter also provides information about another kind of legal agreement that you can prepare *after* you are married — the postnuptial agreement. Although used less often than prenuptial agreements, postnuptials serve very much the same purpose as prenuptials.

Prenups: They're Not Just for the Wealthy Anymore

Traditionally, prenuptial agreements have been associated with very rich people, especially when a wealthy person is marrying someone with a lot less wealth or earning power — something on the order of the Donald Trump and Marla Maples union.

In recent years, however, people of more-average means have begun using these agreements:

- People who have already gone through a difficult and expensive divorce and want to make any future split easier and cheaper.

- Spouses-to-be who own their own businesses and want to protect their enterprise from the potential repercussions of divorce.

- Older professionals headed into marriages with a substantial amount of real estate, stocks, bonds, and other valuable assets.

- Other couples, especially older ones, who want to write their own inheritance rules so that they can ensure that their children from a previous marriage, and not their future spouse's children, inherit certain assets when they die. (By law, in most states, when a spouse dies, the remaining spouse has a legal right to one-third of the deceased's estate, no matter what his or her will says.)

- Couples who want to negotiate the rules of their marriage — how they will share in the housework, what religion their children will be raised in, and other issues related to the management of their marriage and family life. (However, most courts will not enforce such life-style provisions.)

You may feel like you're tempting fate, but working out the details of your divorce before you get married by negotiating a prenuptial agreement can be a smart way to minimize the potential negative financial and emotional repercussions of divorce. Doing most of the end-of-your-marriage negotiating at the start of your relationship — when everything is still rosy — can make your divorce easier, less emotional, and cheaper, and can help protect important assets in the aftermath of divorce (if there is one).

In the prenuptial agreement signed by magician David Copperfield and supermodel Claudia Schiffer, she agreed to never reveal Copperfield's "tricks of the trade" should they divorce.

Broaching the Subject to Your Spouse (Delicately)

You like the idea of a prenuptial agreement, but you're wondering how to broach the subject to your intended. You realize that your soon-to-be spouse may not consider negotiating a prenuptial agreement to be the most auspicious way to begin a marriage.

We can't guarantee a risk-free way to raise the subject. What works for one person may be disastrous for someone else. The right approach for you depends on your individual personalities and on the degree of trust and communication you have already established with one another. Nevertheless, we can give you some general ground rules for opening the discussion:

✔ Be honest without being hurtful about your reasons for wanting a prenuptial. If you sound as though you are being evasive or are lying, or if you appear to be acting out of greed or deceitfulness, you may have a tough time getting to the negotiation stage and you may even derail your marriage before it's begun.

✔ If you are nervous about bringing up the idea of a prenuptial agreement, consider getting some up-front advice from a marriage counselor or therapist.

✔ Be absolutely clear that your desire for a prenuptial agreement says nothing about your love for and commitment to your future spouse.

✔ Explain how your spouse will benefit from the prenuptial agreement.

✔ Avoid becoming defensive or angry if your spouse becomes upset.

✔ If emotions get in the way, schedule a session with a marriage counselor, therapist, or your religious adviser. They can help you work through your emotions and move forward to an understanding about the agreement.

If having a prenuptial agreement is really important to you, be prepared to offer your spouse a financial incentive for going along with what you want. Make that incentive a part of the agreement.

If you and your future spouse try to draft your own prenuptial agreement and reach a stalemate, consider scheduling a session or two with a trained mediator. (Mediation is discussed in detail in Chapter 16.) If mediation helps you resolve your differences and you end up with an agreement, give your draft agreement to an attorney so you can be sure that it complies with your state's legal requirements for prenuptial agreements, thereby making it enforceable. You and your intended should each hire your own attorney for this purpose.

What to Put in Your Prenuptial Agreement

The provisions you include in your agreements should reflect your individual interests and financial concerns. You may have some thoughts already about what to include, and your attorneys can also make some suggestions. In addition, ask yourself the following questions. The answers may give you some fresh ideas.

- ✔ If you're making a sacrifice by agreeing to give up your career to help build up your spouse's career or business, how will you be compensated?

- ✔ How will you be compensated if you agree to be a stay-at-home parent after your marriage when you would really rather work outside the home?

- ✔ Will one of you pay the other alimony in the event your marriage ends? If so, how much will the payments be and how long will they last?

- ✔ Who will pay the legal fees if you get divorced?

- ✔ Who will get the house and any other significant property if you get divorced?

- ✔ How will you deal with inheritance issues?

- ✔ What will you do about your marital debts if you get divorced?

- ✔ How will you treat the income each of you earns during your marriage?

- ✔ If you purchase property together, how will it be titled?

- ✔ How will you share expenses during your marriage?

- ✔ How will your spouse be compensated for any contribution he or she may make to your business?

- ✔ If you intend to support your spouse while he or she goes through law school, medical school, or another training program, how will you be compensated if your marriage ends?

- ✔ Will your spouse have any interest in your business if you get divorced?

- ✔ How will you be compensated if your spouse-to-be has bad credit and, therefore, during at least the early years of your marriage all credit has to be in your name? (You will be responsible for that debt, even if your spouse agrees to pay off some of it should you get a divorce.)

Negotiating the terms of your prenuptial agreement may have an unexpected effect. Depending on what you learn about your future spouse by going through the process, you may be convinced to call off your marriage instead of signing on the bottom line.

After you have prepared your prenuptial agreement, read it periodically to make sure that it continues to reflect your interests and your needs. If things have changed, you and your spouse can agree to amend the agreement or to void it. The amending or voiding process depends on your state law, so talk with an attorney if you are thinking about doing either.

Making Your Prenuptial Agreement Legally Binding

Every state has its own property laws. These laws guide judges when they are making decisions about how to divide up a divorcing couple's joint property and debts. If you and your future spouse write a prenuptial agreement, you can also write your own rules (with the provisos we state next) as long as they are acceptable to both of you.

Like other important agreements related to love, marriage, and divorce, every state has rules for what makes a prenuptial agreement legally binding and enforceable by the court. Those rules usually include the following:

- **The agreement must be in writing.**

- **Both of you must sign your agreement because you want to, not because you are being threatened or coerced.**

- **Your agreement should be negotiated and finalized well before the date of your marriage.**

  This lessens the likelihood that either of you would feel pressured to agree to your partner's requests to avoid jeopardizing your impending marriage. The more distance you can put between the date of your marriage and the signing of the agreement, the better.

- **You must both be involved in negotiating the agreement, although you can use attorneys to do the negotiating for you.**

  Using an attorney greatly increases the enforceability of your agreement if your spouse later tries to contest it down the road.

- **You must be 100-percent forthcoming with one another about what you own and owe.**

  Both of you must be aware of what the other is giving up or getting before you sign the agreement. The more information you share with one another, the better.

✔ **Neither of you should try to gain an advantage over the other by hiding assets you may own.**

For example, you cannot conceal income in order to get your future spouse to agree to a low level of spousal support if you get divorced. The court would view that as fraud.

✔ **You must both sign your prenuptial agreement.**

✔ **Depending on your state, the agreement must be notarized.**

If you or your spouse can prove that one or more of the characteristics just listed were missing from your prenuptial agreement negotiations, the court may change or reverse certain provisions in the agreement or, after holding a hearing, void your prenuptial agreement entirely.

If your prenuptial agreement overwhelmingly favors you to the detriment of your spouse, he or she may be successful at getting the court to declare that the agreement is invalid. Your state may provide other statutory defenses that either spouse can use to contest the legality of a prenuptial agreement down the road. Asking your attorney about these defenses is wise.

Depending on your state, you may be able to include provisions for spousal support in your premarital agreement. However, state family courts are not bound by provisions related to the custody and support of any children you may have during your marriage because those provisions may not be in your children's best interests.

Many attorneys videotape the meeting at which couples are signing their prenuptial agreements. The videotape provides additional proof that the agreement was something that both parties desired and entered into willingly.

Getting Legal Help with Your Agreement

Your state may require that each of you hire your own attorneys to help you during the prenuptial agreement negotiation process. However, even if that's not a requirement in your state, hiring your own attorney is still a good idea any time you negotiate the details of an important legal document that has implications for your financial well-being.

An attorney can help you ensure that the agreement is fair to you and can explain how the agreement can affect you if your marriage ends in divorce. He or she can also make certain that the agreement meets the letter of the law in your state.

Using a prenup to negotiate the terms of your marriage

A prenuptial agreement can be used for more than just setting the terms of your divorce. You can also use a prenup to establish the "rules" of your marriage (however, most courts will not enforce so-called lifestyle provisions). Spending time discussing the seemingly minor issues that can sometimes scuttle a marriage can help to solidify your married relationship. For example, your agreement can address the following potential marriage-busters:

✔ Will you have children? If so, how many and how soon?

✔ Will one of you stay home to care for the children?

✔ If one or the both of you have children from a previous marriage and the children will be living with you or visiting you periodically, what are your expectations of one another regarding the care of your kids?

✔ When is it okay to borrow money and how much debt do you feel comfortable with? How do you feel about credit card debt in particular?

✔ How much will you put into savings each month? Are you going to buy a home together or rent a place to live?

✔ How will you share housework, yard work, the management of your finances, and other household activities?

✔ How will you share your bills?

✔ If you both own your own homes and furniture, where will you live and how will you blend your household items?

✔ How are you going to share the decision making?

✔ If you reach a decision-making impasse or are generally having trouble getting along, will you agree to get counseling?

✔ Where will you spend important holidays — with your family, with your spouse's family, or somewhere else?

✔ If one of you is close to retirement age, what are your plans for the future after you stop working?

Talking out these issues before you get married can increase your confidence in the future success of your marriage. On the other hand, if you and your intended don't see eye-to-eye on the really important issues, you may begin to question the long-term potential of your relationship and rethink the idea of marrying.

The attorney you use should be a family law practitioner with specific experience in the area of prenuptial planning (not all attorneys have this expertise). Depending on the circumstances, you may also need the assistance of a lawyer with special expertise outside the area of family law or the help of other professionals. For example, if you own a business, you may want a business law specialist or a business valuation expert involved in your prenuptial planning. Or, if you want to set up a trust as part of your planning, the assistance of an estate planning attorney is advisable.

You and your spouse should discuss your prenuptial goals and concerns and what each of you thinks is fair before you meet with your attorneys. Then you can determine if writing a prenuptial agreement is even possible. You'll need to identify and categorize the issues you agree on, the issues that need legal clarification, and what you want your attorneys to help negotiate. This up-front work saves you money in the long run.

Using an attorney to help you work out the terms of your prenuptial agreement can cost you anywhere between $1,000 and $100,000, depending on where you live, the complexity of the issues you address in the agreement, and the value of the assets involved. For most couples, the attorney fees are at the low end of the scale. If you consider the cost of a litigated divorce, spending money now on a prenuptial agreement may save you some dollars in the long run.

After You're Married: Drafting a Postnuptial Agreement

Just as its name implies, a *postnuptial agreement* is one that you and your spouse draft after you are married. Although this type of agreement is not as common as a prenuptial agreement, it has been growing in popularity.

Understanding how you can use a postnup agreement

You can use a postnuptial agreement pretty much the same way that you can use a prenuptial agreement. For example:

- If you or your spouse decides to start a business after you are married, you can spell out in a postnuptial agreement what will happen to the business if you get divorced or if you die while you are still married.

  For example, assume that you're going to open a shop. You and your spouse may agree that all of the income your store earns will remain in a business checking account for three months in order to pay the bills. Then, after the three months are up, the income will be divided 50-50 into two separate personal property accounts — one for you and one for your spouse. Or, perhaps you want to word your agreement to ensure that the full value of the business goes to your children when you die and that your spouse will not get any of it.

✔ You can use the postnuptial to ensure that all of your estate goes to your children when you die, instead of a portion of it automatically going to your spouse.

✔ You can use a postnuptial to work out most of the details of your divorce (child custody and child support not included.)

Making the postnup agreement legally binding

State laws regarding what makes a postnuptial agreement legally binding tend to be less well-defined than those that apply to prenuptial agreements. Generally however, the laws mirror one another. Therefore, when you negotiate your postnuptial agreement, abide by all of the same rules that apply to prenuptials in your state, including full disclosure, no coercion, and honesty.

If you want your postnuptial agreement to be legally valid, you're better off negotiating it while your marriage is still on solid ground, not after your relationship begins to fall apart. Otherwise, if you do split up and one of you later contests the legal validity of the agreement, the court may view the post-nup as little more than an effort by one of you to defraud the other. Also, if you file for divorce too soon after you finalized your postnuptial agreement (and what constitutes "too soon" is up to a judge to decide), the agreement may not hold up in court if your soon-to-be-ex challenges it.

Even if your state does not require that you and your spouse use separate attorneys, doing so is a very good idea. Because a postnuptial agreement is relatively rare, using separate attorneys can help ensure that your agreement will stand up in court if one of you contests its legality down the road.

Most states will invalidate a postnuptial agreement if it is proven that the agreement is an attempt to defraud creditors.

Now it belongs to me: The partition agreement

A *partition agreement* is a narrowly-focused legal agreement that married couples can use to legally convert specific marital assets into separate property. With this type of agreement, one spouse gives the other his or her legal interest in the value of a certain marital asset. If the marital asset you partition is real property (such as a house), be sure that all ownership documents (the deed of record if it's real estate) are changed to reflect the new ownership.

Part VI
The Part of Tens

The 5th Wave   By Rich Tennant

"They both traveled a lot and were big Internet users. Finally, three years and two modems later, they broke up due to insufficient bandwidth."

In this part . . .

The Part of Tens contains quick and handy bits of advice and information, packaged ten to a chapter, including:

- ✔ Divorce-related Web sites that put you in touch with a world of other folks who are going through a divorce or have expert advice on divorce

- ✔ Things you can do to help make your children's lives as happy and stable as possible

- ✔ Suggestions for how to put your divorce behind you, get on with your life, and jump back into the social swim

- ✔ Because you never know when you'll meet someone new, tips on how to make your next marriage a happy and lasting one

Chapter 21
Ten Great Divorce Web Sites

*A*lthough surfing the Net is no substitute for solid legal advice, through online browsing you can quickly grab basic information about divorce-related issues and hook up with countless other people facing the same challenges as you. In this chapter, we list some of the best Web sites dedicated to divorce issues.

Divorce Central

Divorce Central covers the legal, emotional, and financial aspects of divorce and offers information about parenting during and after divorce. This site also features a bulletin board where you can post divorce-related questions and a resource guide for locating a support group or ordering reading materials.

You may also want to visit the "The Steam Room," a chat room where you can go if you are *really* mad and just need to vent. You can also visit the "New Dawn Café" where you can relax, make new friends, and maybe even strike up a romance! (If you are really serious about romance, check out the <u>Personals</u> link.) To see what else this site offers, aim your browser to

```
www.divorcecentral.com
```

Divorce Helpline

The stated goal of this Web site is to help divorcing couples "reduce conflict, negotiate an agreement, and stay out of court." To that end, Divorce Helpline offers a solid online primer about the basic issues in a divorce, plenty of helpful worksheets for couples who are trying to minimize their use of attorneys, and a "Directory of Self-Help Services." You can find Divorce Helpline at

www.divorcehelp.com

Divorce Info

Friendly and comprehensive, this Web site claims it's all about providing superior information to help people get through "one of the cruddiest experiences you'll ever face." The information is organized under four main subject headings: "Getting Through It," "Property Division," "Children," and "Life After Divorce." This site is also developing divorce-related information links for every state in the United States. To see what else Divorce Info offers, head to

www.divorceinfo.com

DivorceNet

DivorceNet hooks you up with other people in the same boat, and we're *not* talking about the Love Boat! You can find 17 interactive bulletin boards including some specifically for folks getting divorced in California, Maryland, Massachusetts, and Virginia. This site also features bulletin boards dedicated to issues related to grandparents of divorce, stepfamilies, domestic violence, child custody and support, visitation, and alimony.

You can also check into real-time chat rooms and a reading room and library where you can read back issues of the *Family Law Advisor* newsletter and other divorce-related resources. For more on DivorceNet, cruise over to

www.divorcenet.com

Divorce Online

Sponsored by the American Divorce Information Network, a group of professionals who support an interdisciplinary approach to divorce and other family law issues, this Web site features informative articles on financial, real estate, legal, and social issues related to divorce. Also featured is a "He Said . . . She Said" bulletin board for angry spouses and ex-spouses who need a place to air their gripes.

Depending on where you live, you may be able to use this site to locate professionals in your area who can help you with your divorce (listings are available for only some states). Divorce Online can be found at

```
www.divorce-online.com
```

The Divorce Page

This Web page is the brainchild of Dean Hughson, a business consultant, writer, divorce activist, and the divorced father of three kids who is now happily remarried. Although Hughson is fairly opinionated (and those opinions may not reflect our opinions or those of the publisher of this book), the Divorce Page is definitely worth checking out if you're interested in the rights of divorced dads.

Hughson created his Web site to help "reduce the pain and suffering of people going through a divorce." The Divorce Page offers information on basic divorce issues and specific resources for divorcing fathers, mothers, and children of divorce. Plus, it lists resources for spiritual support, legal help, links to divorce support groups, and even divorce jokes and sound bites of popular songs. You can find this site at

```
http://hughson.com
```

Divorce Source

Touting itself as the comprehensive divorce information network, Divorce Source features ten different interactive bulletin board forums where visitors can share information on everything from saving their marriage to child custody.

This site also offers several divorce chat rooms, a divorce dictionary, links to other resources, and the Family Law Professional Directory that visitors can use to locate attorneys, counselors, appraisers, mediators, financial analysts, and support groups in their area. Divorce Source is located at

www.divorcesource.com

www.divorcesupport.com

Billed as "The divorce page of the Internet," this site has links to pages with information on divorce recovery, child custody, spousal support, domestic violence, visitation rights, state divorce laws, divorce publications, and other information resources on divorce. You can find it at (where else?)

www.divorcesupport.com

Federal Office of Child Support Enforcement

If you're collecting child support, you should bookmark this address. It provides basic information about federal and state laws and programs regarding child-support collection and enforcement, including an online version of the federal *Handbook on Child Support Enforcement*. This site can help you stay up-to-date on important changes in the law. You can also link to your state's Child Support Enforcement program. To access this resource, head to

www.acf.dhhs.gov/programs/CSE/index.html

MSNBC On Air — Divorce at What Cost

Check out the handy online calculator on this Web page. Follow the directions to get an approximate idea of how much your divorce will cost and how you'll fare financially once your divorce is final. *Warning:* An online calculator is no substitute for the professional advice of an attorney or CPA, but it can help ballpark some divorce costs for you. To find out how it works, head for

www.msnbc.com/onair/msnbc/bwilliams/divorcecalc.asp

Chapter 22

Ten Ways to Help Make Everything Okay for Your Kids

- -

In This Chapter

▶ Being there for your children when they need you

▶ Supporting your ex-spouse's parenting efforts

▶ Not burdening your kids with your worries

▶ Agreeing with your ex on the child-rearing basics

▶ Not using your kids as pawns

▶ Keeping your promises

▶ Being sensitive to the issue of dating

▶ Maintaining routines and traditions

▶ Avoiding the "Disneyland Dad" syndrome

- -

*T*hree out of every five divorces involve at least one child under the age of 18. So to say that nearly every child these days knows someone his or her own age whose parents are divorced or divorcing isn't stretching the truth. Even so, few children expect that divorce will happen in *their* family, but when it does, the effects can be devastating.

Children of divorce often feel as if their lives have been turned upside down, with everything that they knew and loved taken away from them. Your divorce is your children's divorce, too. As a parent, you have the responsibility of helping your kids cope with the profound changes that are happening in their lives. This chapter provides suggestions for how you can bring some stability to an otherwise uncertain situation.

For practical advice about how to help your children cope with your divorce while it is happening and afterward, read Vicki Lansky's *Divorce Book for Parents* (Book Peddlers). You can order it by calling 800-255-3379.

Showing Your Children That You Still Love Them

Tell your children that you love them and prove it by your actions. Spend time with them, show them affection, and be ready and willing to listen when they want to talk and share their feelings with you.

At ParentSoup, you can chat with other parents and experts about issues related to your children and your divorce. Head for

www.parentsoup.com

Encouraging Your Kids to Respect and Love Their Other Parent

Give your children permission to love their other parent. Don't paint such a negative picture of your ex that your children feel guilty about their love for their mom or dad. Instead, support your ex-spouse's parenting efforts and speak in positive terms about your ex.

For example, tell your children funny or touching stories about your family, or about how you and their other parent met, or about your former spouse's relatives. Such conversations demonstrate that you are comfortable talking about your ex and will give your children a sense of pride in their family history and roots, something all children need.

Out of Touch: When Parents and Children Lose Contact After Divorce by Geoffrey L. Greif (Oxford University Press) talks about how important it is for children to spend meaningful time with both parents after a divorce in order to feel connected to both their mother and father.

Not Burdening Your Kids with Adult Problems

Treat your children like children, not like grownups. Although your kids may have to assume more responsibilities around the home after your divorce, and may even have to get a job, never forget that they aren't yet adults.

Be careful not to burden them with your problems and avoid sharing your worries with them. If you are going through a rough time, your children will probably sense it and may begin to feel scared about what may happen to them as well. If you're feeling stressed out — perhaps you're concerned about how to pay the bills — let your kids know what's going on but don't go into lurid details. Assure them that no matter what, everything will be all right.

How to Survive Your Parents' Divorce by Nancy O'Keefe Bolick (Franklin Watts, Inc.) is a book you may want to share with your 9-year-old to 12-year-old children. By offering the words and wisdom of children who have survived divorce, the book addresses many common problems children of divorce must face. It also provides advice to young readers about how they can begin their own emotional healing process and a list of additional recommended reading.

Trying to Agree with Your Ex on the Basics

If you and your former spouse are sharing custody, try to agree on the big issues such as curfews, discipline, and grades. Living by one set of rules in one home and by a totally different set of rules in the other can be tough on your children.

On the other hand, if your former spouse does not parent your children as you do, don't complain about it to your children or argue about it with your ex unless his or her parenting style is clearly doing emotional or physical harm to your children.

Making Your Children Feel at Home in Your New Place

If you moved out of your old home and now have a new home or apartment, make sure that your children have a special place there that's all their own. If your finances allow, let them decorate that space. At the very least, make your new home as comfortable as possible for your children so that they will enjoy visiting you.

Your kids will feel much better if you and your ex agree to maintain a supply of clothes, toiletries, and toys for your kids at each of your homes. Then your children don't have to pack and unpack a suitcase each time they travel from one parent's place to the other.

The Healthy Way Web site offers parents a variety of practical advice including specific information on rearing kids in two separate households and helping kids cope with the consequences of divorce. Head to

`www.nt.sympatico.ca/healthyway/HEALTHYWAY/feature_dvc1.html`

Avoiding Manipulation

Avoid arguing with your former spouse in front of your children, using your children as go-betweens if you're fighting with your ex, or trying to prevent your ex from seeing your kids.

If your ex-spouse starts dating, don't attempt to sabotage that relationship or make your children think that you would disapprove of their liking your ex's new girlfriend or boyfriend. Kids can't have too many caring, supportive adults in their lives. Besides, if you act resentful that your former spouse has a new love interest, you're inadvertently giving your kids a lesson in jealous behavior.

If you would like to see divorce through the eyes of children who have been through it and hear their suggestions on how parents can help their kids cope, consider renting the 30-minute, award-winning *Children of Divorce* video from the University of Wisconsin. The cost is $50. For more information, call 800-633-2599 or send an e-mail order to `newist@uwgb.edu`.

Making Good on Your Promises

Keep your promises to your children in order to make their lives as predictable as possible. For example, if you say you'll pick them up at a certain time, be there; if you tell them you're going to do something together, do it. If you have to change your plans, give your children as much notice as possible and, if your ex is agreeable to it, reschedule the planned activity.

If you live too far away from your children to see them regularly, write or call them at least once a week.

Many noncustodial parents dread seeing their children because it is so painful for them to say goodbye and return their children to the other parent at the end of each visitation period. If you are feeling this way, try to take comfort in the fact that over time saying goodbye becomes easier. Don't let these feelings prevent you from seeing your children. It is important that they can depend on spending time with you on a regular basis.

Waiting to Date

Avoid bringing home dates right after your divorce is final and certainly avoid dating several people right away. When you first begin dating, your children may resent your spending time with new people so soon or feel threatened by the presence of the strangers you're dating. For a while, you may want to arrange your dates for when your children are staying with your ex-spouse if you think that will make your children more comfortable. (For more dating advice, turn to Chapter 23.)

If you begin dating someone regularly, your kids may become emotionally attached to that person, treating him or her as a surrogate parent. Be aware that if your relationship ends, your children may have a tough time accepting the fact that it's over (especially if your ex-spouse is no longer an active participant in your children's lives).

Making Your Children's Lives Stable and Predictable

Maintain as many routines, rules, and traditions as you can. Children thrive on predictability. After your divorce, serve their meals at the same time, if possible let them keep their pets, be available to help them with their homework after dinner, and maintain the same standards of discipline.

As much as possible, try to make holidays and other special days like they used to be and don't try to end or interfere in your children's relationships with the parents, brothers, sisters, and other relatives of your former spouse. Your children have already experienced a significant loss — don't compound it by attempting to scuttle new friendships your kids may need and value.

Avoiding the "Super Parent" Syndrome

If you feel guilty about the effect your divorce may have on your kids, or if you're angry because your spouse has custody, don't try to compensate for your feelings by becoming a "Disneyland Dad" (or Mom) who lavishes them with gifts and money or becoming a smothering and over-protective parent.

Try to maintain the same relationship with your children that you had before the divorce. Your kids need predictability and stability right now, not excessive gestures. The best way to provide them with what they need is through your simple love and affection.

Chapter 23

Ten Tips for Putting Your Divorce behind You and Moving On

*I*f you feel like crawling into a hole and hiding until your divorce is over, it's no wonder. But life definitely does go on and things will get better (sooner, rather than later, we hope). You may even fall in love again and your next marriage may be a truly perfect match. To boost your spirits a bit, we offer ten practical tips for moving forward with your life and planning for happier times.

Find an (Adult) Shoulder to Lean On

Find someone with whom you can talk openly and honestly about your situation. It could be a cousin, a brother, a friend, a neighbor — as long as that person is a good listener. Pick someone you trust and someone who has given you good advice in the past.

When your marriage ends, you're likely to have a lot that you want to say even if a great deal of it doesn't seem to make sense. Express your thoughts the safest way you can. In other words, don't rant and rave to your former spouse or to your children. Get rid of the bitterness, the guilt, the sorrow, the disappointment, and the depression so that you can get on with your life.

Be careful not to rely on your special confidant so much that you jeopardize your relationship. Remain sensitive to the time demands and the feelings of that person. Watch for signs that you may be wearing out your welcome — your friend changes the subject or acts impatient whenever you start talking about your former marriage or divorce, is less available to you than in the past, no longer answers the phone, or fails to return your calls.

And, avoid dumping all your worries on your kids. They have their own insecurities right now, and you need you to put up a strong front for them.

Start Keeping a Journal

An excellent way to get a handle on your emotions is by starting a journal. Journalizing is a healthy catharsis and may even make you less reliant on friends and family to help you get your head together.

Spend time each evening after you are done with your work and the kids are in bed writing down everything that is on your mind. Or, you may want to do your writing first thing in the morning, before you begin getting ready for your day.

Write as though you're talking to your best friend or to yourself. Draw pictures to illustrate your thoughts. Every week, read what you wrote the previous week. You may be surprised at the depth (or the silliness) of your emotions, or you may discover that, in just a week, your feelings about things have changed quite a bit.

If Necessary, Seek Counseling

If you're crying all the time, harboring a lot of anger toward your ex, feeling depressed, or having a tough time getting on with your life, you need more than a shoulder to lean on — you need professional counseling. A mental health professional can give you the objective feedback and advice you need to deal with your emotions in a constructive manner.

If you do not already have a mental health professional that you like and respect, your family physician should be able to recommend someone. You may also be able to obtain a referral from your divorce attorney, a trusted friend or relative, or your local mental health association.

Fight the Urge to Return to Your Former Spouse

If you become desperately lonely after your divorce, which happens to many people, stay away from your ex-spouse. Endings should remain as endings. Do not attempt to look for comfort in those old, familiar arms no matter how much you would like to. It's time to move on. You may feel that reconciling is the only way to stop the heartbreak and ease your loneliness, but don't be fooled. None of your old problems will be solved that way.

Focus on Your Work

Your professional life may have suffered while you were going through your divorce. You may have used every ounce of your energy and concentration just to accomplish the most basic tasks of your job and to get through each day. Now that you're divorced, refocusing your energies on your work can help take your mind off your troubles and provide the ordered routine that you need in your life right now. Plus, your professional accomplishments can make you feel good about yourself and may even land you a pay raise or a promotion.

Concentrating on your work can be good temporary therapy but avoid turning into a workaholic to fill a void in your life or burying yourself in your job to avoid confronting your emotions. Now, more than ever, you need balance in your life.

Don't look to your coworkers to provide you with the physical closeness or the emotional understanding that you crave — dating or sleeping with coworkers is dangerous territory. What you want is security, not uncertainty, in your job.

Get in Touch with Your Spiritual Side

If you believe in a higher power, don't be ashamed to pray for guidance and understanding. You may also want to try meditation or yoga, which can give you a renewed sense of calmness and added self-awareness.

Full Catastrophe Living: Using the Wisdom of Your Body and Mind to Face Stress, Pain, and Illness by Jon Kabat-Zinn (Delta Books) explains how meditation can help you cope with both the everyday and unexpected tension in your life. The book was featured on a PBS special, *Bill Moyer's Healing and the Mind.*

Clean Up Your Debts

Try to get debt-free as quickly as possible. Right now, you don't need the extra worry of dealing with unpaid bills and debt collectors. Plus, the sooner you can wipe out your debt, the sooner you can start saving money for the things you really need or want.

If you do not have a spending plan or budget, develop one now. It will help you determine if your monthly income is sufficient to meet your monthly outgo. If your living expenses and debts exceed your income, carefully analyze your expenditures to see which ones you can reduce or eliminate. You may also want to find some ways to earn extra money for a while so that you can get your financial situation under control more quickly. (Chapter 2 provides detailed instructions for developing a personal budget.)

If you have enough income to cover your monthly expenditures and debts, focus on paying off those debts that carry the highest interest rates and service charges. Those usually include credit card debt, retail store charges, and finance company loans.

If you need help preparing a budget or deciding how to deal with your debt, schedule an appointment with the nonprofit Consumer Credit Counseling Service (CCCS) office in your area. If you can't find a listing in your local telephone directory, call the CCCS at 800-388-2227. For practical advice about how to live on what you earn and how to deal with debt, read *Beating the Paycheck to Paycheck Blues* by John Ventura (Dearborn Financial Publishing, Inc.).

If you are in danger of having your car repossessed or your home foreclosed on, or if the IRS or another creditor is preparing to levy against your bank account or seize it altogether, garnish your wages, or seize any of your property, schedule an appointment with a bankruptcy attorney immediately.

Try Something Entirely New

Seek out activities you'll enjoy as a newly single person — join a gym or take a dancing or cooking class where you can meet new people who are also looking for new activities.

Dare to try something that your ex-spouse would never agree to do with you — go skydiving or backpacking, join a rock climbing club, or take that cross-country drive you've always dreamed about. (A change of scenery may be just what the doctor ordered!) If outdoor activities don't sound appealing, discover the artist within you. Painting, sculpting, and photography will keep your hands and mind busy, and you'll have something to show for your efforts.

Save Money by Sharing Your Space

If you are financially strapped, you may consider getting a roommate. By sharing your home or apartment with another adult, you can reduce some of your monthly expenses and your living space may seem less lonely.

First make certain that you and your potential roommate are compatible. Do either of you smoke? Are you more of a Felix (who can't tolerate sloppy habits) than an Oscar (who avoids house cleaning at all costs)? Does your roommate have a steady income? Does he or she keep odd hours? Find out before you end up with another intolerable living arrangement.

Depending on your situation, another option may be to move back in with your parents temporarily. Returning to familiar surroundings where you will be around loved ones can provide you with a safe place to regroup and save money until you're back on your feet.

Jump-Start Your Social Life

Get out of the house and meet new people. Join a support group or a singles club for the formerly married. Meeting other divorced people and doing fun things together is good therapy, not to mention a way to meet people you may want to date.

If you can't locate a support group for divorced people in your area, start your own! New Beginnings (800-567-0122) or Single Parent Resource Center (212-947-0221) are model groups that can provide you with the information and materials to get started.

Dating again when the time is right

At some point you'll want to get back into the social swim. But don't begin dating as soon as the ink has dried on your divorce decree. Most mental health professionals suggest not dating anyone seriously until you have been divorced for at least a year.

Give yourself time to put your former marriage in perspective and to pull yourself together emotionally. Spend time making yourself whole again by rebuilding your self-esteem and creating a healthy life for you and your children. In other words, learn to be happy as a single person. If you do, you are more apt to make better choices when you begin to date.

If you begin dating prematurely, you may end up in a destructive relationship. If your self-esteem is still iffy, you may be more prone to date people who are manipulative, controlling, or abusive. Such people prey on those who feel vulnerable and needy.

Your children's well-being is another very important reason for not dating right away. Your kids may feel threatened by the strangers you're dating so soon after your divorce. They may be fearful that one of them is going to take you away, or replace their other parent, or cause some other unhappiness in their lives.

You may find yourself attracted to people simply because they're polar opposites of your former spouse. For example, if your ex was a total couch potato you may find yourself attracted to people who are perpetually in motion. Just because someone is the complete opposite of your former spouse that's no guarantee that the two of you will get along.

The majority of both divorced men and divorced women usually remarry within three years of getting divorced; and men are more likely than women to get married again.

Finding that certain someone

After you have decided that you are ready to date, you may be in a quandary about how to meet new people, especially if you have been away from the dating scene for some time or didn't date a lot before you were married. Meeting potential dates may require some resourcefulness:

✔ **Tell your friends that you want to start dating.** They may be eager to introduce you to someone, perhaps by inviting both of you to a dinner party or to join them in some other low-stress group activity.

✔ **Take a class.** An auto repair class is usually a good place to meet both men and women.

✔ **Take up a sport.** Joining a softball team or a bowling league that attracts both sexes can be a healthy, relaxed way to meet people you may want to date.

✔ **Volunteer.** Giving your time and energy to a cause you care about can put you in touch with like-minded men and women.

✔ **Join a singles group.** You may be able to find some groups listed in your local yellow pages or your local newspaper. Your place of worship may also have an organized singles group. Look for groups that meet in public places, such as a museum or large restaurant.

✔ **Use a dating service.** Some dating services let you create a video to advertise yourself and preview the videos of other people who have done the same. Some services also sponsor social activities designed to help you meet potential dates and make the initial "getting to know you" process more comfortable. (See the nearby sidebar, "Hey, it's the '90s: Tips on using dating services.")

✔ **Place a personals ad or answer one.** Try running an ad in your local daily paper or singles newspaper or magazine, or answer a few personal ads run by people who sound interesting. For the price of running an ad you may also get to create a recorded message that callers hear when they punch in a special code. When you create your message, don't include your last name, address, or phone number (you probably won't be allowed to do that anyway). Keep your message brief and friendly and mention some of your interests. And be realistic about your expectations.

If you answer someone else's ad, don't read from a script when you leave your message; nothing is a bigger turn-off. Just be yourself and talk about the kinds of things you like to do and leave your first name and a work number or beeper number to call.

If you use personal ads to meet potential dates, for safety reasons always choose a public place for your initial meetings and steer clear of bars. A meeting at a lunch spot, coffee shop, or bookstore is usually a good choice. Do not give anyone you meet through a personal ad your home phone or address until you feel comfortable and safe with that person.

Hey, it's the '90s: Tips on using dating services

If you have been out of the dating scene for a while or have difficulty meeting people of the opposite sex, using a dating service can be a worthwhile option. But watch out: These services are in business to make a profit, so choose a service carefully.

Make sure you're comfortable with the service's approach to matchmaking. Learn as much as you can about the company by reviewing its literature, scheduling an in-person meeting with a dating service representative, and asking for a sample contract to review. Dating services operate in a number of different ways:

- Some maintain photos and information on their clients that you can review. If you want to know more about someone, you can view that person's video. After that, if you're still interested, the service contacts that person, shows him or her your video, and, assuming the attraction is mutual, arranges a meeting.

- Some services use computers to match people up according to their personal profiles. These services will also arrange a meeting between you and your computerized match.

- Some dating services rely on the instincts of their staffers to make a good match between two clients.

After you have found a dating service that appeals to you, ask the following questions:

- What do you charge and what do I get for my money? (Fees can be as high as several thousand dollars.)

- Do you offer optional services (social functions, photography, grooming, or dating advice) and how much are they?

- Under what conditions can I get a refund?

- Can I sign up on a trial basis? (Avoid multiyear contracts.)

- How many clients do you have? What percentage of them are men and what percentage are women?

- Does the information questionnaire ask important questions about a prospective date?

- How long have you been in business? (Fly-by-nights may be out of business before you can use the services you paid for.)

Before you pay, ask for a copy of the service contract. Read it carefully to make certain that it addresses all the items we listed here and that no conflicts exist between what the company representative told you and what the contract says.

And, before you sign anything, call your local Better Business Bureau and the consumer protection office of your state Attorney General's office to find out if any complaints about the service are on file.

Chapter 24

Ten Strategies for Next Time to Keep Divorce at Bay

*B*efore you can get behind the wheel of a car, you must be tested on your driving skills and knowledge of the rules of the road. But no such tests exist to determine your fitness for marriage. Many couples fail to realize that a good marriage doesn't just *happen* — it takes work.

Both parties to a marriage must nurture and care for that relationship. Those of us who manage to figure that out often come to that realization the hard way — through trial and error, living through failed marriages, going through a divorce, and trying again. With that in mind, this chapter offers you several key ingredients that relationship experts tell us are found in just about every successful marriage.

Try Pre-Marriage Counseling to Avoid Surprises

Too often, the euphoric pleasure of falling in love and planning a marriage overshadows the truly important preliminary work you should be doing — ensuring that your new relationship is the real thing and that you both have what is needed to make it work. That means getting to know one another, warts and all, making certain that you share the same basic values and priorities, and building the relationship skills necessary to weather love's slings and arrows after the newness and excitement of your relationship has worn off.

Pre-marriage counseling is an excellent way to get this education. In the past, this counseling was commonly seen as a responsibility of a religious adviser, but growing numbers of marriage counselors, community mental health centers, and colleges are now offering it. Even high schools are getting into the act.

Among other things, pre-marriage counseling can offer you and your future spouse an opportunity to

- Define your goals for marriage.

- Learn what is needed to have a successful marriage and to discuss your fears and concerns in a supportive environment.

- Compare and contrast your individual values and attitudes about such potential marriage-busters as money problems, tough decision making, arguments over housework responsibilities, differences on raising children, and so on.

- Learn conflict management skills so that small problems are less apt to become big ones.

- Understand how to communicate effectively.

In some communities, local religious institutions have adopted a policy of refusing to marry couples who do not first receive formal training on conflict resolution and communication. Some local governments have taken the concept one step further, requiring that couples receive marriage education from a certified professional before they can be married in either a religious or a civil ceremony.

Call the American Association for Marriage and Family Therapy for referrals to organizations in your area who can provide you with pre-marriage counseling and education. The association's toll-free number is 800-374-2638.

Harville Hendrix, Ph.D., has written two excellent books that can help you build the kind of successful marriage most people desire: *A Guide For Couples* (Harper Perennial) and *Getting the Love You Want, Keeping the Love You Find* (PocketBooks). Another excellent resource written from a woman's point of view is *The Dance of Intimacy* by Harriet Goldhor Lerner, Ph.D. (HarperCollins).

For a comprehensive listing of marriage education classes across the country, head to the following Web site:

www.his.com/~cmfce/

Find Some Happily Married Mentors

Another way to prepare for marriage is to be mentored by an older married couple participating in a marriage mentoring program. Marriage mentors meet with engaged couples to tell them what it is *really* like to be married, share their personal stories about married life, and answer their questions. Some marriage mentors also mentor already-marrieds who are struggling with problems in their marriages. Depending on the mentoring program, you may have to pay a small fee to participate.

Although no national marriage mentor organization exists that you can contact, marriage mentor programs are growing in popularity and becoming more widely available throughout the country. Possible sources for such programs include your church, a college or university in your area, and local civic and community organizations. Mental health professionals and social workers who specialize in family or couples counseling also may be able to refer you to a marriage mentor program.

Don't Just Talk — Communicate!

Failure to communicate is at the root of many marriages gone sour. Poor communication manifests itself in many ways. You may have a tough time speaking your mind or broaching uncomfortable subjects with your spouse, or you may have assumptions and expectations that are completely unknown to your marriage partner.

If you want to talk with your spouse about something that you know is a sensitive or difficult issue, carefully choose the time and place for the discussion. You may also want to rehearse what you're going to say to avoid inadvertently using words that may make your spouse angry or defensive.

When you tell your spouse about something that's bothering you, avoid using statements that begin with "you" and asking "why" questions, both of which will almost certainly put your spouse on the defensive. Many mental health professionals suggest writing down a three-part statement that begins with how you feel, followed by what you would like changed, and ending with what you would like your spouse to do instead. For example, "I feel frustrated when you tell me that we're going to the movies, and then you don't get home from work until 10 p.m. I wish you would call me when your plans change."

Men and women tend to differ in their communication styles, which can sometimes cause problems in relationships. If you want help understanding what your spouse is really saying, pick up a copy of Deborah Tannen's best-selling book, *You Just Don't Understand: Women and Men in Conversation* (Ballantine Books).

Make Time for Each Other

Many couples are inseparable at the start of their marriage. But over time, as they get caught up in the day-to-day details of their lives and struggle to balance career and family, they begin to have less and less time for each other. Gradually, they drift apart, emotionally and physically. Then, if problems develop, they may discover that they don't have the will or desire to work things out together.

In this time-deprived, high-pressure culture of ours, most people have too little time for themselves, much less for their spouses. Yet, if you want your marriage to stay healthy, you must create regular opportunities to be together, show that you care for each other, and demonstrate how much you appreciate your spouse's company. Here are some suggestions for showing your spouse how you feel:

- Say "I love you." Don't assume that after you marry your spouse doesn't need to hear those words anymore.

- Hug your spouse at least once a day.

- Eat at least one meal together each day. Talk to one another during your meal and don't watch TV while you're eating.

- Go on a date together at least once a month. Mark the day on your calendar and schedule it just like you would any important meeting or appointment. Your date doesn't need to be expensive. It can involve a walk in the woods, a movie, a picnic, or a drive in the country. What you do is less important than your taking the time to be alone and to enjoy one another.

- Don't sit in front of the TV every night. Instead, have a conversation with your spouse. Do a puzzle together, play a game, or just share the silence and enjoy simply being with one another.

- Don't assume that the way you like your spouse to demonstrate his or her love for you is also what your spouse desires. Ask your spouse to make a list of the caring behaviors he or she would welcome in order to feel loved. Give your spouse a list of your own preferences. You may be surprised at how the two lists compare.

You can lift your spouse's spirits and say you care in little ways — a simple "thank you," a romantic note posted on the bathroom mirror, or a massage after a long workday. One of us has written a two-page love letter to our spouse every day for seven years, starting the day we got engaged.

Need more practical ideas for how to keep the romance and excitement in your marriage? Take the advice of Drs. Lew and Gloria Richfield, marriage and family therapists who themselves have been together for nearly 50 years. They authored *Together Forever! 125 Loving Ways to Have a Vital and Romantic Marriage* (Dell Publishing).

Fight Fair

Fighting in marriage can actually be a healthy way to clear the air and resolve problems. Good fighting is fair fighting. When you fight fair, you avoid personal attacks, insulting language, finger pointing, recriminations, and threats. Any one of those things is apt to put your spouse on the defensive, increase the emotional level of your argument, and make your spouse less willing to listen to what you are saying and less open to compromise. The goal of a fair fight is not to have a winner or a loser, but to resolve your disagreement in a way that makes you both feel good about the outcome.

If your tempers are flaring, take a time-out and cool down. Schedule a date to discuss the subject later when you both will be more calm and collected.

Try New Ways of Resolving Old Problems

In every relationship, certain problems seem to occur time after time. You may find that you always respond to those problems in the same way, whether your response is effective or not. Even if the problems that keep repeating themselves are quite minor, over months and years they can create a considerable amount of anger and resentment in a marriage.

Oftentimes, the solution to recurring problems, both big and small, is to find a new way of dealing with them. The new solution may be quite simple. For example, you like the tube of toothpaste you share with your wife to be squeezed from the bottom and rolled tight as it's used up. Your wife drives you crazy because she is a free-form tube squeezer. You have had countless arguments over the toothpaste tube — you don't know why she can't remember to do what you ask, and she can't understand why you're making such a big deal out of what she considers to be a very petty issue. The solution? Buy two tubes of toothpaste — one for her and one for you.

Want another example of creative problem solving? You and your spouse both work outside the home, and you feel like you're stuck with all the household chores. You don't like cleaning house, doing dishes, or taking care of the laundry any more than your spouse does. What's the solution? List all the chores on a piece of paper. Then take turns signing up for a chore each week or each month, whichever works best, until all of the chores have been assigned. To be fair, alternate who is the first to choose. Another option is to write all of the chores on pieces of paper and take turns picking them out of a bowl. Again, alternate who chooses first.

Although the solution to every recurring problem may not be quite so easy as resolving the toothpaste debate, creative problem solving can work wonders for a marriage.

Maintain Your Sense of Humor

Laughing together is one of the best experiences you can have in a marriage. Find ways to make it happen. Tell jokes, look for the humor in everyday situations, go to a funny movie, recount amusing situations from home or work, or simply smile more often whether you feel like it or not. Making light of a problem is a gentle way of letting your spouse know that something he or she is saying or doing (or *not* saying or doing) is bugging you and it's time to talk about it.

Forgive and Forget

In a relationship as close as marriage, on occasion you're going to get on each other's nerves. Although these minor irritations don't usually signal the end of your marriage, if you overreact by making them more significant than they really are, you can damage your relationship over time.

When your spouse's behavior irritates or angers you, try to understand why. Is it because you had a bad day at work or because you are really worried about one of your children? Does your spouse's behavior remind you of something your ex used to do or remind you of the way one of your parents used to treat you?

For example, in your previous marriage it really bugged you that after your ex got ready for work, the bathroom you shared was a disaster area. Despite numerous requests to tidy up the bathroom so that it would be easier for you to get ready, your ex-spouse consistently left the place a wreck. Although your new spouse is much neater than your ex and much more responsive to your requests, it still irks you whenever you find things out of place.

Try to keep your spouse's behavior in perspective. Ask yourself: "Is what my spouse said or did *really* that important?" Try to remember all of the good things about your spouse. Also, consider the things you do that drive your spouse crazy and how much you've appreciated a forgiving attitude. If your spouse's behavior is really a problem for you, try talking about it together. If the problem is serious, get professional help.

PAIRS is an international program that helps married couples sustain and improve their relationships by learning how to communicate better and resolve anger in a constructive, and not destructive, fashion. Couples participate in PAIRS workshops conducted by trained coaches. To learn more about PAIRS, call (888) PAIRS-4U or visit its Web site at www.pairs.com.

Resolve Problems Sooner Rather Than Later

If you and your spouse have had a fight, it may be up to you to swallow your pride and say, "Let's talk" or "I'm sorry," even if you still feel hurt, vulnerable, or angry. We'll be the first to admit that living by this rule isn't necessarily easy. But resolving your marital differences sooner, and not later, helps minimize the likelihood that your relationship will be infected by hurt feelings, festering anger, and unresolved conflict.

Many marriage counselors advise setting aside time once a week to talk about any problems or miscommunications that may have happened between the two of you. If you seem unable to discuss your problems calmly or resolve an issue that is important to either of you, try a couple's communication workshop or schedule an appointment with a therapist. Many therapists lament that if only they'd seen some couples sooner, they may have been able to save their marriages.

Seeking help to resolve your differences

Some marital problems are too complex, serious, or potentially dangerous to manage on your own. Dealing with those problems may require the help of a mental health professional. If you're experiencing any of the following situations, it may be time to seek some help:

✔ Your spouse has threatened to harm you or your children.

✔ Your children are afraid of your spouse and refuse to be left alone with him or her.

✔ Your spouse is trying to isolate you, cutting you off from your friends, family, or coworkers.

✔ You cannot control your anger and regret the things you do or say when you're upset.

✔ Either one of you is abusing drugs or alcohol.

✔ Your spouse refuses to give up an extramarital affair.

✔ You are thinking about suicide or homicide as a way out of your marriage.

✔ You (or your spouse) are having trouble getting out of bed in the morning, you can't get to sleep at night, or you're exhibiting other signs of depression.

Support Your Spouse's Outside Interests

Some newly marrieds assume that after they become a couple, they have to do everything together. Although "being joined at the hip" with your new husband or wife may be fun at first, after a while at least one of you will want to do things on your own, hang out with your own friends, or take a pass on participating in one of your spouse's favorite activities.

If your spouse suddenly wants to do his or her own thing, don't assume that your spouse loves you any less. And, don't act resentful over your spouse's newfound interest or hobby. Instead, support your spouse in pursuing new interests, maintaining old friendships, and making new ones. Those things that make your spouse happier and more satisfied will produce positive feelings that transfer to your marriage. You may find that your conversations are more interesting and you're laughing more often. You may even discover new things to appreciate about your spouse, which can deepen your love for the person you married.

Attempting to control how your spouse spends every waking hour can make a once-happy marriage feel suffocating and create needless anger and resentment in your relationship. If you're feeling threatened by the changes taking place in your relationship, try to understand why they bother you or make an appointment to talk with a mental health professional about it.

If you sense that your spouse feels saddened or threatened by the activities you want to do by yourself, talk with your spouse about your interests, make sure that your spouse meets your new friends, and reassure him or her with your love and affection that everything is fine in your relationship.

Glossary of Terms

Abandonment: When one spouse moves out of the home the couple shares without the consent of, or against the wishes of, the other spouse.

Action: The legal term for a lawsuit (also called a *cause of action*).

Adversarial divorce: Occurs when the spouses involved cannot come to an agreement about the terms of their divorce.

Affidavit: A written statement of facts. The statement is made under oath and notarized.

Alimony: The payment of money by one spouse to another. Alimony is usually provided for only a limited period of time but can end earlier than the specified period if one spouse dies or remarries. Alimony is taxable income for the spouse who receives it and provides a tax deduction for the spouse who pays it.

Alimony *pendente lite*: A temporary court order for support while a couple's divorce is pending (also called *temporary spousal support*).

Annulment: The legal end to a marriage that has been ruled invalid. States vary in regard to what makes a marriage invalid.

Answer: A formal response to a petition for divorce, separation, or annulment. In the response, the person who is served with the petition admits or denies the allegations made by the petitioner and may also make allegations against the petitioner.

Appeal: The process by which the losing party in a divorce asks a higher court to review the decision of a lower court and determine whether a legal reason exists to order a new trial or to change some aspect of the lower court's decision.

Arbitration: A legally binding resolution to a dispute achieved through a nonjudicial process.

Arrearage: Past due child support or alimony.

Assets: Property of value including but not limited to cash, real estate, vehicles, securities and other investments, fine jewelry, artwork, and other valuables.

Automatic wage deduction: A court order that requires the employer of the parent who is obligated to pay child support to deduct the payments out of the employee's paycheck and send it to the court for distribution to the other parent (also called *income-withholding order*).

Change of venue: A change in the location of a trial, usually from one county to another county within the same state.

Child support: Money paid by one spouse to the other spouse to help meet the financial needs of their minor children. Ordinarily, the support continues until a child turns 18 or 21, depending on the state, although a parent may have to provide support while a child is a full-time college student or attending trade school.

Claim: A charge by one spouse against the other.

COBRA: A federal law that allows individuals who are covered on a medical insurance policy to remain on the policy for a limited period of time and for a certain time after their marriage or employment ends.

Common law marriage: A relationship between a man and a woman that in some states is recognized as a marriage even though no formal ceremony occurred and no license was issued. Common law marriages are formally ended by divorce.

Community property: Property, including money and other assets, acquired during a couple's marriage that is owned equally by both spouses. This concept applies in states with community property laws.

Complaint: The written document or pleading filed with a court to initiate a divorce. It cites a wrong, names the person(s) who allegedly committed the wrong (or in the case of a divorce the name of the other person involved), and describes the relief sought. In a divorce, the complaint will indicate the grounds for the divorce, whether any minor children are involved, and other relevant information (also called a *petition*).

Contempt of court: A willful and deliberate violation of a court order, judgment, or decree (for example, nonpayment of child support or alimony). Spouses who are in contempt of court may be punished by the court.

Contested divorce: A divorce in which the spouses cannot agree on how to resolve all of the issues involved. The court may resolve the issues if the parties have still not settled by the time of the final hearing.

Court order: A written document issued by a court and signed by a judge that orders someone to do something.

Cross-examination: The questioning of a witness by the attorney representing the opposing party to ascertain the truthfulness of what the witness said or to further develop the witness's testimony. Witnesses are cross-examined during a trial.

Custody: The legal right and responsibility to raise a minor child and to make decisions on her or his behalf.

Decree: The final written order in a divorce.

Deed: A legal document that conveys ownership in real estate or other real property.

Default judgment: An order or judgment made on the basis of the plaintiff's information only because the defendant failed to respond, didn't respond on time, or did not appear in court.

Defendant: The person sued for divorce; also known as the *respondent.*

Deposition: Testimony taken outside of court and under oath and subject to examination by all parties to a lawsuit. A stenographer records the testimony and types it up verbatim.

Direct examination: The questioning of a witness on the stand by the attorney representing the spouse on whose behalf the witness is testifying.

Discovery: A process used by attorneys to get at the facts in a divorce prior to trial. Most often discovery gets at financial facts, but depending on the jurisdiction it may also be used to explore other issues. The tools of discovery include depositions, interrogatories, and the production of documents, among others.

Dissolution: The end of a marriage (in other words, a *divorce*). The term does not include annulments.

Emancipation: The age at which a child is treated as a legal adult and his or her parents are no longer responsible for the care of the child. In most states the age is 18, but in some states children are emancipated at 21. A child may become a legal adult at a younger age if he or she marries, joins the military, goes to work full time, or petitions the court to declare him or her an emancipated minor and the court agrees to do so.

Equitable distribution: A legal system of dividing up the value of a divorcing couple's marital property based on what is fair to both of them.

Evidence: Relevant testimony, documents, videos, tape recordings, and other information offered to and accepted by the court to prove or disprove an allegation.

Ex parte: An application for relief from the court made without the other party being present or when the other party is given very short prior notice.

Garnishment: The legal taking of a debtor's money or bank account to pay his or her debt. In a divorce, a parent's wages can be garnished for nonpayment of child support.

Grounds: The legal basis or reason for a divorce.

Guardian *ad litem*: A court-appointed adult, usually a trained social worker, counselor, or other professional who represents the non-legal interests of minor children in a couple's divorce.

Hearing: A proceeding before the court that attempts to resolve an issue through testimony, legal arguments, and the introduction of evidence.

Hold harmless: A situation in which one spouse agrees to assume full responsibility for paying the other spouse's debt and promises to protect that spouse from any loss or expense associated with the debt. *Indemnification* is the same thing as holding someone harmless.

Injunction: A court order prohibiting someone from acting in a way that's likely to harm someone else, either by causing a financial loss for that person or hurting that individual emotionally or physically.

Interrogatories: Written questions formally served by one party in a divorce on someone else (that person may or may not be the other spouse). Interrogatories are served in order to gain information and establish facts related to the issues under dispute in a divorce. Answers to interrogatories must be provided under oath within a set period of time, usually a month.

Joint custody: A situation in which divorced (or separated) parents share custody. They may share legal custody (the right and obligation to make important decisions about their minor children), physical custody (the right and obligation to have their children reside with them), or they may share both legal and physical custody.

Joint property: Property legally owned by two or more persons, a husband and wife for example.

Judgment of divorce: A formal written document that states that a man and a woman are divorced. Also called a *divorce decree* or *decree of dissolution.*

Jurisdiction: The authority of a court to rule on a particular legal matter. Different types of courts have different jurisdictions. For example, state family courts hear issues related to family law, and federal bankruptcy courts hear consumer and business bankruptcy cases.

Legal separation: A legal agreement or court judgment formally authorizing a couple to live apart and spelling out the terms for their living apart. The couple is still married to one another. Not all states recognize legal separations.

Maintenance: Another word for *alimony* or *spousal support.*

Marital property: Property acquired by or earned by a couple during the couple's marriage.

Marital settlement agreement: A written agreement between spouses that spells out their decisions in regard to the division of their marital property and in regard to child support, visitation, and alimony.

Mediation: A popular nonlegal means of resolving a divorce-related dispute with the assistance of a neutral third party. Decisions made in a mediation session are arrived at by mutual agreement and not ordered by a judge.

Motion: A written or oral application to the court asking the court to take a certain action — such as ordering temporary support, custody, or visitation rights, or preventing a spouse from taking or spending assets.

Motion to modify: A written request of the court to change an earlier court order regarding child custody, support, alimony, or other divorce-related decisions.

No-fault divorce: A divorce that is granted with no requirement to prove that one of the spouses was guilty of some marital misconduct.

Noncustodial parent: The parent who does not have physical custody of his or her children. Ordinarily, this parent is obligated to pay child support.

Order: A ruling by the court on a motion that requires the parties in a divorce to do something or not do something or that establishes the parties' rights and responsibilities.

Petition: The legal document filed to initiate a divorce (also called a *complaint*).

Petitioner: The person who files a petition or initiates a couple's divorce proceedings (also called the *plaintiff*).

Pleading: Formal written application to the court for relief and the written response to it. Among other things, pleadings can include petitions, answers, and motions.

Postnuptial agreement: A binding legal agreement between spouses that spells out their present and future rights and responsibilities should they divorce or should one spouse die.

Prenuptial agreement: A binding legal agreement between a couple before they marry that spells out their rights in the event that they later divorce or one of them dies during their marriage.

Pro se: A plaintiff or defendant who is not represented by an attorney.

Qualified Domestic Relations Order (QDRO): A court order that requires a portion of one spouse's retirement benefits to be awarded to the other spouse. The order is directed to the administrator of the retirement benefits.

Real Property: Homes, other buildings, and land and any attachments to those assets.

Respondent: The defendant in a divorce.

Response: A formal written reply by a defendant to respond or answer a complaint.

Retainer: Money paid to an attorney to begin work on a case.

Separate property: Property legally owned by one spouse and not by both spouses.

Settlement: A written agreement between spouses resolving the issues in their divorce.

Sole custody: When only one parent has custody of the children.

Subpoena: A legal document served on a witness requiring that he or she appear in court. Ignoring a subpoena can result in punishment by the court.

Summons: A written notification to the defendant in a lawsuit that the lawsuit has been filed and that a response is needed (also called a *citation*).

Testimony: Statements provided by a witness under oath during a deposition or in court.

Transcript: A typed record of the trial or deposition proceedings.

Trial: A formal court hearing presided over by a judge to resolve the issues in a pleading or complaint.

Uncontested divorce: A divorce in which there are no issues to be resolved.

Visitation: The legal right of the noncustodial parent to spend time with his or her children.

Index

•••

(continued)

postnuptial agreements, 41, 114
  basic description of, 293, 335
  commingling assets and, 118
  copies of, 214, 227
  discussing, 295
  drafting, 300–302
  how you can use, 300–301
  legally binding, rules for, 301–302
prenuptial agreements, 41, 49
  basic description of, 293–294,
      295–299, 336
  commingling assets and, 118
  copies of, 214, 227
  discussing, 295
  establishing the rules of your marriage
      with, 299
  getting legal help with, 298–300
  legally binding, rules for, 297–298
  property division and, 114, 118
  what to put in, 296–297
pretrial conferences/hearings, 58, 244–246
pretrial motions, 55, 84, 244
priorities, deciding on, 83
privacy, 220, 234
private investigators, 286
probate, 263
profit sharing plans, 79, 123–129
profit-and-loss statements, 81, 131
promises, keeping, 312–313
property. *See also* marital property;
      separate property
  guardians, 263
  law, 25–28
  personal, finding a safe place for, 86–87
  taxes, 121, 122
protective orders, 16–17, 42
psychological examinations, 21, 248
psychological treatment, 146, 149, 160,
      163. *See also* counseling
  in the case of depression, 105
  mediation and, 13
psychologists, as expert witnesses,
      248–249
Public Health Department, 254

• Q •

QRDOs (Qualified Domestic Relations
      Order), 126, 127, 262, 336
Quicken, 29
"quickie" divorces, 45
Quinn, Jane Bryant, 30

• R •

real estate. *See also* home
  accounting for, 80
  agents/brokers, 121, 248–249
  alimony payments and, 48
  appraisers, 120
  investments, 23
rebound marriages, 106
Rebuilding When a Relationship Ends
      (Fisher), 272
rebuttals, 253
reconciliation, after separation, 68, 71–72
re-cross examinations, 253
redirect, 253
rehabilitation programs, substance
      abuse, 17
rehabilitative alimony, 136–137. *See also*
      alimony
rejection, feelings of, 96, 102
religion. *See also* religious advisors
  anti-divorce sentiment and, 9
  Catholicism, 15, 63, 64
  child custody and, 157
  exploring spirituality, 108, 318
  separation and, 63
religious advisors, 11, 108, 159. *See also*
      religion
  attorney referrals through, 209
  as mediators, 232–233
rent, 24, 144
residency requirements, 45
respondents, 53, 336
retainers, 212, 336
retaliation, avoiding, 278
retirement benefits, 41, 170
  borrowing against, 87
  dividing up, 123–129

(continued)

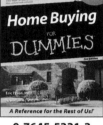

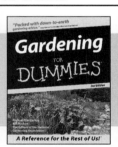